A Microsoft® Excel
Companion for **Business Statistics**

3rd Edition

David L. Eldredge

Murray State University

THOMSON
———✶———™
SOUTH-WESTERN

WEST

Australia · Canada · Mexico · Singapore · Spain · United Kingdom · United States

THOMSON

SOUTH-WESTERN

A Microsoft Excel Companion for Business Statistics, 3e

David Eldredge

VP/Editorial Director:
Jack W. Calhoun

VP/Editor-in-Chief:
George Werthman

Acquisitions Editor:
Charles McCormick

Developmental Editor:
Alisa Madden

Marketing Manager:
Larry Qualls

Production Editor:
Stephanie Blydenburgh

Technology Project Editor:
Christine A. Wittmer

Manufacturing Coordinator:
Diane Lohman

Printer:
West Group
Eagan, MN

Design Project Manager:
Rick Moore

Cover Designer:
Rick Moore

For permission to use material from this
text or product, submit a request online
at http://www.thomsonrights.com.

For more information
contact South-Western,
5191 Natorp Boulevard,
Mason, Ohio 45040.
Or you can visit our Internet site at:
http://www.swlearning.com

BRIEF CONTENTS

CONTENTS

PREFACE

The type of computer software that is most commonly used for data analysis within business and industrial organizations is spreadsheet software. Current windows-based spreadsheet software comes with a number of built-in features for performing statistical analysis. Since the majority of the graduates of our business schools will mainly use spreadsheets for analysis in their subsequent careers, most of them will benefit from a familiarity with the use of the statistical features of spreadsheet software.

A number of years ago, I concluded that if we as business statistics professors do not familiarize our students with these capabilities, they may never discover them. Accordingly as an experiment in the spring 1995 semester, I switched from the use of dedicated statistical software (e.g., Minitab, SPSS, SAS) to the use of spreadsheet software for my business statistics courses. The experiment was a success. I have used spreadsheet software as the sole software support for all the statistic courses I have taught since that time. Consequently, it pleases me to be able to share the results of some of my experiences with you through the contents of this manual.

In considering the use of this manual you may have a number of questions. We have tried to anticipate some of these. The answers to them follow.

What Is The Purpose Of This Manual? The title of this manual, *A Microsoft Excel Companion for Business Statistics*, implies the three aspects of its purpose. First, it presents step-by-step instructions for using Excel for statistical analysis. The instructions are complimented by figures of computer screen captures. These show data input, menus, dialog boxes and statistical results. Second, this manual is designed for use in conjunction with a textbook. For example, the manual does not include end-of-the-chapter exercises. Our intent is for you the student to work through a topic within this manual and then apply Excel to similar examples and exercises from your textbook. Third, this manual is focused on the area of business statistics. Although there are similarities in the application of statistical analysis to many areas, our orientation through our examples is to the use of statistical analysis for business and industrial organizations.

Which Textbooks Does It Support? The manual has been designed for use with most business statistics textbooks. This is possible for at least two reasons. First, there is a large degree of consistency among business statistics textbooks. The topics included and the organization of these topics is quite similar for many textbooks. Second, this manual uses a modular approach in the presentation of topics. As a result, it is relatively easy to identify the unit within this manual that corresponds to the topical coverage of a particular textbook.

Do I Need This Manual If My Textbook Covers Excel? Many of the currently published business statistics textbooks incorporate the use of Excel directly within them. However, oftentimes the instructions provided are not in sufficient detail for those students who do not have a good working knowledge of Excel. This manual presents detailed instructions and many figures showing the computer screen as the user will see it. This level of detail as needed by some users usually is not presented within the covers of a business statistics textbook. If the specific instructions and visual guidance provided within this manual were added to the typical business statistics textbook, its length would certainly become substantial if not prohibitive.

Which Statistical Topics Are Supported By This Manual? The topics within this manual include most of those you will find within your textbook. The manual covers (1) the charts, graphs and numerical measures of descriptive statistics, (2) discrete and continuous probability distributions, (3) sampling distributions, (4) the point estimates, confidence intervals and hypothesis testing of introductory inferential statistics, (5) hypothesis tests utilizing the chi-square statistic, (6) the multivariate analysis approaches of the analysis of variance, regression analysis and time series forecasting, and (7) quality control charts. Chapter topics found within business statistics textbooks that are not supported within this manual include (1) probability concepts, (2) nonparametric statistics other than the chi-square statistic, (3) index numbers and (4) decision analysis.

Is Additional Software Required? No. Our approach is to use only the inherent capabilities of Excel. That is, we rely totally on the computing, charting, statistical analysis tools, statistical functions and other features that are included within Excel as it is distributed to customers. We do not rely on add-ins, special macro functions, or special worksheets. All you need is Excel in order to construct all the worksheets within this manual. In addition, the CD included with this manual contains files of all the worksheets developed within this manual. These can serve as templates for solving statistical problems. Thus, you also have the option of solving your problems without going through the development given within the manual.

Which Versions of Excel Are Supported? The manual supports the two most recent versions of Excel running under the Microsoft® Windows operating system. These include **Excel 2002**, the Excel component of **Microsoft Office XP, and Excel 2000**. The manual has been developed using Excel 2002. It can be run with Windows XP, Windows 2000 or Windows 98. The small differences between Excel 2002 and Excel 2000 are summarized in Appendix D. In addition, Excel 97, the version prior to Excel 2000, has very few differences from Excel 2000 and can be used with this manual or with the second edition of this manual. If you are using an even earlier version, either Excel 95 or Excel 5, you would be better served by using the first edition of this manual. The first edition is written using Excel 95 with boxed notes to indicate any differences it has with Excel 97 and with Excel 5.

What Level of Excel Knowledge Is Required? The primary purpose of this manual is to introduce you to the statistical capabilities of Excel. However, it is written assuming some readers will not have had prior experience with Windows and/or Excel. Accordingly, Chapter 1 includes an introduction to the Windows environment and an introduction to Excel. These sections are not a complete guide to either Windows or Excel. However, they present sufficient material for most persons to be able to begin using Excel for statistical analyses.

Will The Worksheets I Develop Always Look Like Those Shown In the Manual? As you work through the example analyses of this manual, you will develop your own Excel worksheets for performing the required computations and charting we demonstrate. Although your worksheets will generally resemble those given in the manual, you may detect differences. Some differences arise from additional editing and formatting that we have done in order to make the figures more understandable to the readers of this manual. In some instances we have enlarged charts and column widths, and others we have added borders to cells and used different font style such as italics or boldface. These sorts of cosmetic changes can be made by you but are not necessary for understanding the statistical analyses presented.

Should I Just Use the Worksheets Given On the CD? As previously mentioned, a CD containing files of all the worksheets developed within this manual is included with it. However, if your objective is to learn to use Excel for solving statistical problems, you should follow the manual's instructions for developing the worksheets yourself. You will become much more Excel proficient through this approach as opposed to using the worksheet templates developed by us. On the other hand, some of the worksheets require a considerable number of Excel operations to develop. Particular examples include the chi-square test of independence worksheet of Section 9.2 in Chapter 9, the five quality control chart worksheets of Chapter 12 and the Box Plot chart procedures presented in Appendix C. For such worksheets, you may well wish to forego the experience of developing them for the expedience of using the templates we have developed.

Acknowledgements

I need to thank a number of persons for bringing this project to completion. First, is Glen Garrett. He was our ever-faithful Thomson Sales Representative at Murray State University for a number of years. I am grateful to Glen for his friendship and service over the years, and for his recommendation of me for a related publishing project that preceded this manual. Second, I would like to thank Professor Ken Black of the University of Houston—Clear Lake. Ken has become a co-author and friend as the result of his acceptance of me for that prior project.

This manual has benefited from others that came before it. In particular, my friend Mike Middleton's *Data Analysis Using Microsoft Excel*, Kenneth N. Berk and Patrick Carey's *Data Analysis with Microsoft Excel*, and John L. Neufeld's *Learning Business Statistics with Microsoft Excel*.

I would like to acknowledge the input from a number of "Business Stat" students at Murray State University. Their observations and recommendations in response to their use of the prior manual have been useful in a number of instances. In similar fashion, I must thank Professor Debbie Newell of Union University and her accounting students who identified needed corrections to Chapter 10 of the prior edition.

My thanks also to the project team at Thomson South-Western under the direction of Senior Acquisitions editor Charles McCormick, Jr. Their assistance has been not only helpful, but necessary, for the completion of this project.

Finally, your use of this manual may result in comments, corrections, criticisms and suggestions for improving it. I would greatly appreciate hearing of these from you.

David L. Eldredge
Department of Computer Science and Information Systems
652 Business Building, South
Murray State University
Murray, Kentucky 42071-3314

Dave.Eldredge@Murraystate.Edu

This effort is dedicated to my wife of those many years, Judy, and to all my family for their constant love and support.

CHAPTER 1. INTRODUCTION TO STATISTICS WITH EXCEL

The most powerful general-purpose managerial software available for data analysis in business and industry is spreadsheet software. Currently, the most widely used spreadsheet program is Microsoft® Excel. Businesses and industries have used Excel throughout their organizations for their computational, charting and data management needs for years. Beyond these three uses, Excel includes a number of features that provide the capability for easily conducting many statistical analyses. The purpose of this manual is to introduce you to these features that facilitate the computing and charting requirements of your study and use of statistics.

A number of versions of Excel are available for various types of computers under various operating systems. The Excel version used in this manual is **Excel 2002** running under the Microsoft® Windows operating system. Excel 2002 is a component of **Microsoft Office XP**. Office XP may be run under Windows 98 or later versions of Windows. This manual also fully supports the immediately prior version of Excel, Excel 2000. The presentation within this manual is for Excel 2002. However, the few small differences encountered when using Excel 2000 are summarized in Appendix D. In passing we might note that Excel 97, the version prior to Excel 2000, can be used with this manual with few differences. However, prior versions such as Excel 95 and earlier would be more difficult to use with this manual.

We begin below in **Section 1.1** with a brief overview of some WINDOWS features for those persons who are unfamiliar with Windows. In **Section 1.2** we introduce EXCEL and provide some initial instruction in its use for those who are unfamiliar with it. These first two sections are not meant to be a complete guide to either Windows or Excel. They merely present enough material to get you started. To become proficient you may need to refer to other books and resources. One of these further resources can be the extensive on-line HELP SYSTEM provided by Excel and Windows. An introduction to Excel's help system is presented in **Section 1.3**. This is followed in **Section 1.4** by an introduction to the features of Excel that we use in this manual to facilitate statistical analyses. These include DATA ANALYSIS TOOLS, STATISTICAL FUNCTIONS, the CHART WIZARD, the TRENDLINE feature for charts and the PIVOT TABLE WIZARD. We continue in **Section 1.5** with a presentation of a number of worksheet practices that will help to make your worksheets more effective for you and any others who might use them. Finally, **Section 1.6** discusses the use of this manual as a companion to your study of a business statistics textbook.

1.1 USING WINDOWS

The first thing you need to know about Windows is how to start (or launch) the software. For most computer systems, Windows will automatically start when you turn on the computer and the monitor. If you are using a computer on a network, you may be prompted to enter your assigned user name and password. If so, you should key in your user name from the keyboard, press the **Tab** key on the keyboard, key in your password and press the **Enter** key. The resulting presentation on the screen is called the Windows *desktop*. It displays a number of small pictures called icons and a number of buttons that facilitate your communication with your computer.

A pointing device is used to select the icons and buttons on the desktop. The most common pointing device is called a mouse. The movement of the mouse in your hand causes a corresponding movement of a mouse pointer on the computer screen. There are five mouse techniques you will be using to communicate with your computer.

- **Point**—moving the mouse until the on-screen pointer is touching the object on the desktop which you wish to select
- **Click**—quickly pressing and releasing the **left** mouse button once
- **Double Click**—quickly pressing and releasing the **left** mouse button twice in rapid succession
- **Drag**—pointing to an object, pressing and holding down the **left** mouse button, moving the mouse pointer to a new location and releasing the mouse button
- **Right Click**—quickly pressing and releasing the **right** mouse button once

After you have started Windows and understand the operation of the mouse, you are ready to start (or launch) Excel. In later chapters we refer to the following as the **Start-Up Procedure.**

START-UP PROCEDURE

1. Point and click the **Start** button in the lower left corner of your Windows desktop. The Windows *Start* menu will open.
2. Point to **All Programs** (Windows XP) or to **Programs** (Windows 2000 and 98) and the *Programs menu* will appear to the right of the Windows *Start* menu.
3. Point to **Office XP** (or Office 2000) on the menu and *Office menu* will appear to the right listing the Office XP components. *(This Step 3 may not be necessary for your computer system).*
4. Point and click the selection **Microsoft Excel** and the Excel window will appear.

Alternatively you may
Double click on the Excel icon on the Windows desktop if one is shown.

Your resulting Excel window should be similar to that shown in Figure 1.1. If your window does not fill the entire screen, you should change it to a full-screen presentation. Click on the **Maximize** button that is at the very top right of the window. It is the second button from the right at the top.

Although your window should generally resemble that of Figure 1.1, some of the details may differ slightly **(for Excel 2000 see Figure D.1 of Appendix D)**. One reason for this is that Excel allows modifications to be made to the appearance of its window. For example as you use Excel 2002, the window will display the Excel features that you primarily use.

Figure 1.1 Excel Window

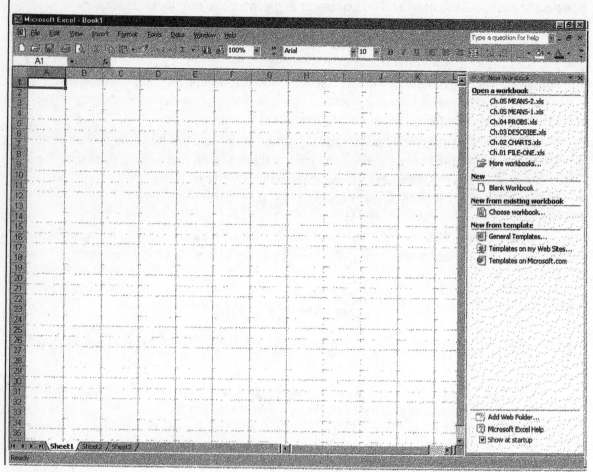

1.2 USING EXCEL

We will introduce Excel by discussing three major topics within this section. They include first a description of the parts that make up the Excel window. Next we will discuss the use of dialog boxes for communicating with Excel and last how to perform a number of Excel basic tasks.

1.2.1 The Excel Window

If this is your first look at an Excel window such as Figure 1.1, you may feel a sense of panic! How can you ever come to grasp the use of such a complex appearing presentation?

Three thoughts may help you overcome your feeling of panic. First, Excel has many features that you will never need to use. Second, it has more than one way to complete most actions. Consequently, it is not necessary for you to know everything about Excel in order to make effective use of it. Third, the window is organized into lines starting at the top with the line labeled as *Microsoft Excel—Book1* on the left side of Figure 1.1. Our consideration of the window is simplified by starting at the top and considering the important aspects of each line one at a time.

The top line of the Excel window is called the **Title Bar.** The *Microsoft Excel* label refers to the computer software program being used and the label *Book1* is the default name for what Excel calls a *Workbook*. A workbook is made up of one or more *Worksheets*. Each worksheet may be used to represent data and descriptive text, to perform computations and to display charts. A worksheet is divided into *columns* which are labeled as *A, B, C* and so on, and divided into *rows* which are labeled as *1, 2, 3* and so on. The intersection of a row and a column forms a *cell* in which you can enter values, text, formulas or functions (special predefined formulas). The first of these worksheets within the *Book1* workbook is displayed in Figure 1.1. You may access additional worksheets by pointing and clicking on the tabs labeled **Sheet2** and **Sheet3** at the bottom of the worksheet.

There are other names you may hear used when someone is referring to a workbook. These include spreadsheet, file and worksheet. However, the term *Spreadsheet* actually refers to the category of software which includes Excel, *File* refers to the workbook as saved on a computer's hard disk drive, CD or diskette, and *Worksheet* is an element of an Excel workbook.

As you view the title bar of the Excel window note it includes the previously mentioned **Maximize** button (second button from the right). In addition it includes the button for closing Excel. The **Close** button is the first button on the right

The second line down in the Excel window is called the **Menu Bar**. It provides nine or more different menus usually starting on the left with the selection **File** and ending on the right with **Help**. Excel commands are organized into pull-down menus. You pull down (or open) a menu by pointing and clicking on a name on the menu bar. After you open a menu, you point and click to choose a command from the list of commands presented on it. We will be using items from the menu bar many times in this manual. In addition to the menu selections, the menu bar includes the *Ask a Question* box **(not available in Excel 2000)**. Section 1.3 below discusses the use of this resource. Finally on the far right of the menu bar are the buttons for maximizing and closing the *Book1* workbook window. These are in addition to the buttons on the *title bar* for maximizing and the closing the Excel itself.

Excel includes 20 of what is called toolbars **(Excel 2000 has 15).** Each toolbar includes buttons identified with icons representing commands, and also boxes that list available options. The toolbars allow you to select frequently used commands and options more quickly than you can by using the menus. The third line of Figure 1.1 shows the two toolbars that are most frequently used and most frequently displayed in the Excel window. On the left is the **Standard Toolbar** on the right is the **Formatting Toolbar.**

To determine the purpose of each element of a tool bar, point to the icon or box. A small descriptor of one or so words will appear below the toolbar element. These are called *ToolTips*. To select a command, you should point and click on the appropriate toolbar icon. To select an option from a toolbar list box, point and click on the down-pointing arrow on the right side of the box. A drop-down list will appear with the possible options. You select an option by pointing and clicking on it.

The fourth line from the top in Figure 1.1 provides two pieces of information about the cell within the worksheet that is called the **Active Cell** or **Cell Pointer**. It is that cell which is ready to have its contents entered or modified. It is identified on the worksheet with a heavy border around it. In Figure 1.1 you will note that the active cell is cell A1. If you point and click on another cell in the worksheet, the active cell will change to the cell you clicked. The area on the right of the fourth line is called the **Formula Bar.** It shows the contents of the active cell and can be used for entering or editing the contents of the cell. On the left side of the fourth line is the **Name Box**. It displays the cell address for the active cell. In between these two elements is an icon labeled as *fx*. It provides access to the *Insert Function* resource. Its use will be discussed below in subsection 1.4.2.

Below the name box and formula bar is the active worksheet window on the left and the *Task Pane* window (may not appear on your screen) on the right (**Excel 2000 does not include Task Panes**). As previously mentioned, the worksheet window consists of rows and columns. The intersection of a row and a column defines a cell. The column letters above the cells and row numbers to the left of the cells provide an address (or name) for each cell. This row of letters starting with *A* and ending with *L* in Figure 1.1 and the column of numbers starting with *1* and ending with *35* are sometimes called the **Worksheet Frame.** Directly below the worksheet on the left are the **Sheet Tabs**. As mentioned above, additional worksheets within the workbook are made active by pointing and clicking on the tabs labeled as **Sheet2**, **Sheet3** and so on.

Your worksheet can include more rows and/or columns than just those displayed on your screen. In fact, the Excel worksheet can include up to 256 columns labeled A though Z, then AA through AZ, BA through BZ and so on up to IA through IV (eye-vee). In addition, it can have 65,536 rows labeled 1 though 65,536. As previously pointed out, Figure 1.1 displays only columns A though L and rows 1 through 35. Your computer screen may display more or fewer columns and rows. The number shown depends on a number of considerations such as your version of Excel, the size of your monitor, the size of the window, the toolbars displayed and so on.

In order to display different areas of the active worksheet, the Excel window provides two scroll bars. The first is on the very right side of the worksheet itself. It is called the **Vertical Scroll Bar** and can be identified by the upward pointing arrow at its very top right and a downward pointed arrow at the very bottom right. To view a lower part of the active worksheet, move the mouse pointer to the bottom arrow on the vertical scroll bar. Press and hold down the left mouse button. Note that the row identifiers on the left of the worksheet are increased. A similar procedure using the top arrow on the vertical scroll bar will reverse the process.

The window also includes a **Horizontal Scroll Bar**. It is shown on the right in the row displaying the sheet tabs. The right pointing arrow at the right of the scroll bar can be used to scroll to right of the active worksheet. The left pointing arrow at the left of the scroll bar can be used to scroll back to the left. You may wish to try this scroll bar also.

To the right of the worksheet window is the *Task Pane* window (may not appear on your screen). The task pane provides easy access to commonly used commands. The task pane of Figure 1.1 is the *New Workbook* task pane. It facilitates opening Excel workbooks stored on your computer. As you develop a worksheet, different task panes may be displayed. In addition to the *New Workbook* pane of Figure 1.1, you may encounter three others, the *Clipboard*, the *Search* and the *Insert Clip Art* task panes. At the top right of the task pane window is a *Close* button which can be used to eliminate the task pane. Next to the close button is *Other Task Panes* arrow. Clicking on it allows access to the other three types of task panes. If you wish to eliminate all task panes from appearing, click on **View** on the menu bar and click on **Task Pane** on the pull-down menu to eliminate the check mark. On the other hand, if your opening Excel screen doesn't include the *New Workbook* task pane, click on **View** and click on **Task Pane** to add a check mark.

The line below the sheet tabs and horizontal scroll bar, displays the **Status Bar.** It includes three elements. The **Mode Indicator** on the left of the status bar indicates what Excel is prepared to do next. In Figure 1.1 it displays *Ready*. To the right of the mode indicator is the **AutoCalculate Area**. It provides the capability to obtain a quick sum of selected cells. Five other functions are available by right clicking in the AutoCalculate area. Finally, the right side of the status bar provides **Key Indicators**. It shows the status of some keys such as the *Caps Lock* and *Num Lock*. Press your Caps Lock key to demonstrate this part of the status bar.

This completes our review of the elements of the Excel window. As you have explored these elements, you may have noted that the mouse pointer changes shape when it is moved from one part of the window to another. When the mouse pointer is within the worksheet, its shape is a block plus sign. When the pointer is over an icon, sheet tab or scroll bar, its shape is an upward pointing block arrow. When it is over the formula bar, its shape is an I-beam and so on. The mouse pointer can take on over a dozen different shapes. Generally the shape of the pointer indicates what action is to be taken by you.

1.2.2 Excel Dialog Boxes

Dialog boxes are displayed in the Excel window so you can enter information required by an Excel command. You may have noticed when you select a pull-down menu from the menu bar, the name of some of the commands on the menu are followed by ellipsis (…). These indicate that the command requires you to enter information through a dialog box. In addition, some commands accessed through toolbars will present a dialog box for additional information. Figure 1.2 presents an example Excel dialog box. If you wish to view this specific dialog box on your computer screen, click **Tools** from the menu bar and **Options** from the subsequent pull-down menu.

Like the Excel window, a dialog box may seem complex to you at first. However, Excel dialog boxes are all made up of a standard set of elements, called controls. In fact, Windows itself and all Window programs are made up of these same standard controls. We have listed the eight standard controls in Table 1.1 on page 9. The table also gives a brief description and identifies example controls shown in Figure 1.2 **(for Excel 2000 see Figure D.2 of Appendix D).**

Figure 1.2 Elements of Dialog Boxes

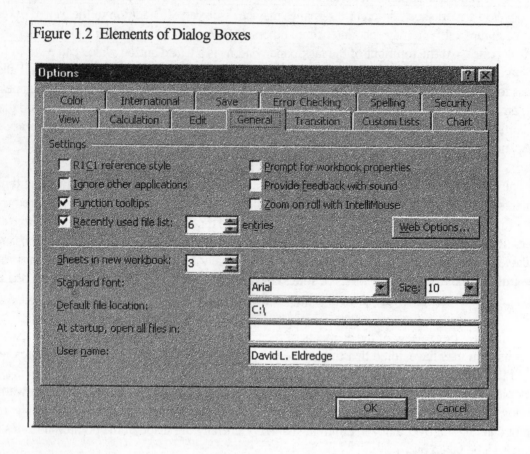

In our analysis procedures throughout this manual we will use these eight names to tell you how to respond to various dialog boxes. Accordingly, you may wish to refer back to Table 1.1 as you work through this manual. Perhaps a photocopy of this table for future reference would be helpful to you. At this point, see if you can locate on Figure 1.2 or on your computer screen the examples listed in the right column of Table 1.1.

Sometimes a dialog box will cover over something you want to see on the screen. You can move the box by pointing to the colored (usually blue) title bar (labeled as *Options* in Figure 1.2) at the top of the box and dragging it with the mouse to a new position on the screen.

Many dialog boxes include a *Collapse Dialog Box* button. It has an upward pointing red arrow and is located on the right side of text boxes. If you click it, the dialog box is collapsed and only the text box is displayed. The required data can be entered into the text box by keying or dragging. Then click the *Redisplay Dialog Box* button. It has a downward pointing arrow on the right side of the text box. The original dialog box will then be restored. Refer to Figure 2.3 of the next chapter for an example of the collapse dialog box. See if you can identify the three in this figure.

Table 1.1 Dialog Box Controls

CONTROL	DESCRIPTION	FIGURE 1.2 EXAMPLES
Tab	A button that resembles a file folder tab at the top of a dialog box. Clicking a tab displays a different page in the dialog box.	Thirteen **tabs** beginning with *View* and ending with *Security*
Text Box	A data entry area for text or numbers. Move the mouse pointer to the text box and it changes to the I-beam shape. Click and type the appropriate entry.	**Text box** labeled as *User Name* with the entry *David L. Eldredge*
List Box	A scrolling list of specified choices. Click on the up or down arrow on the right side of the list to scroll through it. Then click on your choice. The selected item appears in highlighted text.	Figure 1.2 does not include. Click on *Custom Lists* tab. Its dialog box includes a **list box** labeled *Custom lists.*
Drop-Down List Box	A list box that does not display its scrolling list until you click on the down arrow on the right side of its displayed text box. Click on your choice and the selected item appears in the text box above the list.	**Drop-down list box** labeled as *Size* with the entry *10.*
Command Button	A large rectangular button that executes or cancels a dialog box. In addition, some command buttons have ellipsis that indicate it will open an additional dialog box.	**Command buttons** labeled as *OK* and *Cancel*
Check Box	A square box for selecting an option. A check mark in a check box indicates the option is selected. Click on the check box to select or deselect the option. You can select more than one check box.	**Check boxes** under the label *Settings*. The check box labeled as *Recently used file list* is selected.
Option Button	A round button for selecting an option (also called a radio button). A dark circle in an option button indicates the option is selected. Click on the option button to select the option. To deselect an option, click on another option button. You can only select one option from a group of options.	Figure 1.2 does not include. Click on *Calculation* tab. Its dialog box includes three **option buttons** under the label *Calculation.* Only one is to be selected.
Spinner	A box displaying a number with an up and a down arrow to the right of the box. Click on the arrows to make changes in the number by increments of one.	**Spinner** is labeled as *Sheets in New Workbook* and its current value is *3.*

The dialog boxes for complex operations are presented as Wizards. A **Wizard** is a sequence of dialog boxes that simplifies the operation by guiding you through the process step by step. The title bar for each dialog box in the series designates it as *Step X of N* where X and N will be numbers. The dialog box for each step asks you to enter information through the controls of Table 1.1. Generally, Wizard dialog boxes include a command button labeled *Back* to go back one step and make revisions. Another command button is labeled *Next* which steps forward to the next step. Others are labeled with a question mark in a balloon for *Help*, with *Cancel* and with *Finish*. Refer to later Figures 1.7 and 1.9 for the first steps of two Wizards we will be using in this manual.

1.2.3 Excel Basic Tasks

Now that you have some familiarity with the Excel Window and with the use of dialog boxes, we will consider a number of basic Excel tasks. You will need to use all of these during the development of your worksheets for performing statistical analyses in this manual. Most of these tasks can be done in more than one way. Generally, we will take the approach of using the simplest way. For example, saving a workbook by clicking the **Save** icon instead of clicking **File** on the menu bar and then **Save** on the subsequent pull-down menu.

To begin you should go through the **Start-up Procedure** of Section 1.1. The result will be a blank worksheet similar to Figure 1.1. You are now ready to perform the following tasks.

1. **Moving Around a Worksheet.** Before entering or modifying the contents of a particular cell, you need to make that cell the *Active Cell (Cell Pointer)*. You can select the cell to be active with either the mouse or the keyboard. To use the mouse point and click on the cell. Use the mouse to make cell B1 the active cell.

   If the cell is not currently displayed on the screen, the vertical and horizontal scroll bars can be used to display the area containing the cell, and then the mouse used to point and click. Now make cell P40 the active cell.

   In addition to the mouse, Excel allows the use of the keyboard to move around a worksheet. The most frequently used keys are (1) the four **arrow** keys which move one cell up, down, left or right, (2) the **Page Up (PgUp)** and **Page Down (PgDn)** keys which move up or down one full screen, (3) the **Home** key which moves to column A of the current row, and (4) the **Crtl** key and **Home** key pushed simultaneously which moves to cell A1. You should now try all four of these sets of keys for moving around the worksheet.

2. **Entering Text (Labels).** As previously mentioned, you may enter values, text, formulas and functions (predefined formulas) in each cell of a worksheet. Although text may be used as data, usually it is used to label or identify the data in a worksheet as we do in what follows. Make cell B1 the active cell and use the keyboard to enter the worksheet title: **CHAPTER ONE WORKBOOK.** Press the down arrow to make cell B2 the active cell and key in **Your Name** (use your actual name). Select cell A3 by using the arrow keys or the mouse pointer. Key in **Today's Date** (use the actual date). Select cell D3 and enter a file name to use for saving the workbook, say, **FILE-ONE.xls.** Select cell A5 and key in the label **Numbers.** Your worksheet will resemble that of Figure 1.3 although yours will have your name and the date. Also, Figure 1.3 shows the results of the following steps in this procedure.

3. **Entering Values (Numbers).** Values or numbers are the major entries in most worksheets. Select cell A6, key the number **1** and use the down arrow (or press the **Enter** key) to move the cell pointer to cell A7. Key the number **2** and move to cell A8. Continue down the column until you have entered the number **5.**

Figure 1.3 File-One Worksheet

	A	B	C	D	E	F
1		CHAPTER ONE WORKBOOK				
2		Your Name				
3	Today's Date			FILE-ONE.xls		
4						
5	NUMBERS			NUMBERS		
6	10			10		
7	2			2		
8	3			3		
9	4			4		
10	5			5		
11						
12	24			24		
13						

4. **Entering Formulas.** Formulas provide the true power of spreadsheet software such as Excel. To demonstrate, select cell A12. Use the keyboard to enter **=A6+A7+A8+A9+A10** and press **Enter**. The value shown in A12 is 15, the sum of the values in cells A6 through A10. Change the value in A6 to **10** and notice A12 displays the new total, 24 as shown in Figure 1.3. Select cell A12 again and notice that your equation is displayed in the formula bar. Formulas use the common mathematical symbols of **+** for addition, **-** for subtraction, ***** for multiplication, **/** for division and **^** for raising a number to a power.

5. **Copying Cell Contents.** You can copy text, values, formulas and functions from one cell to another and from one worksheet to another. You can copy the contents of one cell at a time or the contents of a group of cells at one time. Click on cell A5 and drag through cell A10. Notice that these cells are highlighted. Next click on the **Copy** icon. It looks like two sheets of paper with the top right corner turned down. It is the seventh icon from the left on the standard toolbar in Figure 1.1. This copies the contents of the selected cells to an Excel feature called the **Clipboard**. Next click on cell D5. Finally click on the **Paste** icon. It looks like a clipboard and a sheet of paper and is the eighth icon from the left on the standard toolbar in Figure 1.1. This copies the contents of the clipboard to cells D5 through D10.

A *Clipboard* icon will be shown about in cell E11. This feature of Excel is a *Smart Tag* which shows options available to you **(not available in Excel 2000)**. When you use paste, the Smart Tag provides five options for formatting the copied material. A number of different Smart Tags are available in Excel. If you wish to eliminate a Smart Tag, press the **Esc** (Escape) key.

Now repeat this process to copy the formula in cell A12 to cell D12. Notice the contents of D12 as shown in the *formula bar*. The formula was copied but the cell addresses in the formula were changed from A6 through A10 to D6 through D10. This is the result of a feature called **relative addressing** for cells that will be useful in future chapters. Another form of addressing called **absolute addressing** will be discussed when needed later in this manual.

If your worksheet had the New Workbook task pane displayed on the right of the worksheet, you will notice this second copy operation caused the *Clipboard* task pane to be displayed.

6. **Saving a Workbook.** As you develop your workbook, it is temporarily held in the computer's memory. This copy is erased when the computer is turned off. For permanent storage, you need to save your workbook on an external storage media such as a diskette. To accomplish this put a diskette in the disk drive that is appropriate for your computer system. For this discussion, we will assume it is drive A. Point and click on the **Save** icon. It looks like a diskette and is the third icon from the left on the standard toolbar in Figure 1.1. A dialog box entitled *Save As* will appear. You must complete three actions. First click on the arrow to the right of the drop-down list box labeled *Save in,* and click on the **3½ Floppy (A:).** Second, click in the far left of the text box labeled *File Name.* Use the **Delete** key to eliminate the default file name given and then key your file name, **FILE-ONE.** Excel will add the extension or suffix *.xls*. Finally, click on the **Save** command button. The light on the A drive should come on briefly as your file is saved to the diskette in that drive.

7. **Closing a Workbook.** Click the **Close** button which is the first button on the right of the *menu bar*. Alternatively, you can click **File** on the menu bar and then **Close** on the pull-down menu. The result will be that the menu bar, the toolbars and so on will continue to be shown on the screen but the worksheet will be deleted from the screen. If you had not saved the workbook, a dialog box will open reminding you to save your workbook. If you wished to now work on a new workbook, you would click the **New Workbook** icon. It looks like a single piece of paper with its upper right corner turned down and is the first icon on the left of the standard toolbar in Figure 1.1.

8. **Retrieving a Workbook.** The above steps have had you create a worksheet, save it to a diskette and than erase it from the computer's memory. We will now read it back into the memory from the diskette file. Click on the **Open** icon. It looks like an open file folder and is the second icon from the left on the standard toolbar in Figure 1.1. In the resulting dialog box click on the arrow to right of the drop-down list box labeled as *Look in* and click on **3½ Floppy (A:).** A list of files will be displayed in a box under the *Look in* list box and one (perhaps the only one) should be *FILE-ONE.xls*. Click on **FILE-ONE.xls** and then on the **Open** command button (alternatively you can double click on FILE-ONE.xls). Your workbook will be loaded into the computer and appear on the screen.

9. **Printing a Worksheet.** You also will want to print your worksheets. Click on the **Print** icon. It looks like a printer and is the fourth icon from the left on the standard toolbar in Figure 1.1. Your worksheet will be printed.

You can improve the readability of your worksheet by including on your printout the worksheet frame (the row and column headings) and the worksheet gridlines. To select these two options before printing, click on **File** from the menu bar and click on **Page Setup** from the pull-down menu. The Page Setup dialog box that appears has four dialog tabs. Click on the **Sheet** tab. Use the mouse pointer to place a check in the **Gridlines** check box and the **Row and Column Headings** check box. Finish by clicking the **OK** command button. Now select the print icon to print the revised worksheet.

10. **Exiting Excel.** A three-step procedure is recommended for exiting Excel. First save the workbook again (number 6 above). Second, close the workbook (number 7). Third exit Excel by clicking the **Close** button (first button on the right of the *title bar*). Alternatively, you could click on **File** from the menu bar and then **Exit** from the subsequent pull-down menu. The result will be a return to the Windows screen.

11. **Exiting Windows.** Click the **Start** button in the lower left corner of the window to obtain the *Start* menu. If you are using

* *Windows XP*, click on **Turn Off Computer** at the bottom of the *Start* menu. In the resulting dialog box, click the **Turn Off** button.

* *Windows 2000*, click on **Shut Down** at the bottom of the *Start* menu. In the resulting dialog box, make sure the **Shut Down** option is shown in the drop-down list box. Click **OK**.

* *Windows 98*, click on **Shut Down** at the bottom of the *Start* menu. In the resulting dialog box, select the option button labeled **Shut down.** Click **OK**.

Your computer system will either automatically shut down or the message *It's now safe to turn off your computer* will be displayed. You may then turn off your computer and monitor.

If you are new to Windows and Excel, Sections 1.1 and 1.2 should have presented enough information for you to be able to use them at a basic level. A higher level of proficiency will be yours through repeated use and exploration of Excel's capabilities. In addition, Excel provides help through the on-line capabilities discussed next.

1.3 USING HELP

It is not possible for most persons (perhaps any person) to remember all the commands, menus, buttons, tools, functions and other details of using Excel. The developers of Excel have anticipated this problem and provide a number of on-line (available as you are using Excel) aids for helping your memory. We discuss a number of these below.

The first of these is the previously mentioned **ToolTips**. These are displayed when you move the mouse pointer to an icon or button and do not press a mouse button for a second or two. A descriptor of one or more words will then be displayed near the icon or button.

A second convenient help feature is the **Ask a Question Box** on the right side of the menu bar **(not available in Excel 2000)**. You can click in the box, type a question (or just enter a word or phrase) and press **Enter**. A drop-down list presents topics of possible help to you. Click on the most appropriate topic. The **Microsoft Excel Help System** window will open on the right of the screen. The right half of this help window provides information about your question. The left side of this window provides three means of searching for further help. The **Contents** tab provides access to help topics by general category. The **Answer Wizard** tab serves the same function as the *Ask a Question Box* and the **Index** tab provides an index to all help topics.

A third help feature is the **Office Assistant.** It is an animated graphic in the form of a paper clip (see upper right of Figure 1.4). To activate it, click on the **Microsoft Excel Help** icon on the Standard toolbar. This icon is in the form of a question mark within a cartoon balloon.

The Office Assistant can help you in two ways. First, you can have it respond with a list of topics that relate to an entry you give it. Within a balloon, it presents the question *What would you like to do*? Near the bottom of the balloon is a text box for you to key in your entry. Your entry can be a word, a phrase or a question. Next you click on the button labeled **Search**. A list of possible help topics will be presented. Click the most appropriate topic and a help screen will be provided. You may print the help screen and close after you are through with it.

The second way the Office Assistant can help you is by monitoring your work and accumulating tips on how you might better do your work. You can view the tips at any time by activating the Office Assistant. When a light bulb is shown above the Office Assistant, you may click it to view the most recent tip.

A fourth help feature is the **What's This?** command on **Help** menu as shown in Figure 1.4. When you click on *What's This?* the mouse pointer changes to a question mark and an upward pointing block arrow. Move the mouse pointer to a button on a toolbar and click the left mouse button. A help window will open that explains in more detail then a *ToolTip* the use of the toolbar button you selected. If you again click the mouse button, the help window will disappear. This help function is also available for items on the pull-down menus from the menu bar. First click the *What's This?* from the **Help** menu. Next select a menu from the menu bar and finally click on the menu selection from the pull-down menu. A help window will open for this menu selection. Click again to close the help window.

A fifth source of help is provided within many dialog boxes. Some dialog boxes have a **Question Mark** box (see the top right of Figure 1.2). A click on the question mark box changes the mouse pointer to question mark and a upward pointing block arrow. Point and click to controls in the dialog box in order to activate a help window. Many dialog boxes have Help command buttons as shown in Figures 1.5 and 1.6.

Figure 1.4 Excel Help Menu

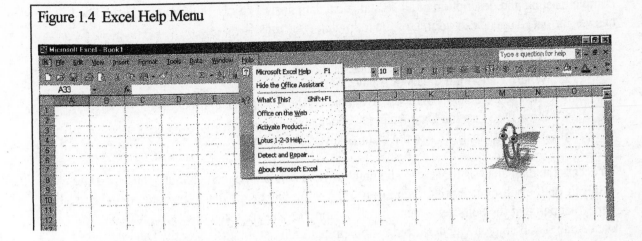

The pull-down menu of Figure 1.4 includes some additional help features that may be helpful to you. The **Office on the Web** selection displays a Microsoft Web page that includes up-to-date Excel information. Your computer must be connected to the Internet to use this command.

The **Lotus 1-2-3 Help** is for spreadsheet users who are familiar with Lotus 1-2-3 but not with Excel. To assist such persons, the developers of Excel allow you to enter Lotus 1-2-3 commands and functions, and obtain the equivalent for Excel through this help feature.

The **Detect and Repair** feature is used when Excel is not running properly or is generating errors. It will automatically find and fix errors.

1.4 USING EXCEL'S STATISTICAL FEATURES

Excel includes a number of features that facilitate the computation and charting requirements for statistical analyses. Primary among these are 18 DATA ANALYSIS TOOLS and the 80 STATISTICAL FUNCTIONS. Both of these features are used throughout this manual for facilitating statistical analysis. Three additional Excel features that support specific aspects of statistical analysis within this manual include the CHART WIZARD, the TRENDLINE feature of charts and the PIVOT TABLE WIZARD.

1.4.1 Data Analysis Tools

Excel includes 19 **data analysis tools**. One of them provides *Fourier Analysis* for engineering applications. The remaining 18 provide statistical analyses beginning with ANOVA: SINGLE-FACTOR and ending with z-TEST: TWO SAMPLES FOR MEANS. We demonstrate the use of all but one of these within the following chapters of this manual. In addition, Appendix A presents a complete listing and description of all 18 statistical data analysis tools. Utilizing a question-and-answer format, Appendix A addresses the following questions.

1. What Are the Data Analysis Tools?
2. Where Can I Find the Data Analysis Tools?
3. Are the Data Analysis Tools Available on the Computer I Am Using?
4. How Do I Use the Data Analysis Tools?
5. For What Analyses Are the Data Analysis Tools Used?

To access the data analysis tools, you should click on **Tools** on the menu bar and click on **Data Analysis** on the subsequent pull-down menu. The result will be the dialog box shown in Figure 1.5. It may happen that the pull-down menu for the computer you are using does not include the entry Data Analysis. If so, you will need to do some preparation before accessing the Data Analysis dialog box. The details of the necessary preparation are found in Appendix A under the discussion for *Question 3* in the above list.

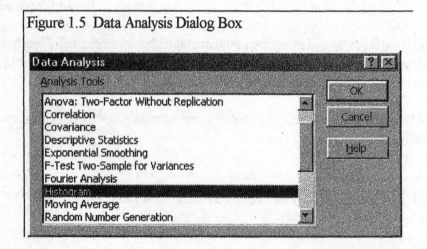

Figure 1.5 Data Analysis Dialog Box

From the dialog box of Figure 1.5, you click on the tool you wish to use. If the one you wish to use is not displayed in the list box, you click on the vertical scroll bar arrow on the right of the box to scroll to it. After you have selected the tool you wish to use, click the **OK** button. The result will be a second dialog box allowing you to enter the specific ranges and values for your data analysis problem. You may wish to try selecting a tool and viewing its dialog box. For example, refer to Figure 2.3 in Chapter 2 to see the dialog box for the HISTOGRAM data analysis tool.

The discussion in Appendix A of *Question 5* in the previous list gives a short description of the use of each of the statistical tools. In addition, it classifies the tools into six categories beginning with *Descriptive Statistics* and ending with *Time Series Forecasting*. The chapter(s) within this manual that demonstrates each statistical tool is (are) also noted.

You may wish to explore the purpose and use of some of these tools at this time through the Help System. First, select the analysis tool of interest from the Data Analysis dialog box (Figure 1.5). Then in the subsequent dialog box click on the **Help** command button.

1.4.2 Statistical Functions

There are hundreds of built-in functions (predefined formulas) in Excel. Eighty are classified as **Statistical Functions** beginning with AVEDEV and ending with ZTEST. We use many of these within this manual. In addition, Appendix B presents a complete listing and description of all the statistical functions. Again we use a question-and-answer format and address the following.

1. What Are the Statistical Functions?
2. How Do the Statistical Functions and the Data Analysis Tools Differ?
3. How Do I Use the Statistical Functions?
4. For What Analyses Are the Statistical Functions Used?

The Statistical Functions both supplement and duplicate the analysis capabilities of the Data Analysis Tools. However there are a number of differences that are presented in the discussion in Appendix B of *Question 2* of above list. The primary difference is that the results from the *Tools* usually are numbers and the results from the *Functions* are formulas.

Access to the statistical functions is facilitated through Excel's INSERT FUNCTION command. It has an icon labeled with the symbol *fx*. It is between the name box and formula box. Click on the icon and the dialog box of Figure 1.6 will be displayed. Next click on the category **Statistical** from the drop-down list box that is labeled as *Or select a category*. As a result the scrolling list box at the bottom will present the 80 statistical functions. You can scroll through the list to find the function you wish to use. Next click on the function you wish to use and a second dialog box will be shown. For example, refer to Figure 3.8 of Chapter 3 to see the dialog box for the function VARP that computes the population variance.

The discussion in Appendix B of *Question 4* in the previous list gives a short description of the use of each of the statistical functions. In addition, we have classified the functions into fifteen categories beginning with *Descriptive Statistics—Measures of Central Location* and ending with *Regression and Correlation—Exponential Regression Analysis*.

You will note in Figure 1.6 below the boxes, a brief description of the function that is highlighted in the lower list. Much greater detail about the selected function can be obtained by clicking on the **Help on this function** label in the lower left corner of the dialog box. This will activate the **Microsoft Excel Help System** discussed in the prior section. You may wish to explore the help facility for one or more functions of interest to you at this time.

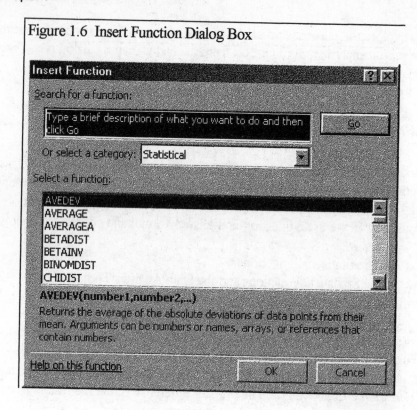

Figure 1.6 Insert Function Dialog Box

1.4.3 Other Statistical Features

Graphs and charts are effective in summarizing and visually presenting statistical data. Excel's CHART WIZARD makes the development of graphs and charts somewhat easy. It provides 14 *standard chart types*. Furthermore, each of these standard chart types has from two to seven *chart sub-types* to provide variations in the presentation of the chart type. In addition, Excel is distributed with 20 *custom chart types* and you may add to that list of custom chart types as demonstrated in Appendix C.

The CHART WIZARD is accessed with a mouse click on its icon on the standard toolbar. Its icon depicts a bar/column chart (see Figure 1.1 to the left of the number *100%*). A click on the icon will result in the first of four dialog boxes that make up the Chart Wizard. The Step 1 dialog box is shown in Figure 1.7. You may wish to try this on your computer. If the **Standard Types** tab is not in front as shown in Figure 1.7, click on it.

Figure 1.7 shows the names for 11 of the 14 Chart Types in the scrolling list on the left. The remaining three are at the bottom of the scrolling list and are hidden from view. These three are the *Cylinder*, the *Cone* and the *Pyramid* charts. All three resemble a three-dimensional bar/column chart with the bars either in the form of a cylinder, cone or pyramid.

The CHART WIZARD is presented in detail in Section 2.2 of the next chapter. In addition, it is used in Chapters 4, 10, 11 and 12.

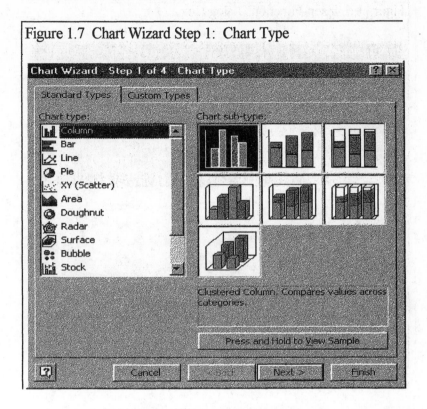

Figure 1.7 Chart Wizard Step 1: Chart Type

A second additional Excel resource that is useful for statistical analyses is the TRENDLINE feature of charts. It helps you to easily find the best relationship for data plotted on a chart. The relationship can be one of six forms: linear, logarithmic, polynomial, power, exponential or moving average as indicated in Figure 1.8. Trendline computes the equation for the relationship. The equation together with a measure of the goodness of the fit of the line to the data can be shown on the chart.

You can add trendlines to seven of the fourteen standard types of charts available from the Chart Wizard. These include the unstacked, two-dimensional versions of the area, bar, bubble, column, line, stock and XY (Scatter) charts. The Trendline feature is accessed by first activating a chart for editing by clicking inside the chart. This action results in the addition of the *Chart* menu to the menu bar. Next select the **Chart** menu and the **Add Trendline** selection from the subsequent pull-down menu. The result will be as shown in Figure 1.8. Trendline is presented in detail in Section 10.1 of Chapter 10. In addition, Trendline is used in Chapter 11.

The third additional Excel feature for statistical analysis we use within this manual is the PIVOT TABLE WIZARD. A pivot table is a tabular summary of a list of data. The summary presented by a pivot table can be data sums, frequency counts, averages, maximums, minimums, standard deviations and so on. The Pivot Table feature is accessed by selecting **Data** from the menu bar and **PivotTable and PivotChart** from the subsequent pull-down menu. The result is the first of three dialog boxes as shown in Figure 1.9.

Figure 1.8 Add Trendline Dialog Box

Figure 1.9 PivotTable and PivotChart Wizard Step 1

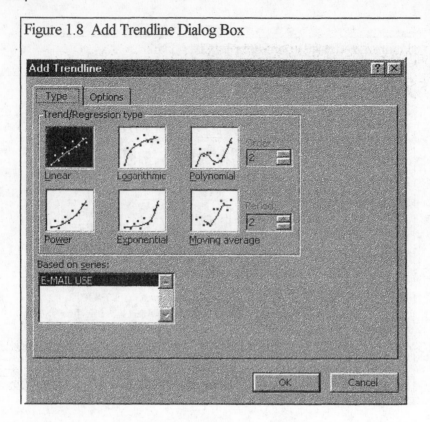

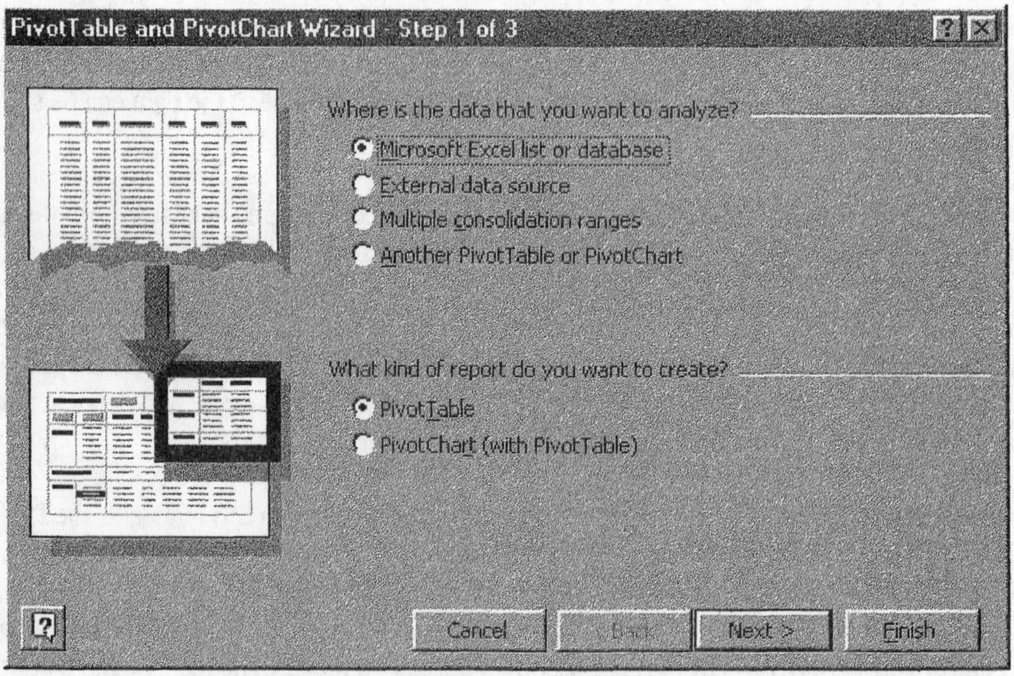

The primary advantage a Pivot Table has over a manually entered summary table is that it is interactive. This means (1) the table changes automatically as the source data on which it is based changes and (2) you can change the view of the source data to see more details or calculate different summaries. We demonstrate the PIVOT TABLE WIZARD in Section 9.3 of Chapter 9 to compute frequency count of data for qualitative variables.

1.5 USING GOOD WORKSHEET PRACTICES

The process of developing and maintaining an effective worksheet involves the activities of planning, building, testing and protecting.

Planning for the development of a worksheet requires that you take some time considering the worksheet before you sit down at the computer. You need to decide

1. What the purpose of worksheet is,
2. What the inputs are,
3. What the outputs are to be, and
4. What the intermediate computational and charting requirements are.

Once you have identified these major elements of the worksheet, you should make a rough sketch of the layout of all these elements. An effective worksheet will usually have separate areas for different uses, and will have a vertical layout as opposed to horizontal. For example, the worksheet can begin with identification material, and below it might be an area that contains all the input data. The area devoted to computations might be below the input data and the final results below the computations. In some instances, this order of identification material, followed by input, followed by computations and then by outputs might be reordered to meet the specific requirements.

As you get into actually building the worksheet you may have to revise parts of this initial plan. The plan provides a starting place for building the worksheet.

Building the worksheet involves entering textual material (labels), values (numbers), formulas, functions, and charts. For your worksheet to be effective, you need to make sure it is understandable to you and to any others who have the need to use at it. To accomplish this consider the following guidelines.

- Begin the worksheet with suitable **Identification Material**—(1) a title or short description of the worksheet, (2) your name, (3) the date and (4) the file name for saving the worksheet.
- Use labels to identify all inputs, intermediate results and final outputs.
- Use currency, comma and integer (whole numbers) format wherever appropriate.
- Use uppercase and lower case letters as you would in a written report.
- Use bold, italics and underlining where appropriate for emphasis.
- Generally put data in columns if it is appropriate.

- Use consistent alignment and formatting.
- Write clear formulas by perhaps dividing complicated computations into more than one cell.
- Add *Cell Comments* to cells that need further explanations. (Click on **Insert** on the menu bar, click on **Comment**, type your note and click. A red triangle in upper right corner of the cell indicates the presence of the comment. It will be displayed on the screen when the mouse pointer is over the cell. It can also be printed.)
- Enlarge charts above the default size.
- Use the on-line help system to answer questions that might arise.

Testing the worksheet involves using input data for which the output values are known. These known output values are then compared to the worksheet output to determine if the formulas are correct. The test input values can be actual values for which the results are known or can be values for which the results can easily be calculated by hand. If the worksheet has computational options, all the possible options should be tested. Without a verification of your worksheet, you cannot be assured it is without errors.

Protecting your worksheet from hardware and software failures should begin as you are building the worksheet and continue through out its use. Protecting your investment of time and mental energy involves.

- Saving your worksheet frequently as you are building it and after it is completed.
- Keeping backup copies of your worksheet file on one or more diskettes.
- Keeping a printout of the worksheet.
- Keeping a second printout of the worksheet showing the formulas, the row and column headings and cell comments. (To display the formulas and comments on the screen, click on **Tools** on the menu bar, click on **Options** and click on the **View** tab. Under *Comments* select the option button for **Comments & indicator** and under *Window Options* select the **Formula** check box and click on **OK**. Next to prepare for printing, click on **File** from the menu bar, **Page Setup,** and **Sheet**. On the Sheet dialog box check **Gridlines,** and **Row and Column Headings.** From the *Comments* drop-down list box select either **At end of sheet** or **As displayed on sheet**. Then print the worksheet.)
- Not giving anyone (including your professor) your only diskette with your worksheet file.

It is safe to say that almost all computer users will experience some problem that can be reduced by adhering to the above guidelines.

1.6 USING THIS MANUAL WITH YOUR TEXTBOOK ⸻

As stated in the first paragraph of this chapter, *The purpose of this manual is to introduce you to the (Excel) features that facilitate the computing and charting requirements of your study and use of statistics.* The built-in capabilities of Excel allow you to easily computerize many of the methods in the textbook you may be studying.

This manual can be used as a companion to many business statistics textbooks. This is possible because there is a consistency in the organization and flow of most, although not all, of the material presented in business statistics textbooks. The typical book will have the following organization.

1. A chapter or two of **introduction** covering the importance of statistics, some basic definitions, the types of data and sources of data.

2. One, two or three-chapter presentation of **descriptive statistics** covering graphical and numerical methods.

3. One, two or three-chapter presentation of **probability and probability distributions** both discrete and continuous.

4. A chapter or part of a chapter presentation of **sampling distributions**.

5. Three or so chapters covering **statistical inference** (estimation and testing) for means, proportions and variances for one population and two populations.

6. A chapter on the **analysis of variance**.

7. One, two or three chapters on **regression analysis**.

8. A chapter or two on **time series forecasting** sometimes including a presentation of index numbers.

9. Perhaps a chapter on **nonparametric statistics**.

10. Perhaps a chapter on **decision analysis**.

In addition to these topics, a typical textbook may have a chapter on the uses of the **chi-square statistic** and another chapter on **statistical quality control**. The placement of these two chapters in the above sequence is not as consistent among textbooks.

If you open your textbook to the *Contents* listing at the front, you may notice your textbook adheres to the above sequence of topics to a large degree.

This manual also follows the above sequence. However, we did have some decisions to make with regard to the coverage of statistical inference for the one and two population situations (*number 5* in the above list). Some textbooks cover point estimates and confidence intervals separate from hypothesis testing. Others lump them together. Some cover the statistical inference of means with that for variances. Others put the statistical inference for proportions with means. Some cover the one population and two population situations together, others do not. Our approach is to present these topics modularly so the manual can be used with any of these different textbook organizations.

We present one chapter for the statistical inference of means, one for proportions and one for variances. Within each of these three chapters the one population and two population situations are covered in separate sections. Each section has subsections for point estimates with confidence intervals and for hypothesis testing. Accordingly, you should be able to easily identify the parts of this manual that match up with topics in your textbook by referring to the *Contents* listing at the beginning of this manual.

We also had decisions to make for the placement of the chi-square chapter. We have elected to place the chi-square chapter after the chapters dealing primarily with single variable statistical analysis (through Chapter 8) and before those dealing with two or more variable statistical analysis. We do so since the chi-square chapter begins with single variable analysis and ends with two-variable analysis.

Finally, the quality control chapter was placed at the end. We did so since this seems to be the most popular location for the business statistics textbooks we have reviewed. The resulting sequence of chapters for this manual is given by the *Brief Contents* on page iii.

Since our intent is that this manual is to be used in conjunction with a statistics textbook, we have not included end-of-the-chapter exercises. Once you have worked your way through a topic within this manual, you should be able to apply Excel to similar examples and exercises from your book.

As you work through the example analyses of this manual, you will develop your own Excel worksheets for performing the required computations and charting we demonstrate. Although your worksheets will generally resemble those given in the manual, you may detect some small differences. The differences arise from additional editing and formatting which we have done in order to make the figures more understandable to the readers of this manual. In some instances we have enlarged charts and column widths, and others we have added borders to cells and used different font style such as italics or boldface. These sorts of cosmetic changes can be made by you but are not necessary for understanding the statistical analyses presented.

Finally, let us point out that all the Excel worksheets developed in this manual are included on the CD at the back of the book. This allows for some flexibility in how you use this manual. If you wish to learn how to develop such Excel worksheets, you should work through the step-by-step procedures of this manual. On the other hand, if you wish to perform the analysis represented by a particular worksheet in this manual, you may want to just use the appropriate worksheet from the CD.

CHAPTER 2. DESCRIPTIVE GRAPHS AND CHARTS

Descriptive graphs and charts are easily developed using two Excel features. The first is the HISTOGRAM data analysis tool presented in **Section 2.1**. This tool first computes a frequency distribution for a data set of one variable and then can be used to create a histogram and an ogive for the distribution. The second Excel feature for graphs and charts is the CHART WIZARD presented in **Section 2.2**. It provides the capability to create many different chart types. In Section 2.2 we demonstrate its use for constructing frequency polygons, bar/column charts and pie charts for single variable data sets. In addition, we demonstrate its use for creating a scatter diagram for a data set of two quantitative variables.

2.1 THE HISTOGRAM ANALYSIS TOOL

The HISTOGRAM tool has the capability to create (1) a frequency distribution, (2) a histogram, (3) an ogive (a cumulative relative frequency polygon) and (4) a histogram sorted in descending frequency order (called a Pareto Chart). To demonstrate the development of a frequency distribution, a histogram and an ogive consider the following example.

To earn money for school expenses, the three daughters in the Waspork family, Kei, Lei and Dei, decided to open and run a stand selling shaved ice cones near the shopping mall in their hometown of The Meadowlands. Their mother, Kriti, constructed the stand and purchased the needed equipment. The girls have now been in business for 50 days. The 50 values of Table 2.1 are the number of cones sold each day.

Table 2.1 Number of Cones Sold Each Day									
42	30	26	36	32	32	34	26	57	50
30	55	58	30	37	58	50	64	30	52
53	49	40	33	30	43	47	46	49	32
50	61	40	31	32	30	31	40	40	60
52	74	28	37	23	29	35	43	25	54

2.1.1 Frequency Distribution

The first step in developing a frequency distribution is to specify the classes (intervals) for the distribution. The complete specification of the classes includes (1) the number of classes, (2) the width of the classes and (3) the beginning value for the first class. In Excel the classes are called bins. If the bins are not specified, Excel will automatically set the number of bins approximately equal to the square root of the number of values in the data set.   In addition it will set the width of each of the classes equal to the difference between the largest data value and smallest data value divided by the number of classes. Finally, the beginning value for the first class will be set equal to the lowest data value. The result is a quick look at the frequency distribution for the data set. However, it oftentimes is difficult to interpret.

Consequently, it is **strongly suggested that you specify the classes/bins** for your data set. Begin by selecting the number of classes/bins to be between 5 and 20. As a rule of thumb use 5 classes for a sample of 25 or less, up to 7 classes for a sample of 50, up to 10 classes for a sample of 100 and up to 20 classes for a sample of 400 or more. Next identify the largest and the smallest values in the data set. The two Excel functions MIN and MAX can be used to determine these two values for a large data set. The class width should be approximately equal to the difference between the largest and smallest values divided by the number of classes/bins. However the interpretation of the results will usually be made easier if the width is adjusted to be a multiple of the numbers two, five or ten.

To demonstrate this process, suppose we decide to first consider five bins for the fifty data values in Table 2.1. We then note that the largest value is 74 and the smallest is 23 so the difference is equal to 51. If we were to use five bins, the class width could be 51 / 5 = 10.2. However, if the number of classes is increased to six, the width could be reduced to ten, a multiple of 2, 5 and 10. Furthermore, if the beginning value for the first bin is made 20 (not 23), the resulting six bins would be 20 to 30, 30 to 40, 40 to 50, 50 to 60, 60 to 70 and 70 to 80.   Most persons would find these classes/bins easier to understand then the eight bins of 23 and less, 23 to 30.28571, 30.28571 to 37.57143, and so on which Excel would automatically set up for this example.

To specify the classes/bins in Excel we would enter into the worksheet the *upper* value for each class/bin. To obtain the six bins specified above for our example, we would enter the six values of 30, 40, 50, 60, 70 and 80 into the worksheet. Using these six values Excel would determine the frequencies for the bins of *30 and less, greater than 30 to 40, greater than 40 to 50,* and so to *greater than 70 to 80*.   In addition, Excel would automatically include a bin of *greater than 80*. For this example, this last bin will be empty. Oftentimes it is helpful to also have an empty bin at the beginning of the distribution. This is the approach we demonstrate in Figure 2.1 where we have entered the seven bin values of **20, 30, 40, 50, 60, 70** and **80**. Using these seven values, the HISTOGRAM analysis tool would determine the frequencies for the 6 classes/bins we wanted plus an empty bin at the beginning for values of 20 and less and an empty bin at the end for values greater than 80.

The following steps describe how to use the HISTOGRAM analysis tool for this example.

1. Use the **Start-up Procedure** given in Section 1.1 of Chapter 1 to start Excel.

2. Open a new Excel workbook and enter the **Identification Material** as discussed in Section 1.5 of Chapter 1. Specifically enter the worksheet title in cell B1, your name in B2, the date in A3 and the file name you wish to use in D3 such as CHARTS.xls.

3. Enter the label **No. Sold** in Cell A5 and the values for the 50 sales values from Table 2.1 in cells A6 through A55 as shown in Figure 2.1.

4. Enter the label **Bin** in Cell C5 and the values **20,30, . . . 80** in cells C6 through C12.

5. Use the **Saving a Workbook** procedure (Step 6 in Subsection 1.2.3 of Chapter 1) to save your workbook under the file name **CHARTS** (Excel will add the xls suffix). Saving your workbook after you have put some effort into it, will frequently save you effort later.

6. From the menu bar select **Tools** and then **Data Analysis** from the subsequent pull-down menu as shown in Figure 2.1. The Data Analysis dialog box as shown in Figure 2.2 will then appear. Select **Histogram** from the scrolling list and then click on the command

Figure 2.1 Example Data and Tools Pull-Down Menu

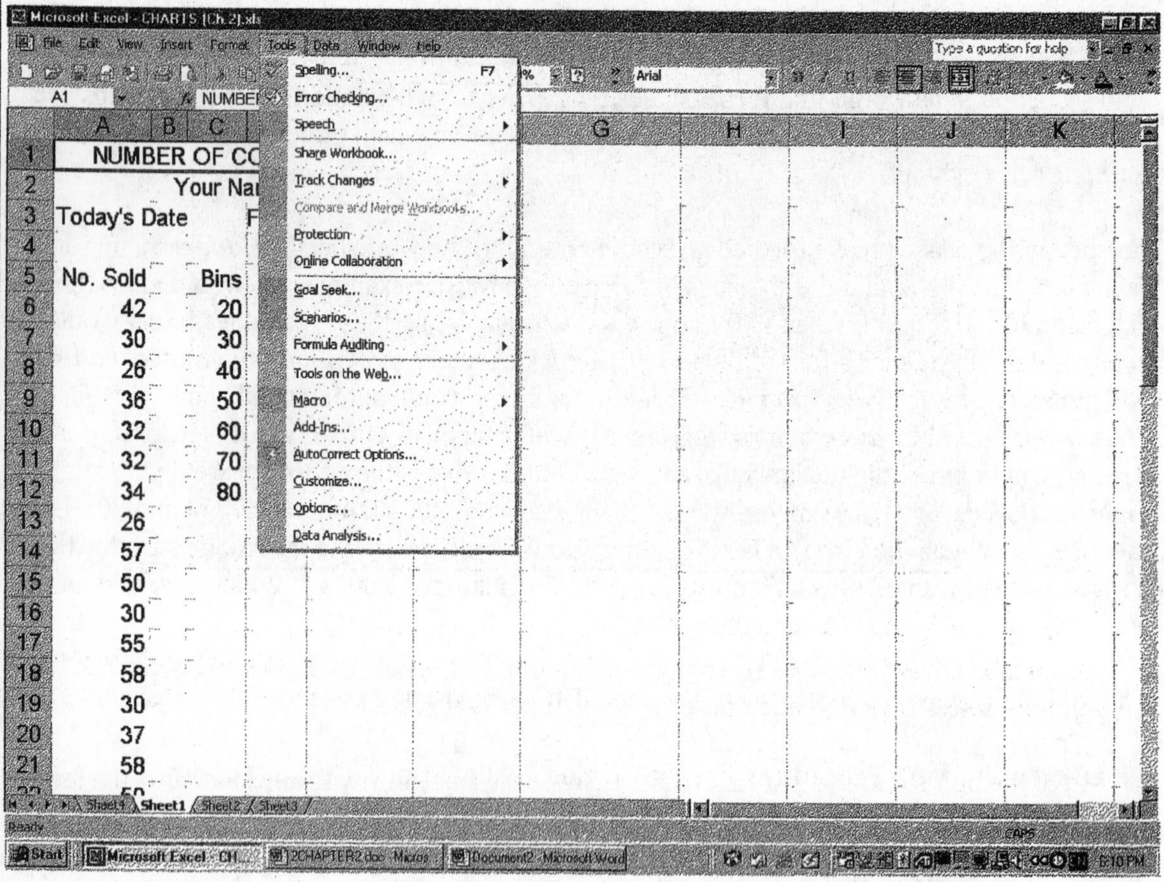

Figure 2.2 Data Analysis Dialog Box

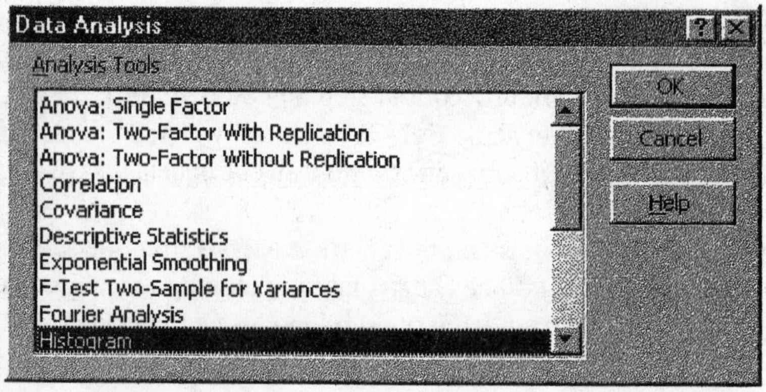

Figure 2.3 Histogram Dialog Box

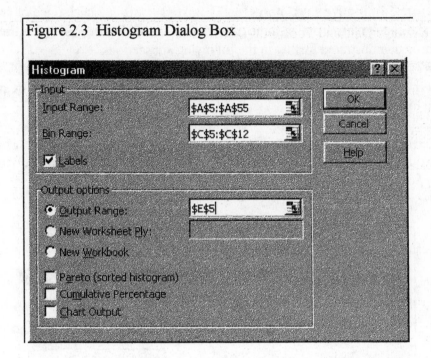

button labeled as **OK**. The Histogram dialog box will appear as shown in Figure 2.3. You will now select the input and output options for HISTOGRAM.

7. Move the pointer to the text box to the right of the label **Input Range** and click the left mouse button. Enter the range of cells for the data including the label in cell A5. You may either key the range **A5:A55** or click on cell A5 and drag to cell A55. (Note Excel automatically adds the $ signs to indicate absolute addresses if you use the drag operation.)

8. Move the pointer to the text box to the right of the label **Bin Range** and click the left mouse button. Enter the range of cells for the bins including the label in cell C5. You may either key **C5:C12** or click on cell C5 and drag to cell C12.

9. Move the pointer to the **Labels** check box and click the left mouse button once or twice to get a check mark in the box. This tells HISTOGRAM that the two ranges above include the labels in cells A5 and C5.

10. Move the pointer to the **Output Range** option button and click once or twice to get a dot in the button.

11. Move to the **Output Range** text box and click once and enter the cell address of E5 to specify the upper-left cell of for the Histogram output.

12. Sequentially move the pointer to the last three check boxes labeled as **Pareto (sorted histogram), Cumulative Percentage,** and **Chart Output** and click once or twice to **remove** the check mark from all three of these boxes (see Figure 2.3). The use of these selections is demonstrated further in the following subsections.

13. Click on the **OK** command button and Excel will compute and display the frequency values shown in Figure 2.4.

These results show the frequency distribution using the six classes of *20 to 30* through *70 to 80*. In addition, they indicate that no values are *equal to or less than 20* and no values are *greater than 80*.

Figure 2.4 Frequency Distribution Results

	A	B	C	D	E	F	G
1	NUMBER OF CONES SOLD						
2			Your Name				
3	Today's Date			File: CHART.xls			
4							
5	No. Sold		Bins		Bins	Frequency	
6	42		20		20	0	
7	30		30		30	12	
8	26		40		40	16	
9	36		50		50	10	
10	32		60		60	9	
11	32		70		70	2	
12	34		80		80	1	
13	26				More	0	
14	57						
15	50						
16	30						

2.1.2 Histogram

 The procedure for producing a histogram in addition to a frequency distribution is exactly like steps one through thirteen above with one exception. The change involves Step 12. In order to additionally get a histogram, the check box for **Chart Output** should have a check mark in it. To demonstrate, again use the **Tools/ Data Analysis/ Histogram/ OK** command sequence to call up the HISTOGRAM dialog box as you did for Figure 2.3. Your prior input and output selections may still be shown. If not, reenter them. In addition, use the mouse button to add the check mark to the box for **Chart Output.** Click on **OK** and Excel will present a dialog box asking for permission to overwrite the output range. Select **OK** and the results of Figure 2.5 will appear.

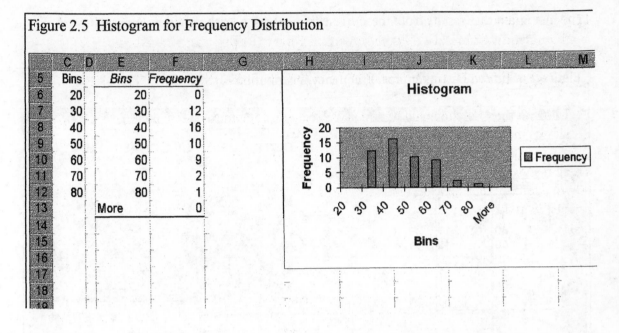

Figure 2.5 Histogram for Frequency Distribution

If your analysis is for your use only, the format of the histogram of Figure 2.5 may be satisfactory. However, if you wish to present your histogram to others, you may wish to edit it with more finished looking features. As examples of possible editing, consider the following.

1. To enlarge the histogram, click inside the histogram and eight sizing handles (black squares in the corners and midpoints of the outside border) will appear as shown in Figure 2.6. Move the mouse pointer to the bottom center sizing handle. The mouse pointer will become a two-headed arrow. Drag the sizing handle to row 20. Next point and drag the right center sizing handle to column M.

2. To give the histogram a different title, click on the current title, *Histogram*. Sizing handles will appear around a box surrounding the title. Key a new title such as **Distribution of Cones Sold** and press the **Enter** key.

3. To change the X-axis title, click on the current title *Bins* and key in a new title such as **Class Endpoints**. Press the **Enter** key.

4. Since only one set of data is plotted, a legend is not needed. Click on the legend box that contains the word **Frequency**. Press the **Delete** key.

5. Traditionally histograms do not have space between their bars although bar graphs do. To make this change, click on one of the bars. Small squares will appear on all the bars to show they are ready to be edited. Click on **Format** on the menu bar. Click on **Selected Data Series** from the pull-down menu. Click on the **Options** dialog tab. Use the **Gap Width** spinner to change from 150% to 0%.

The histogram that results from these five editing steps is as shown in Figure 2.6.

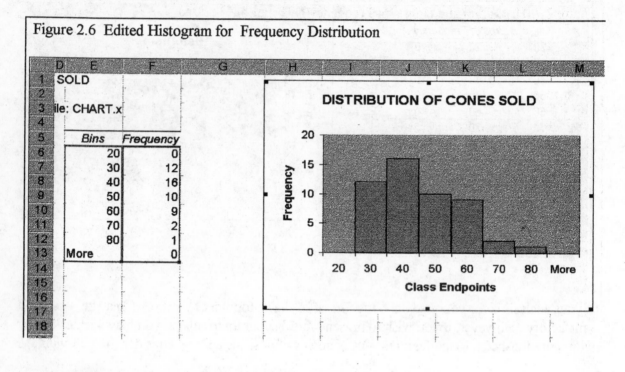

Figure 2.6 Edited Histogram for Frequency Distribution

2.1.3 Ogive

The procedure for adding an ogive to the output of the HISTOGRAM tool also requires changing only one input to the 13-step procedure of Subsection 2.1.1 above. Again the change involves Step 12. In order to compute the cumulative relative frequencies (cumulative percentages), the check box for **Cumulative Percentage** in the Histogram dialog box should have a check mark in it.   To demonstrate, again call up the HISTOGRAM dialog box as shown in Figure 2.3. This time use the mouse to add the check mark to the box for **Cumulative Percentage**. Click on **OK** and give permission to overwrite the output data. Excel will create a second chart on top of the first as shown in Figure 2.7.

If you would like, you can eliminate the first chart by clicking inside the first chart but outside the second chart. The sizing handles will appear for the first chart to indicate it has been selected. Next press the **Delete** key. Alternatively, you can click on the second chart and use the sizing handles for it to expand it to completely cover the first chart.

As you will note in Figure 2.7, the cumulative percentages have been added to Column G. The accompanying chart is a combination of a histogram and a plot of the cumulative percentages. The axis for the histogram is on the left and the axis for the cumulative percentages of the ogive is on the right. Again you can edit the chart to give it a more finished look.

Figure 2.7 Histogram and Ogive for Frequency Distribution

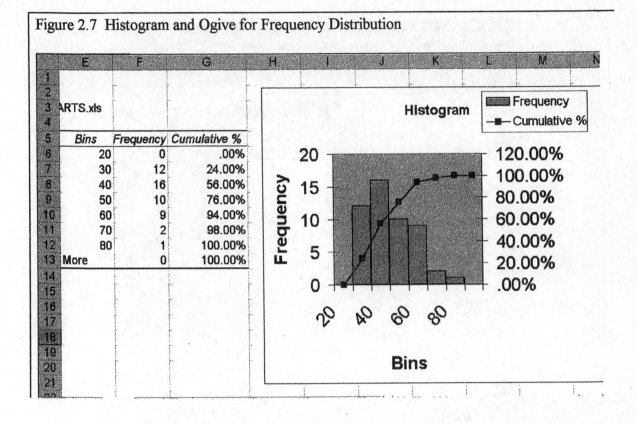

2.2 THE CHART WIZARD

Excel's feature called the CHART WIZARD can be used to create 14 chart types. Eleven of these are listed in the scrolling list on the left of Figure 2.8. The remaining three are at the bottom of the scrolling list and are hidden from view. These three are the *Cylinder*, the *Cone* and the *Pyramid* charts. All three resemble a three-dimensional bar/column chart with the bars either in the form of a cylinder, cone or pyramid.

We demonstrate the use of four of these fourteen chart types in Section 2.2. Subsection 2.2.1 demonstrates the use of a *XY (Scatter)* chart for constructing a frequency polygon for the *Cones Sold* example. Subsection 2.2.4 demonstrates the Chart Wizard's use for constructing a scatter diagram for that example. In Subsection 2.2.2 a new example is introduced. It is used to create a *Bar* chart, a *Column* chart and a *Pie* chart. In addition, Subsections 2.2.2 and 2.2.3 demonstrate three-dimensional sub-types for the Bar, Column and Pie charts.

Figure 2.8 Chart Wizard Step 1: Chart Types

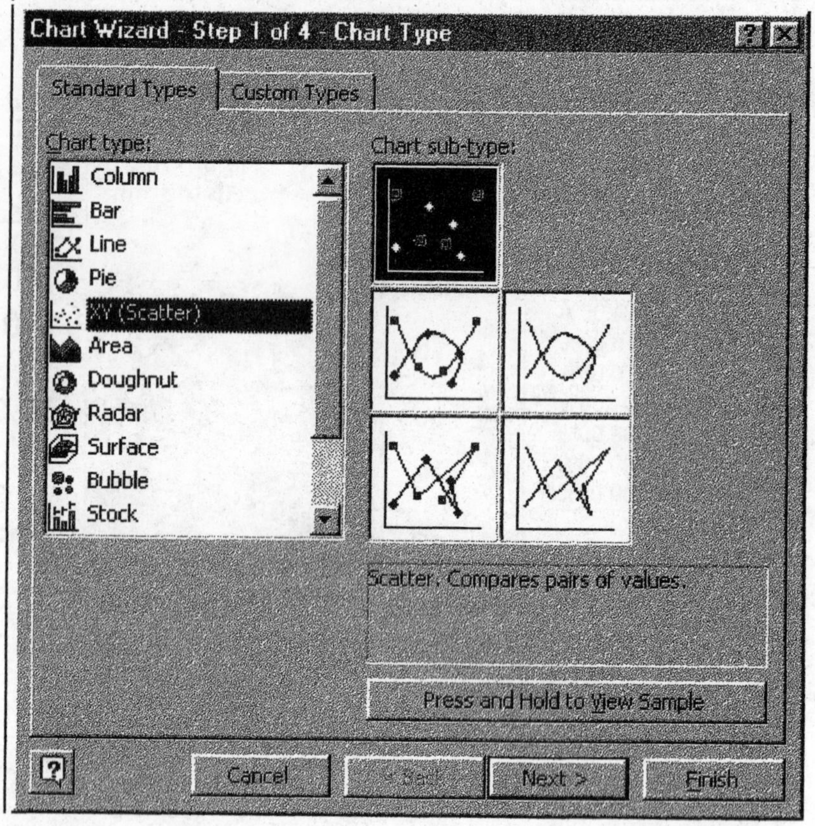

2.2.1 Frequency Polygon

The XY (Scatter) chart can be used to create a frequency polygon for the *Cones Sold* example used throughout Section 2.1 above. You would proceed in the following manner.

1. Move the cell pointer to cell E25 of the *Charts* workbook and enter the label **Midpoint** and to F25 and enter the label **Frequency**.

2. In cells E26 through E33 enter the midpoints for the classes/bins of cells E6 through E13 as **15, 25, 35, . . . , 85**.

3. Copy the frequency values from cells F6 through F13 to cells F26 through F33. (You may wish to refer ahead to Figure 2.13 to see the results of Steps 1, 2 and 3.)

4. Highlight the range of cells from E26 through F33 by dragging through them.

5. Move the pointer to the CHART WIZARD icon on the standard toolbar and click once. The *Chart Wizard — Step 1 of 4—Chart Type* dialog box will appear as shown in Figure 2.8 above. If the **Standard Types** tab is not in front, click it.

6. Use the mouse to select the **XY (Scatter)** chart and then select the sub-type in the lower left corner of the Chart sub-types. See Figure 2.9.   Click on the **Next** command button. The *Chart Wizard — Step 2 of 4—Chart Source Data* dialog box will be displayed as shown in Figure 2.10.

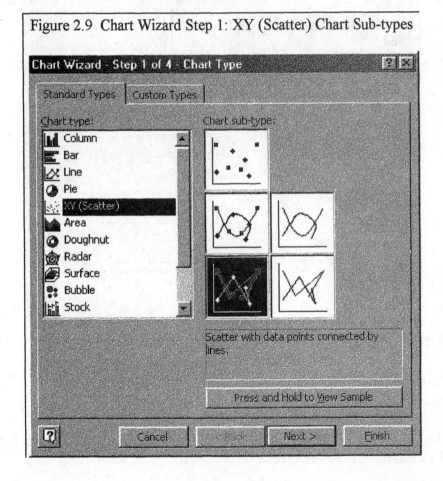

Figure 2.9 Chart Wizard Step 1: XY (Scatter) Chart Sub-types

7. If the **Data Range** tab is not in front, click it. Check to make sure the data range is given as E26:F33 (as noted in Figure 2.10, *Sheet1* may be referenced and the range given as absolute cell references). Make sure **Columns** option button is selected for *Series in*. Click on the **Next** command button. The *Chart Wizard — Step 3 of 4—Chart Options* dialog box of Figure 2.11 will be displayed.

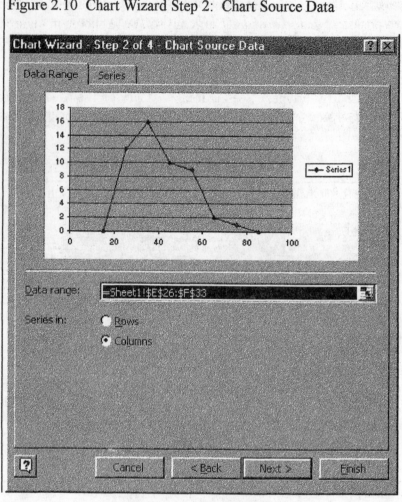

Figure 2.10 Chart Wizard Step 2: Chart Source Data

8. Click on the **Titles** tab if it is not in front. Move the mouse pointer to the **Chart title** text box and click. Enter the title *FREQUENCY POLYGON*. Enter *Class Midpoint* for the **Value (X) axis** and enter *Frequency* for **Value (Y) axis** as shown in Figure 2.11.

9. Click on the **Axes** tab. Select the check boxes for both the **Value (X) axis** and **Value (Y) axis**.

10. Click on the **Gridlines** tab. None of the four check boxes should be selected.

11. Click on the **Legend** tab. The check box *Show legend* should not be selected.

12. Click on the **Data Labels** tab. None of the boxes under the words **Label Contains** should be checked **(Excel 2000-App. D)** .Click on the **Next** command button. The result will be the *Chart Wizard — Step 4 of 4—Chart Location* dialog box as shown in Figure 2.12.

13. Click on the option **As object in.** Click on the **Finish** command button. Click and drag
the chart to a position beside the data. The result will be as shown in Figure 2.13.

Figure 2.11 Chart Wizard Step 3: Chart Options

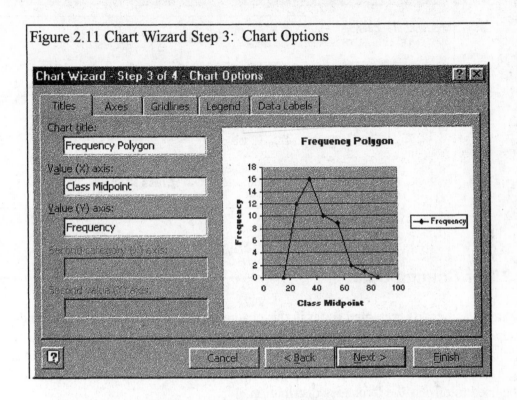

Figure 2.12 Chart Wizard Step 4: Chart Location

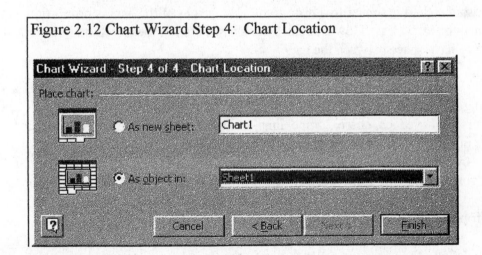

You may wish to enlarge the chart as you did to get Figure 2.6.

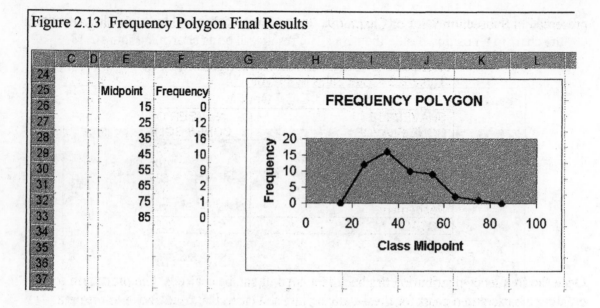

Figure 2.13 Frequency Polygon Final Results

	Midpoint	Frequency
26	15	0
27	25	12
28	35	16
29	45	10
30	55	9
31	65	2
32	75	1
33	85	0

2.2.2 Bar/Column Chart

The graphs and charts presented so far in this chapter included histograms, ogives and frequency polygons. These are used to display a frequency distribution for **quantitative** or numerical variables (measured on an interval or ratio measurement scale). For **qualitative** or categorical variables (measured on a nominal or ordinal scale) a bar/column chart or pie chart can be used to display the frequency distribution.

A bar/column chart is similar to a histogram. The height of the bars is proportional to the frequency for each class. However since the classes are not measured on a numerical scale, it is usual to have space between the bars.

As an example, let us revisit Kei, Lei and Dei, the three sisters who are running a stand selling shaved ice cones near the shopping mall in their hometown. The sisters sell five flavors of shaved ice, cherry, grape, lime, orange and peppermint. During their first 50 days in business they sold a total of 2066 cones. Table 2.2 presents a tabulation of these sales by flavor. These data represent a frequency distribution for a qualitative or categorical variable. Consequently, the previous procedures of this chapter for the development of a histogram, an ogive and a frequency polygon would not be appropriate.

The tabulation of sales data in order to obtain the frequency distribution of Table 2.2 can be done by hand. However, if the sales data are within an Excel worksheet, Excel has a feature that can determine the frequency distribution. The feature isn't the HISTOGRAM analysis tool because it is appropriate for only quantitative data. The feature is the PIVOT TABLE WIZARD. The use of it to tabulate a one variable frequency count such as that of Table 2.2 is presented in Subsection 9.3.1 of Chapter 9. This is particularly useful tool for large data sets.

Table 2.2 Cone Sales by Flavor	
SHAVED ICE CONE FLAVOR	NUMBER OF CONES SOLD
Cherry	330
Grape	186
Lime	537
Orange	269
Peppermint	744
TOTAL	2066

Once the frequency distribution has been tabulated, it can be charted. The procedure for creating a bar/column chart for these data is quite similar to that used above to create a frequency polygon. We will continue with the Excel workbook from the prior example.

1. Click on the **Sheet2** tab at the bottom of the window. This will allow you to create a second worksheet for this second example within the workbook entitled *CHARTS*.

2. Enter the data labels **Flavor** in cell A5 and **Number** in cell B5. Enter the names of the five flavors in cells A6 through A10 and the five frequency values in cells B6 through B10. As a check on your data entry, you can enter the equation =**SUM(B6:B10)** in cell B11 to see if the total is correct. Refer to later Figure 2.16 to see the results of this step.

3. Highlight the range of cells from A6 through B10 by dragging through them.

4. Move the pointer to the CHART WIZARD icon on the standard toolbar and click once. The *Chart Wizard — Step 1 of 4—Chart Type* dialog box will appear as previously shown in Figure 2.8. If the **Standard Types** tab is not in front, click it.

5. Use the mouse to select the **Column** chart and then select the sub-type in the upper left corner of the Chart sub-types. Click on the **Next** command button. The *Chart Wizard — Step 2 of 4—Chart Source Data* dialog box will be displayed as shown in Figure 2.14.

6. If the **Data Range** tab is not in front, click it. Check to make sure the data range is given as A6:B10 (as shown in Figure 2.14, *Sheet2* may be referenced and the range given as absolute cell references). Make sure **Columns** option button is selected for *Series in*. Click on the **Next** command button. The *Chart Wizard — Step 3 of 4—Chart Options* dialog box of Figure 2.15 will be displayed.

7. Click on the **Titles** tab. Move the mouse pointer to the **Chart title** text box and click. Enter the title *CONE SALES BY FLAVOR*. Enter *Cone Flavor* for the **Category (X) Axis**

and enter *Number Sold* for **Value (Y) Axis** as shown in Figure 2.15.

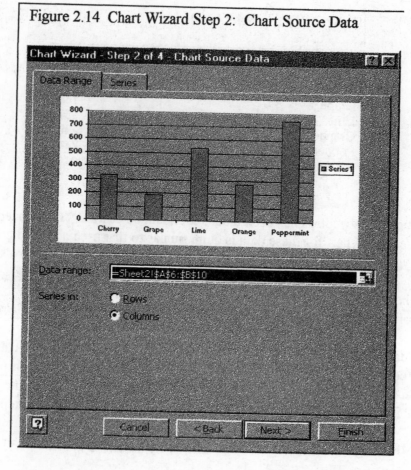

Figure 2.14 Chart Wizard Step 2: Chart Source Data

8. Click on the **Axes** tab. Select the check boxes for both the **Category (X) axis** and **Value (Y) axis.**

9. Click on the **Gridlines** tab. None of the four check boxes should be selected.

10. Click on the **Legend** tab. The check box *Show legend* should not be selected.

11. Click on the **Data Labels** tab. None of the boxes under the words **Label Contains** should be checked **(Excel 2000-App. D)**. Click on the **Next** command button. The result will be the *Chart Wizard — Step 4 of 4—Chart Location* dialog box as shown previously in Figure 2.12 except **Sheet 2** will be displayed in the box labeled **As object in**.

12. Click on the option **As object** in. Click on the **Finish** command button. Click and drag the chart to a position beside the data. The result will be as shown in Figure 2.16.

Figure 2.15 Chart Wizard Step 3: Chart Options

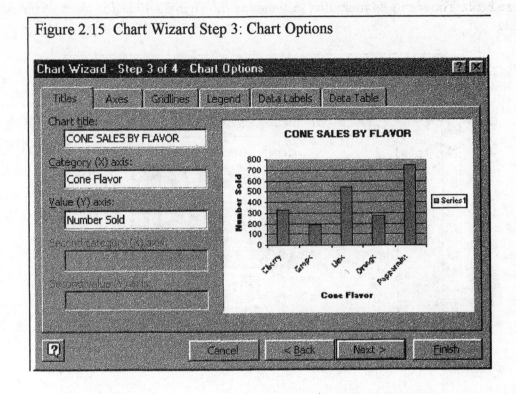

Figure 2. 16 Column Chart Final Results

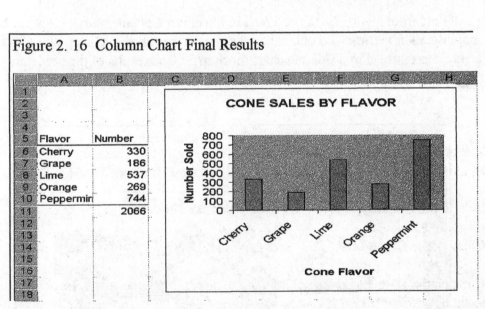

To obtain a three-dimensional version of the column chart of Figure 2.16, you should repeat the steps directly above with just a few changes. *First change*, start with Step 3 of the above procedure. *Second*, for Step 5 select the chart sub-type shown on far left of the second row. *Third*, for Steps 7 and 8 the axes will be **X** and **Z** instead of X and Y. The result is shown in

Figure 2.17. The X axis of your chart may differ from Figure 2.17 as the result of our further editing of it.

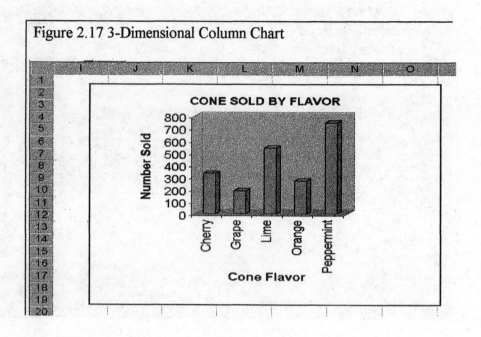

Figure 2.17 3-Dimensional Column Chart

As you will note from Figure 2.8, a *Bar chart* in Excel is a *Column chart* except the bars are horizontal instead of vertical. To obtain bar chart, again repeat the 12-step procedure but select a **Bar** chart instead of a Column chart for Step 5. The results of the procedure will be as shown in Figure 2.18. Note that the X and Y axes are reversed.

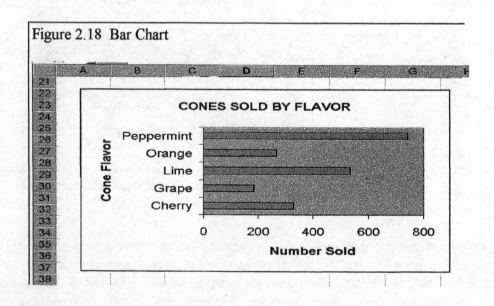

Figure 2.18 Bar Chart

Finally, suppose you wished to obtain the three-dimensional version of a Bar chart. Again repeat the procedure but for Step 5 select the chart sub-type shown on far left of the second row. The results will be as shown in Figure 2.19.

The four charts of Figures 2.16 through 2.19 provide similar but different representations of the same set of qualitative or categorical data.

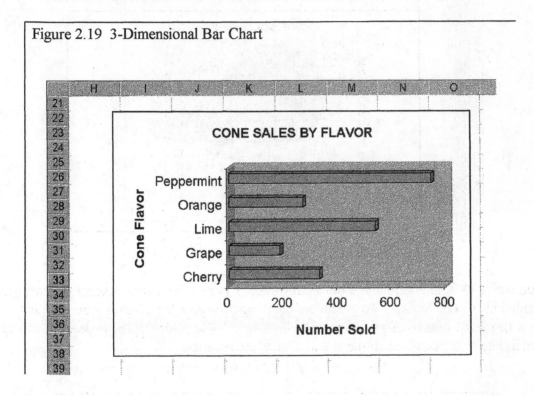

Figure 2.19 3-Dimensional Bar Chart

2.2.3 Pie Chart

A pie chart is used for representing percentages and relative frequencies usually for qualitative variables. The CHART WIZARD can be used to also create a pie chart for the *Cones Sold* example of the prior subsection.

As a test of your knowledge of the CHART WIZARD use it to create a pie chart of the data of Table 2.2. The results should be as given in Figure 2.20. Two of the specifications for this chart include do not check **Show legend** for the *Legend* dialog box and do check both **Category Name** and **Percentage** for the *Data Label* dialog box given for *Chart Wizard—Step 3 of 4—Chart Options* **(Excel 2000-App. D)**.

As a further test of your use of CHART WIZARD, construct the 3-D Pie chart of Figure 2.21.

Figure 2.20 Pie Chart

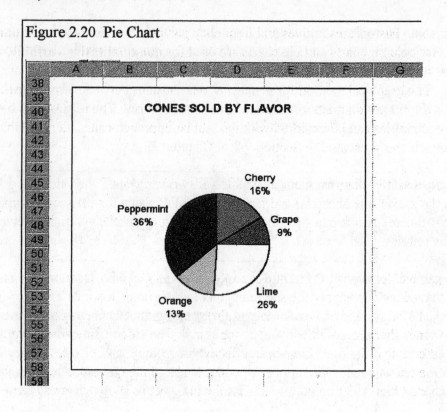

Figure 2.21 3-Dimensional Pie Chart

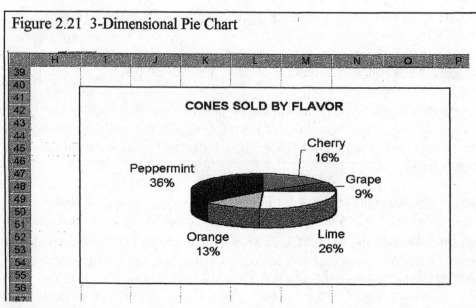

2.2.4 Scatter Diagram

The graphs and charts discussed so far in this chapter included histograms, ogives, frequency polygons, bar/column charts and pie charts. These are used to display a frequency distribution for one variable. Histograms, ogives and frequency polygons are used for **one quantitative variable.** Bar/column charts and pie charts are used for **one qualitative variable.** Oftentimes for business and industry problems, it is desired to determine how two variables are related to each other. The graphical method for displaying relationships between **two quantitative variables** is the scatter diagram as presented in this subsection. The relationship between **two qualitative variables** can be explored with the tabular approach called a cross-tabulation or contingency table as presented in Section 9.2 of Chapter 9.

We construct a scatter diagram from the values for two variables. The value for one variable is plotted on the x-axis (the abscissa) and the corresponding value for the second variable on the y-axis (the ordinate). Each pair of values for the x-variable and the y-variable determines one point on the graph.

As an example, let us visit for a third time Kei, Lei and Dei who are running a stand selling shaved ice cones near the shopping mall in their home town of The Meadowlands. For the last 10 days, they have distributed fliers throughout the metropolitan area of The Meadowlands that promote their shaved ice stand. The enterprising sisters would now like to determine if the fliers have been effective in promoting cone sales. They have entered the ten values for the number of cones sold and the corresponding ten values for the number of fliers distributed into an Excel worksheet as shown in later Figure 2.23.

The procedure for constructing a scatter diagram for these data is the following.

1. Click on the **Sheet3** tab at the bottom of the window. This will allow you to create a third worksheet for this example within the workbook entitled *CHARTS*.

2. Enter the data labels **No. of Fliers** in cell A5 for the x-variable and **No. Sold** in cell B5 for the y-variable. Enter the ten values for the number of fliers in cells A6 through A15 and the ten corresponding sales values in cells B6 through B15. Refer ahead to Figure 2.23 to see these results.

3. Highlight the range of cells from A5 through B15 by dragging through them.

4. Move the pointer to the CHART WIZARD icon on the standard toolbar and click once. The *Chart Wizard — Step 1 of 4—Chart Type* dialog box will appear as shown in previous Figure 2.8. If the **Standard Types** tab is not in front, click on it.

5. Use the mouse to select the **XY (Scatter)** chart and then select the sub-type in the top row of the Chart sub-types. Again you may refer to Figure 2.8. Click on the **Next** command button. The *Chart Wizard — Step 2 of 4—Chart Source Data* dialog box will be displayed as previously shown in Figure 2.10.

6.   If the **Data Range** tab is not in front, click on it. Check to make sure the data range is given as A5:B15 (*Sheet3* may be referenced and the range given as absolute cell references). Make sure the **Columns** option button is selected for *Series in*. Click on the **Next** command button. The *Chart Wizard — Step 3 of 4—Chart Options* dialog box of Figure 2.22 will be displayed.

7.   Click on the **Titles** tab if it is not in front. Move the mouse pointer to the **Chart title** text box and click. Enter the title *PROMOTION EFFECT ON CONE SALES*. Enter *Number of Fliers* for the **Value (X) Axis** and enter *Number Sold* for **Value (Y) Axis** as shown in Figure 2.22.

8.   Click on the **Axes** tab. Select the check boxes for both the **Value (X) axis** and **Value (Y) axis**.

9.   Click on the **Gridlines** tab. None of the four check boxes should be selected.

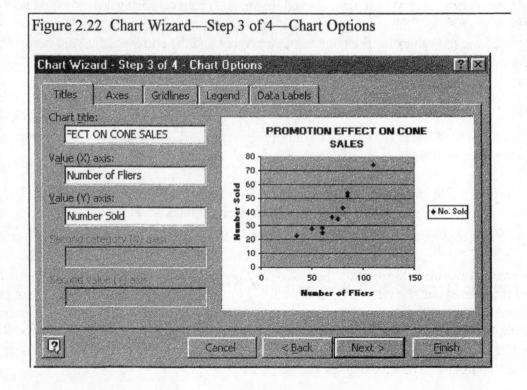

Figure 2.22 Chart Wizard—Step 3 of 4—Chart Options

10.   Click on the **Legend** tab. The check box *Show legend* should not be selected.

11.   Click on the **Data Labels** tab. None of the boxes under the words **Label Contains** should be checked **(Excel 2000-App. D)**.

12. Click on the **Next** command button. The result will be the *Chart Wizard — Step 4 of 4— Chart Location* dialog box as previously shown in Figure 2.12.

13. Click on the option **As object in.** Click on the **Finish** command button. Click and drag the chart to a position beside the data. The result will be as shown in Figure 2.23.

Figure 2.23 Scatter Diagram Final Results

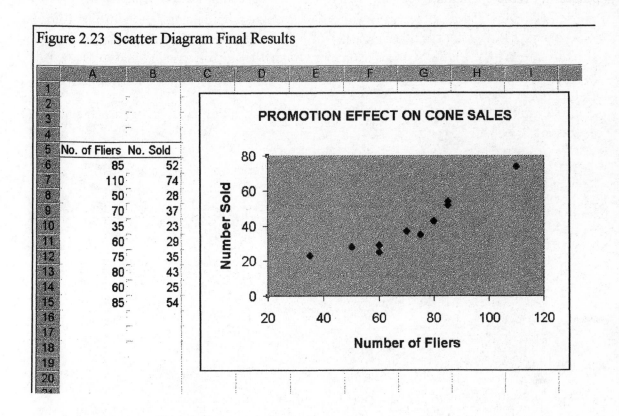

As with previous charts you may wish to enlarge and edit the chart.

The chart of Figure 2.23 suggests there may be a positive relationship between the number of fliers distributed and the number of cones sold. Furthermore, it suggests the relationship may be linear. It doesn't appear to be a perfect linear relationship since all the points do not lie on a straight line. However, all the points look as if they will be close to a straight line. We will consider further such relationships in Chapter 10 where we will use regression analysis to find the *best* straight-line relationship for such data sets.

If you have completed all the instructions of Section 2.2, you have used four of the chart types available through the CHART WIZARD. In addition, the histogram-ogive chart of Figure 2.7 in Section 2.1 is an example of a **Line-Column Combination** chart available as *Custom Type* chart from the CHART WIZARD. Your experience with these charts should prepare you to use other chart types that are available. You may wish to experiment with some of these other types. In addition, the CHART WIZARD will also be used in chapters 4, 10, 11 and 12 for charting.

At this time you may wish to save your Excel workbook one last time and perhaps print the results. You will then need to close your workbook and exit Excel. If you need to review the process for these operations, you may wish to review Subsection 1.2.3 of Chapter 1.

CHAPTER 3. DESCRIPTIVE NUMERICAL MEASURES

3.1 The DESCRIPTIVE STATISTICS Analysis Tool
    3.1.1 Measures of Location
    3.1.2 Measures of Variability
    3.1.3 Measures of Shape
    3.1.4 Other Descriptive Measures

3.2 The RANK AND PERCENTILE Analysis Tool

3.3 Descriptive Statistical Functions
    3.3.1 Population Variance
    3.3.2 Population Standard Deviation
    3.3.3 Mean Absolute Deviation
    3.3.4 Z Score

3.4 Combinations of Statistical Functions
    3.4.1 Coefficient of Variation
    3.4.2 Interquartile Range
    3.4.3 Pearson's Coefficient of Skewness
    3.4.4 Box Plot

3.5 Measures of Association Between Two Variables
    3.5.1 The COVARIANCE Analysis Tool
    3.5.2 The CORRELATION Analysis Tool

Excel includes two Data Analysis Tools that compute numerical measures for summarizing a data set for one quantitative variable. The first of these two analysis tools, DESCRIPTIVE STATISTICS, computes and displays most of the usual statistical measures of location, variability and shape for ungrouped data. It is presented in **Section 3.1**. The second tool is RANK AND PERCENTILE as discussed in **Section 3.2**. This tool displays the original data values sorted in ascending order and gives the rank and percentile for each data value.

Section 3.3 discusses four additional descriptive statistics that can be computed by individual statistical functions. **Section 3.4** shows how to combine two or more individual statistical functions in order to compute four further descriptive statistic measures. Finally, **Section 3.5** presents two Data Analysis Tools that compute measures of association between two quantitative variables.

3.1 THE DESCRIPTIVE STATISTICS ANALYSIS TOOL ———

The easiest way to obtain values for a number of the most common descriptive statistical measures is to use Excel's analysis tool DESCRIPTIVE STATISTICS. To demonstrate the use of this tool we will consider the following example.

The DeeLee Trucking Company delivers freight in and about Humid City. The number of tons of freight DeeLee has delivered the past 24 days is shown in Table 3.1. DeeLee would like to summarize these data using the usual statistical measures for location, variability and shape.

Table 3.1 DeeLee Freight Delivered in Tons

45	39	41	46	44	44	41	43
40	40	43	37	44	46	46	43
44	37	43	35	45	48	46	44

The following steps describe how to use the DESCRIPTIVE STATISTICS analysis tool for this example.

1. Use the **Start-up Procedure** of Section 1.1 of Chapter 1 to start Excel.

2. Open a new Excel workbook and enter the **Identification Material** (discussed in Section 1.5 of Chapter 1). In particular, enter the worksheet title in cell B1, your name in cell B2, the date in A3 and the file name you wish to use in D3 such as DESCRIBE.xls.

3. Enter the label **FREIGHT** in cell A5 and the 24 freight delivery values in cells A6 through A29 as shown in Figure 3.1.

Figure 3.1 Example Data and Tools Pull-Down Menu

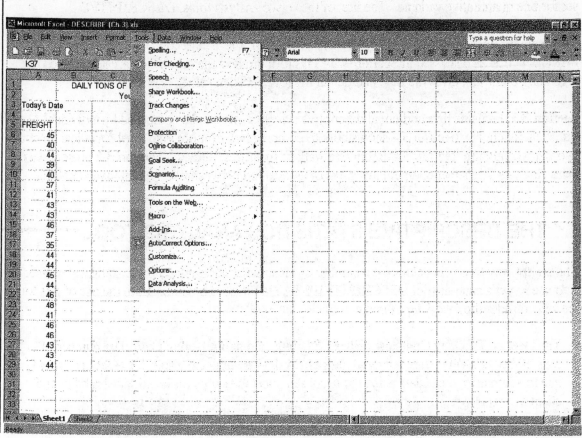

4. Use the **Saving a Workbook** procedure (Step 6 in Subsection 1.2.3 of Chapter 1) to save your workbook using the file name DESCRIBE.

5. From the menu bar select **Tools** and then **Data Analysis** from the subsequent pull-down menu as shown in Figure 3.1. The *Data Analysis* dialog box of Figure 3.2 will be shown on the screen.

6. Select **Descriptive Statistics** from the scrolling list and then click on the command button labeled **OK.** The *Descriptive Statistics* dialog box will be displayed as shown in Figure 3.3.

7. Next you will enter the input and the output options for the Descriptive Statistics analysis tool. Begin by selecting the options on the left hand side of the Descriptive Statistics dialog box. Specifically, select the first input option by clicking the left mouse button once or twice in the check box to the left of the words **Labels in the First Row** to get a check mark in the box.

8. Select the first output option by clicking once on the option button to the left of the words **Output Range** in order to place a dot in the button. Also, click once or twice in the checkbox for **Summary Statistics,** for **Confidence Level for the Mean,** for **kth largest** and for **kth**

smallest to get a check mark in each box. See Figure 3.3.

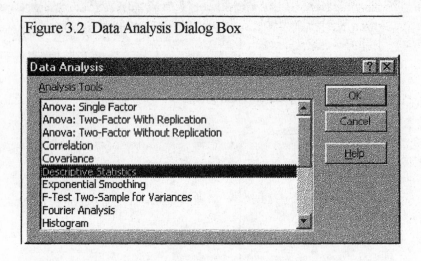

Figure 3.2 Data Analysis Dialog Box

Figure 3.3 Descriptive Statistics Dialog Box

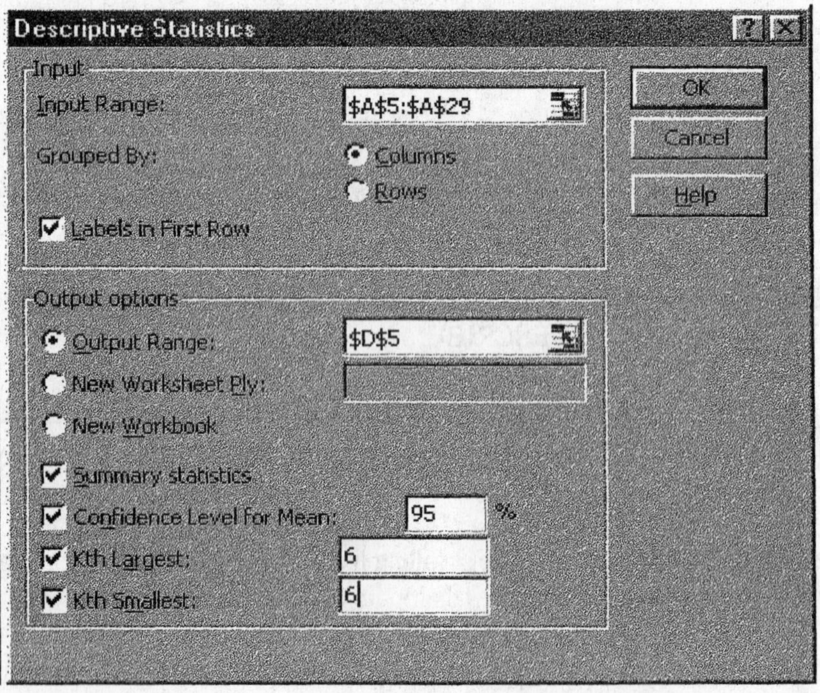

9. Move the mouse pointer to the textbox to the right of **Input Range** and click the left mouse button. Enter the range of cells for the data including the label in cell A5. You may either type A5:A29 or click on cell A5 and drag to cell A29. Excel automatically adds $ signs to the cell addresses to indicate absolute addresses when you use the dragging operation. Press the **Tab** key to proceed to the next dialog box field. Select **Columns** for the **Grouped By** input since

the data are in a column.

10. Press the tab key three times to move the cursor to the **Output Range** text box and enter the upper left cell for the location of the output results. For this example enter **D5**.

11. Press the tab key three more times to move the cursor to the **Confidence Level for Mean** text box. Enter **95** in order to obtain the 95% confidence interval (confidence intervals are discussed in Chapter 5).

12. Tab twice to the **Kth Largest** text box and enter **6** in order to obtain the approximate value for the third quartile or 75th percentile (6th largest of 24 data points). Tab twice to **Kth Smallest** text box enter **6** to obtain the approximate value for the first quartile or 25th percentile (6th smallest of 24 data points). (Exact values for the third and first quartiles can be computed using the individual statistical function QUARTILE as discussed in Section 3.4 below.)

13. Click on **OK** and Excel will compute and display the values as shown in Figure 3.4. (Note the width of column D has been increased so labels appear in full.)

Figure 3.4 Descriptive Statistics Results

	A	B	C	D	E	F
1		DAILY TONS OF FREIGHT DELIVERED				
2			Your Name			
3	Today's Date			File: DESCRIBE.xls		
4						
5	FREIGHT			*FREIGHT*		
6	45					
7	40			Mean	42.66667	
8	44			Standard Error	0.672079	
9	39			Median	43.5	
10	40			Mode	44	
11	37			Standard Deviation	3.292504	
12	41			Sample Variance	10.84058	
13	43			Kurtosis	0.02077	
14	43			Skewness	-0.76248	
15	46			Range	13	
16	37			Minimum	35	
17	35			Maximum	48	
18	44			Sum	1024	
19	44			Count	24	
20	45			Largest(6)	45	
21	44			Smallest(6)	40	
22	46			Confidence Level(95.0%)	1.3903	
23	48					

---

14. Use the **Saving a Workbook** procedure (Step 6 in Subsection 1.2.3 of Chapter 1) to save your worksheet.

The descriptive statistics results given in Figure 3.4 present measures of location, measures of variability, measures of shape and some additional descriptive measures. These are discussed in the following four subsections.

3.1.1 Measures of Location

The measures of location include values for the **mean** in cell E7, the **median** in cell E9 and the **mode** in cell E10.   In addition, cells E20 and E21 show the approximate values for the **third** and **first quartiles**.

3.1.2 Measures of Variability

The most frequently used measures of variability are the **sample standard deviation**, the **sample variance** and the **range** as given respectively in cells E11, E12 and E15 of Figure 3.4.

3.1.3 Measures of Shape

The results of Figure 3.4 also include measures of shape. A value for **skewness** is given in cell E14 and a value for **kurtosis** in cell E13. The value for skewness is based on the differences around the mean raised to the third power. The value for kurtosis is based on the differences around the mean raised to the fourth power.

For a further explanation access *Help* for the Excel statistical functions SKEW and KURT. Help for these two functions is accessed by clicking the INSERT FUNCTION icon (labeled as *fx* on the fourth line of the Excel worksheet as shown in Figure 3.1). The result will be the dialog box shown in later Figure 3.7. For it, select **Statistical** from the drop-down list box labeled *Or select a category* and select **SKEW** or **KURT** from the box labeled *Select a function.* Finally click on the label *Help on this function* found in the lower left corner of the box **(Excel 2000-App. D).**

An alternate measure of skewness is Pearson's Coefficient of Skewness that is somewhat simpler to compute and is perhaps a more usual measure of skewness. It is presented in Section 3.4 below.

3.1.4 Other Descriptive Measures

Figure 3.4 includes six additional outputs. Cell E8 contains the value for the **standard error**. It is equal to the sample standard deviation divided by the square root of the sample size. It is used for computing confidence intervals and conducting hypothesis tests as discussed later in Chapter 5. Cells E16 through E19 present the values for the **smallest value** of the sample, the **largest value**, the **sum** of all the values and the **number of values** in the sample. The final output given in cell E22 is the **half-width** for the 95% confidence interval that is also discussed in Chapter 5.

3.2 THE RANK AND PERCENTILE ANALYSIS TOOL

A second Data Analysis Tool that computes numerical measures for summarizing a data set of one quantitative variable is named RANK AND PERCENTILE. Again the data of Table 3.1 will be used to demonstrate this analysis tool.

The following steps will result in a new table within the worksheet with the data values given in descending order.

1. From the menu bar select **Tools** and then select **Data Analysis** from the subsequent pull-down menu. The Data Analysis dialog box (Figure 3.2) will then appear. Scroll down the list and select **Rank and Percentile** and then **OK** in order to obtain the *Rank and Percentile* dialog box as shown in Figure 3.5.

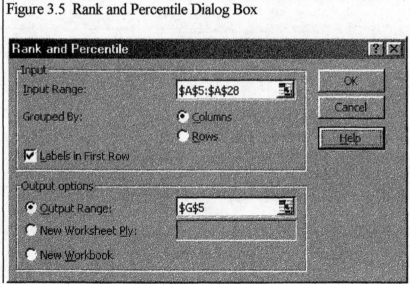

Figure 3.5 Rank and Percentile Dialog Box

2. Next fill in the Inputs and Output options as you did starting with Step 7 of the procedure given in Section 3.1. For the **Output Range** enter **G5**.

3. Click on **OK** and Excel will compute and display the values as shown in Figure 3.6.

The results are given in columns G through J. The original data values, given in column H, are now sorted in descending order. The numbers in column G indicate which data value is in each row. The values in columns I and J present the rank and percentile for each data value.

Figure 3.6 Rank and Percentile Results

	A	B	C	D	E	F	G	H	I	J
5	FREIGHT			*FREIGHT*			*Point*	*FREIGHT*	*Rank*	*Percent*
6	45						18	48	1	100.00%
7	40			Mean	42.666667		10	46	2	82.60%
8	44			Standard Error	0.6720795		17	46	2	82.60%
9	39			Median	43.5		20	46	2	82.60%
10	40			Mode	44		21	46	2	82.60%
11	37			Standard Deviation	3.2925036		1	45	6	73.90%
12	41			Sample Variance	10.84058		15	45	6	73.90%
13	43			Kurtosis	0.0207696		3	44	8	52.10%
14	43			Skewness	-0.762475		13	44	8	52.10%
15	46			Range	13		14	44	8	52.10%
16	37			Minimum	35		16	44	8	52.10%
17	35			Maximum	48		24	44	8	52.10%
18	44			Sum	1024		8	43	13	34.70%
19	44			Count	24		9	43	13	34.70%
20	45			Largest(6)	45		22	43	13	34.70%
21	44			Smallest(6)	40		23	43	13	34.70%
22	46			Confidence Level(95.0%)	1.3903004		7	41	17	26.00%
23	48						19	41	17	26.00%
24	41						2	40	19	17.30%
25	46						5	40	19	17.30%
26	46						4	39	21	13.00%
27	43						6	37	22	4.30%
28	43						11	37	22	4.30%
29	44						12	35	24	.00%

3.3 DESCRIPTIVE STATISTICAL FUNCTIONS

In addition to the Data Analysis Tools for performing statistical analysis, Excel has 80 individual functions for computing statistical values. These functions are listed in Appendix B by the category of analysis each supports. As presented in Appendix B, 36 of the 80 functions are listed in one of the six categories representing descriptive statistics. These 36 functions both duplicate and supplement the analytical capabilities of the three descriptive statistics data analysis tools, HISTOGRAM, DESCRIPTIVE STATISTICS and RANK AND PERCENTILE.

For example, the statistical functions AVERAGE, MEDIAN, MODE, STDEV and VAR compute values for the mean, median, mode, sample standard deviation and sample variance respectively. The DESCRIPTIVE STATISTICS analysis tool also computes values for these five descriptive numerical measures. However, a number of the descriptive numerical measures provided by statistical functions are not computed by the Descriptive Statistics tool. We demonstrate some of these additional measures through the presentation of four individual functions. The first three of these four are the population variance, the population standard deviation and the mean absolute deviation. They provide additional measures of variability. The fourth, the z-score, provides a measure of position.

3.3.1 Population Variance

One of the statistical functions is VARP. It computes the *population* **variance (*N* in the denominator)** as opposed to the *sample* **variance (*n-1* in the denominator).** You may recall that the sample variance was computed in Figure 3.4 through use of the DESCRIPTIVE STATISTICS tool. It also can be computed by the function VAR.

To determine the population variance using the VARP function, we perform the following steps.

1. Enter the label **Population Variance** in cell D24.

2. Move the worksheet pointer to cell E24 and click the INSERT FUNCTION icon. It is labeled with the symbol *fx* on the fourth line of the Excel worksheet as shown in Figure 3.1. The result should be the dialog box shown in Figure 3.7 **(Excel 2000-App. D).**

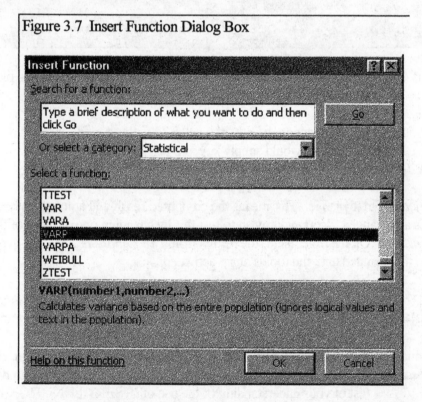

Figure 3.7 Insert Function Dialog Box

3. Select **Statistical** from the drop-down list box labeled *Or select a category*.

4. Scroll to and click on **VARP** in the scrolling list labeled *Select a function*.

5. Click on the **OK** button and the VARP dialog box as shown in Figure 3.8 will be presented.

6. Enter the range of values for the input data by either keying in the range or by clicking and dragging through cells A6 through A29. Notice that the value for the population variance,

10.38888889, is displayed both in the middle and at the bottom of the dialog box.

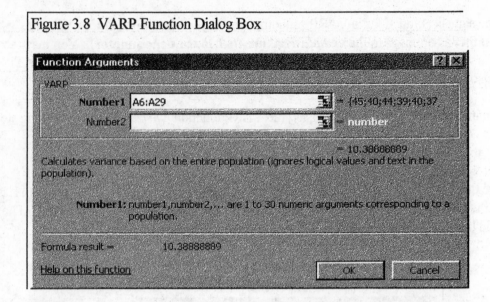

Figure 3.8 VARP Function Dialog Box

7. Click on the **OK** button. The function VARP with the range A6 through A29 is placed in cell E24. The cell displays the value for the function. Figure 3.9 shows this result.

Alternatively, you may key the function directly into cell E24 without going through the dialog boxes of Figures 3.7 and 3.8. You would simply key into cell E24 the expression **=VARP(A6:A29)**. The result would be the same as that shown in Figure 3.9.

Most Excel *functions* are dynamic. This means the computed result will automatically change as the input values are changed. You might wish to test this by changing one or more of the values in cells A6 through A29. On the other hand, the results from *Data Analysis Tools* are generally static. The results are not changed until the tool is again activated.

3.3.2 Population Standard Deviation

Another individual function, STDEVP, computes the ***population standard deviation.*** It is in contrast to the *sample standard deviation* given in Figure 3.4. It can also be computed by the function STDEV. As a test of your understanding of the use of INSERT FUNCTION button, repeat the seven steps given above for the population variance to compute the population standard deviation in cell E25 with a label in cell D25. Refer to Figure 3.9 to see the result.

3.3.3 Mean Absolute Deviation

Another measure of variability that can be obtained through the use of these same seven steps is the **Mean Absolute Deviation (MAD)**. The function that computes it is AVEDEV. Use this function to compute the value for MAD in cell E26 with its label in cell D26. See Figure 3.9 for the result.

Figure 3.9 VARP, STDEVP and AVEDEV Function Results

	A	B	C	D	E	F	G	H	I	J
5	FREIGHT			FREIGHT			Point	FREIGHT	Rank	Percent
6	45						18	48	1	100.00%
7	40			Mean	42.66667		10	46	2	82.60%
8	44			Standard Error	0.672079		17	46	2	82.60%
9	39			Median	43.5		20	46	2	82.60%
10	40			Mode	44		21	46	2	82.60%
11	37			Standard Deviation	3.292504		1	45	6	73.90%
12	41			Sample Variance	10.84058		15	45	6	73.90%
13	43			Kurtosis	0.02077		3	44	8	52.10%
14	43			Skewness	-0.76248		13	44	8	52.10%
15	46			Range	13		14	44	8	52.10%
16	37			Minimum	35		16	44	8	52.10%
17	35			Maximum	48		24	44	8	52.10%
18	44			Sum	1024		8	43	13	34.70%
19	44			Count	24		9	43	13	34.70%
20	45			Largest(6)	45		22	43	13	34.70%
21	44			Smallest(6)	40		23	43	13	34.70%
22	46			Confidence Level(95.0%)	1.3903		7	41	17	26.00%
23	48						19	41	17	26.00%
24	41			Population Variance	10.38889		2	40	19	17.30%
25	46			Population Std. Dev.	3.22318		5	40	19	17.30%
26	46			Mean Absolute Deviation	2.611111		4	39	21	13.00%
27	43						6	37	22	4.30%
28	43						11	37	22	4.30%
29	44						12	35	24	.00%
30										

3.3.4 z-Score

A measure of position for a data value relative to the other values in a data set is provided by its **z-score**. The z-score for a data value is equal to the number of standard deviations it is above or below the mean of the data set. The Excel function which computes a z-score is STANDARDIZE.

To compute the z-score for each data value of the *DeeLee* example proceed as follows.

1. Enter the label **z-Score** in cell B5 and move the cell pointer to cell B6.

2. Click the INSERT FUNCTION button, *fx*, with the left mouse button. The result should be as previously shown in Figure 3.7 **(Excel 2000-App. D).**

3. Select **Statistical** from the drop-down list box labeled *Or select a category*. Scroll to and click on **STANDARDIZE** in the list labeled *Select a function*. Click **OK** to obtain Figure 3.10.

4. Click on the value in cell **A6** to enter the cell address for the x value.

Figure 3.10 STANDARDIZE Function Dialog Box

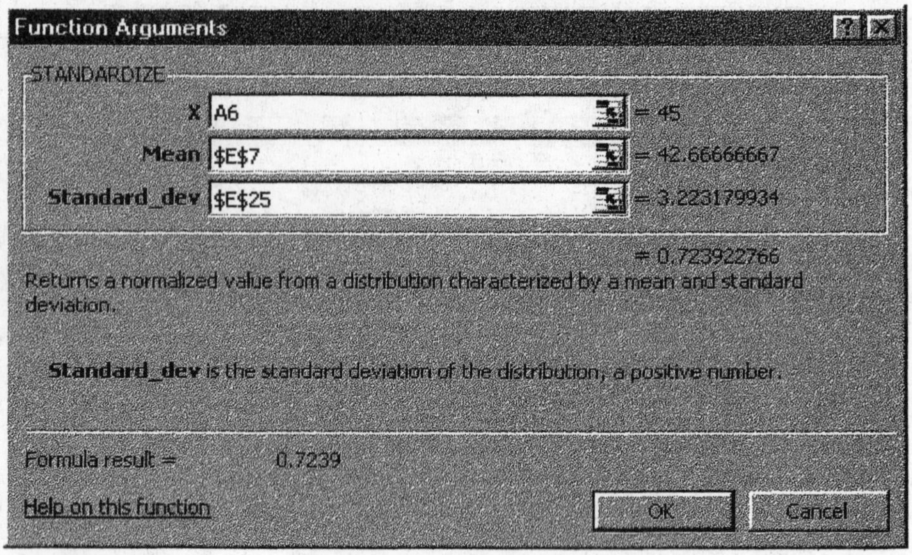

5. Press the **Tab** key to move to the text box for the mean. Key the cell address for the mean, **E7**, and press the **F4** key on top row of your keyboard. Pressing the F4 key changes the cell address from a relative address to an absolute address. The **$** sign before the column letter and before the row number indicate it is an absolute address. An absolute cell address is needed when the contents of a cell are to be copied and the cell address is to remain unchanged.

6. Press the **Tab** key to move to the standard deviation text box, labeled as **Standard_dev**. Key the cell address **E25** and press the **F4** key to make it an absolute address.

7. Click **OK**. The result will be the z-score for the data value in cell A6.

8. Click on the **Copy** button. Click and drag through cells B7 through B29.

9. Click on the **Paste** button. The result will be the z-scores in column B for each of the values in cells A7 through A29. These are shown in Figure 3.11.

3.4 COMBINATIONS OF STATISTICAL FUNCTIONS ⎯⎯⎯

Two or more individual statistical functions can be combined to compute additional descriptive numerical measures. Four of these commonly presented in business statistics textbooks include the coefficient of variation, the interquartile range, Pearson's coefficient of skewness and the box plot. The first two of these provide additional measures of variability. The third gives another numerical measure of shape, and the fourth provides a pictorial summary of the shape of a data set. A box plot is also called a *box and whisker plot*.

Figure 3.11 Z-Score Results

	A	B	C	D	E	F
5	FREIGHT			FREIGHT		
6	45	0.7239				
7	40	-0.8273		Mean	42.66667	
8	44	0.4137		Standard Error	0.672079	
9	39	-1.1376		Median	43.5	
10	40	-0.8273		Mode	44	
11	37	-1.7581		Standard Deviation	3.292504	
12	41	-0.5171		Sample Variance	10.84058	
13	43	0.1034		Kurtosis	0.02077	
14	43	0.1034		Skewness	-0.76248	
15	46	1.0342		Range	13	
16	37	-1.7581		Minimum	35	
17	35	-2.3786		Maximum	48	
18	44	0.4137		Sum	1024	
19	44	0.4137		Count	24	
20	45	0.7239		Largest(6)	45	
21	44	0.4137		Smallest(6)	40	
22	46	1.0342		Confidence Level(95.0%)	1.3903	
23	48	1.6547				
24	41	-0.5171		Population Variance	10.38889	
25	46	1.0342		Population Std. Dev.	3.22318	
26	46	1.0342		Mean Absolute Deviation	2.611111	
27	43	0.1034				
28	43	0.1034				
29	44	0.4137				

3.4.1 Coefficient of Variation

The **coefficient of variation** measures the relative variability in a data set by dividing the population standard deviation by the mean and multiplying the result by 100. This computation can be performed in Excel by using the statistical function STDEVP to obtain the population standard deviation and the function AVERAGE to obtain the mean. Continuing with the worksheet from above, we will proceed as follows.

1. Enter the label **Coefficient Variation** in cell D28. Move the worksheet pointer to cell E28.

2. Click the INSERT FUNCTION icon, *fx*, with the left mouse button. The computer will show the INSERT FUNCTION dialog box as given in Figure 3.7 **(Excel 2000-App. D).**

3. Click on the function category **Statistical**. Scroll to and click on the function **STDEVP** and click on the **OK** button to obtain the dialog box of Figure 3.12.

4. Enter or click and drag through cells A6 to A29 and click **OK**. The population standard deviation will be displayed in cell E28.

5. Press the **F2** key in the top row of your keyboard to enter the edit mode.

6. Key in a slash after the right-most parenthesis of the STDEVP function in cell E28 to indicate the population standard deviation is to be divided by the mean.

Figure 3.12 STDEVP Function Dialog Box

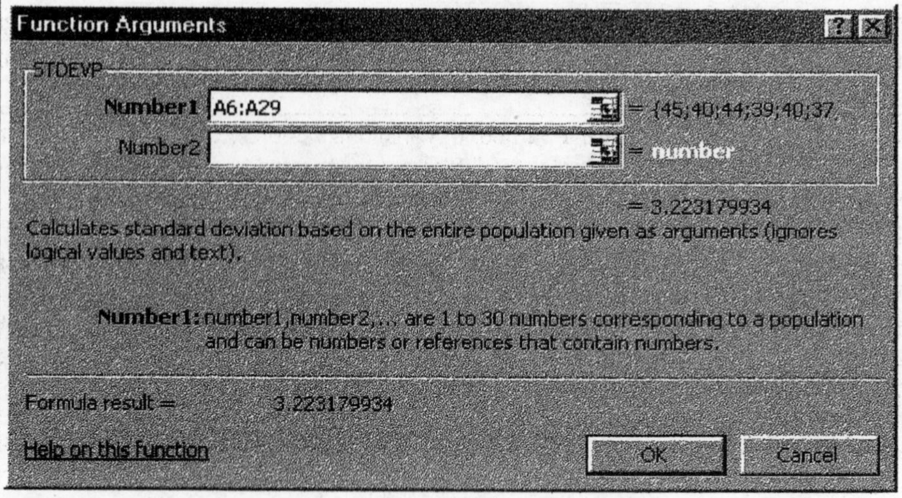

Function Arguments	? X
STDEVP	
Number1	A6:A29	= {45;40;44;39;40;37;
Number2		= number
	= 3.223179934

Calculates standard deviation based on the entire population given as arguments (ignores logical values and text).

Number1: number1,number2,... are 1 to 30 numbers corresponding to a population and can be numbers or references that contain numbers.

Formula result =   3.223179934

Help on this function   OK   Cancel

7. To compute the mean repeat Steps 2, 3 and 4 above but use the statistical function AVERAGE instead of STDEVP.

8. Press the **F2** key again and key in an * (asterisk) at the end of the AVERAGE function to indicate the result is to be multiplied.

9. Key in the number 100 and press the **Enter** key for the final result as shown in Figure 13.13.

Figure 3.13 Results for Coefficient of Variation, Interquartile Range,
              Pearson's Coefficient of Skewness and 5-Number Summary

	A	B	C	D	E	F
23	48	1.6547				
24	41	-0.5171		Population Variance	10.38889	
25	46	1.0342		Population Std. Dev.	3.22318	
26	46	1.0342		Mean Absolute Deviation	2.611111	
27	43	0.1034				
28	43	0.1034		Coefficient of Variation	7.554328	
29	44	0.4137		Interquartile Range	4.25	
30				Coefficient of Skewness	-0.77563	
31						
32				FIVE-NUMBER SUMMARY		
33				Smallest Value	35	
34				First Quartile	40.75	
35				Median	43.5	
36				Third Quartile	45	
37				Largest Value	48	

We could have computed the coefficient of variation more simply by dividing the value in cell E25 by the value in E7 and multiplying by 100. However, we presented the above procedure to demonstrate how to combine two or more statistical functions when they have not been computed separately within the worksheet.

3.4.2 Interquartile Range

Another measure of variability, the **interquartile range** is found by subtracting the first quartile from the third quartile. Excel's function QUARTILE can be used to obtain these two values.

> **QUARTILE Function Note:** There are a number of variations in the conventions used to compute quartiles. The conventions used by Excel may differ from those used in your textbook. If they do differ, the results will oftentimes be the same and sometimes differ by at most one item. For example, textbooks oftentimes define the first quartile as the $[(n + 1) / 4]^{th}$ item in the ordered array of data values. However, Excel defines the first quartile as the $[(n + 3) / 4]^{th}$ item. A little algebraic manipulation shows that Excel's definition is always 0.5 greater than the first definition. Thus, the result after any needed rounding will oftentimes be the same and sometimes differ by at most one item. Similarly, the third quartile is often defined in textbooks as the $[3(n + 1) / 4]^{th}$ item as opposed to Excel's definition of $[(3n + 1) / 4]^{th}$. Excel's definition for the third quartile will always be 0.5 less than the first definition. Again after rounding the result will either be the same or will differ by at the most one item. Excel's definition of the second quartile, the median, is the usual $[(n + 1) / 2]^{th}$.

The following is the procedure for determining the interquartile range for the *DeeLee* example data set using Excel's statistical function QUARTILE.

1. Enter the label **Interquartile Range** in cell D29 and move the worksheet pointer to cell E29.

2. Click the INSERT FUNCTION button, *fx*, with the left mouse button. The result should be the INSERT FUNCTION dialog box as shown in previous Figure 3.7 **(Excel 2000-App. D)**.

3. Click on the function category **Statistical**. Scroll to and click on the function **QUARTILE.** Click on **OK** and the result will be as shown in Figure 3.14.

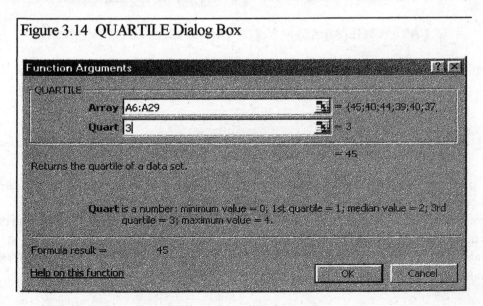

Figure 3.14 QUARTILE Dialog Box

4. Enter or click and drag through cells A6 to A29.

5. Click on the textbox to the right of the **Quart** label and enter the number **3** to designate the third quartile. Click on **OK**.

6. Press the **F2** key to enter the edit mode.

7. Key in a minus at the end of the QUARTILE function.

8. Repeat Steps 2 through 5 for the first quartile by using the number **1** in place of the **3** in step 5.

9. Press the **Enter** key and the results as shown in cell E29 of Figure 3.13 should appear in your worksheet.

3.4.3 Pearson's Coefficient of Skewness

As previously mentioned in Section 3.1, the DESCRIPTIVE STATISTICS analysis tool computes a measure of skewness as the third power of the deviations about the mean. It provides a measure of the shape of a data set. Another measure of skewness is **Pearson's coefficient of skewness**. It is computed by multiplying the difference between the mean and median times 3, and dividing the result by the standard deviation. The three statistical functions AVERAGE, MEDIAN and STDEVP can be combined to obtain a value for this measure in the following manner.

1. Enter the label **Coefficient of Skewness** in cell D30.

2. In cell E30 enter the following formula. Although you may use the INSERT FUNCTION to enter the three functions, it is perhaps easier to simply key the formula into the cell.

   = 3 * (AVERAGE(A6:A29) - MEDIAN(A6:A29)) / STDEVP(A6:A29)

Your results should appear as shown in cell E30 of Figure 3.13. Note the value differs slightly from the previous measure of skewness given in cell E14 .

3.4.4 Box Plot

The **box plot**, also called the box and whisker plot, provides a pictorial representation of the shape of a data set. It graphically shows the two extreme values for a data set, the center of the data set and the variability of the data set. It is constructed using a **five-number summary** for the data set. The five numbers are the median, the first quartile, the third quartile, the smallest value and the largest value. These all can be found with the statistical function QUARTILE (see **QUARTILE Function Note** in Subsection 3.4.2 above). We proceed in the following manner.

1. Key the labels *FIVE-NUMBER SUMMARY, Smallest Value, First Quartile, Median, Third Quartile and Largest Value* in cells D32 through D37 respectively.

2. In cells E33 through E37 key the following five QUARTILE expressions.

$$=QUARTILE(A6:A29,0)$$
$$=QUARTILE(A6:A29,1)$$
$$=QUARTILE(A6:A29,2)$$
$$=QUARTILE(A6:A29,3)$$
$$=QUARTILE(A6:A29,4)$$

The resulting five values as shown in Figure 3.13 can be used to draw the Box Plot either by hand or with Excel.

Although Excel does not include a feature for converting these five numbers into a box plot, we have developed a worksheet that does so. It is included on the CD accompanying this manual under the file name *Boxplot.xls*. For those readers who wish to **develop** their own box plot worksheet, we give the procedure for its development in Section C.1 of Appendix C.

The procedure for the **use** of *Boxplot.xls* worksheet to construct a box plot is the following.

1. Start Excel and load the *Boxplot.xls* file from the textbook CD. Enter the **Identification Material** in the appropriate places on the worksheet.

2. Enter or copy your data into Column A starting in Cell A6. Make sure there are no other data values in *Column A* leftover from a prior data set. (The worksheet is setup to accept up to 100 data values. You can increase this by editing the ranges of the formulas in cells D6 to D10.)

3. The box plot will automatically appear at the right of the worksheet. However, the entire box plot may not be displayed for your particular set of data. It may be necessary to first adjust the minimum and/or the maximum values for the axes. Click on the X-axis to ready it for editing.

4. Next click on **Format** on the menu bar and then **Selected Axis** on the subsequent pull-down menu. (Alternatively, you could **right** click the X-axis and select **Format Axis** from the resulting shortcut menu.)

5. Click on the dialog box tab labeled **Scale**. Change the minimum and the maximum values to appropriate values. Use the *Smallest Value* and *Largest Value* given on the worksheet as guides. Click on **OK** to obtain your final box plot. Refer to Figure C.4 of Appendix C to view the box plot for the example of this section.

It is possible to save the *Boxplot* file as a built-in custom chart in your copy of Excel. Thus, it would always be available to you without the need for the *Boxplot.xls* workbook. In Appendix C, we present the procedure for saving and using such a custom chart in Section C.2.

3.5 MEASURES OF ASSOCIATION
BETWEEN TWO VARIABLES

In the process of using the *Data Analysis Tools* and *Statistical Functions* presented so far in this chapter, you have computed a large number of different statistics. All of these are used to summarize a data set of **one quantitative** variable. Oftentimes for business problems we wish to determine how **two quantitative** variables are related to each other. In Chapter 2 we presented the scatter diagram for graphically displaying such a relationship. In this section of Chapter 3, we will present two data analysis tools, and three statistical functions for computing two measures of the relationship between two quantitative variables, the covariance and the coefficient of correlation.

3.5.1 The COVARIANCE Analysis Tool

As an example, let us revisit the DeeLee Trucking Company. Suppose DeeLee feels there is a relationship between the maintenance cost for trucks and the number of delivery stops trucks make. DeeLee has compiled the maintenance cost and the number of stops made for 12 trucks. He has entered the 12 pairs of values into cells A6 through B17 of an Excel worksheet as shown in Figure 3.15.

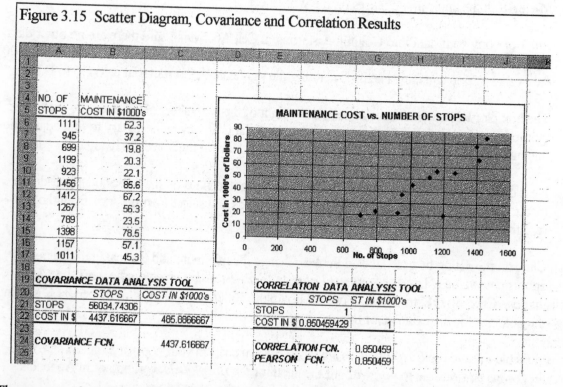

Figure 3.15 Scatter Diagram, Covariance and Correlation Results

The process of analyzing these data should begin with the construction of a scatter diagram to graphically illustrate the relationship between the two variables. We will use the procedure of Subsection 2.2.4 of Chapter 2 to construct a scatter diagram.

1. Click on the **Sheet2** tab at the bottom of the window. This will allow you to create a second worksheet for this second example within the workbook entitled DESCRIBE.

2. Enter the data labels **No. of Stops** and **Maintenance Cost in $1000's** as shown in Figure 3.15. Also enter the 12 pairs of data values in cells A6 through B17.

3. Use steps 3 through 13 of Section 2.2.4 in Chapter 2 to create the scatter diagram of Figure 3.15.

4. From the menu bar select **Tools** and next select **Data Analysis** from the pull-down menu and then select **Covariance** from the scrolling list. Finally select **OK** to obtain the *Covariance* dialog box as shown in Figure 3.16.

5. Make the entries given in Figure 3.16. These include (a) the input range, (b) the grouped by column option button, (c) the labels in first row check box, (d) the output range option button and (e) the output range.

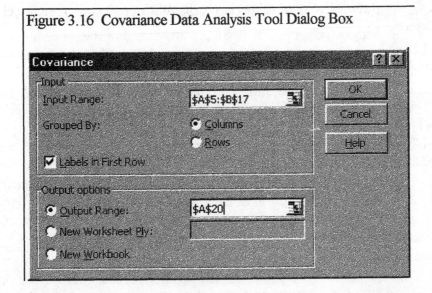

Figure 3.16 Covariance Data Analysis Tool Dialog Box

The results are as displayed in cells A20 through C22 of Figure 3.15. The label directly above these cells has been added for clarification. The value of 4437.74306 is the value of covariance for the two variables *No. of Stops* and *Maintenance Cost*. It is the **population covariance** (N in the denominator, not n - 1). The values given in cells B21 and C22 are the **population variance** values for the *No. of Stops* and the *Maintenance Cost* respectively. To convert these three values to their corresponding **sample** values multiply each of them by the value of the expression N / (n - 1).

As we have previously noted, Excel also has built-in statistical functions for computing the statistical results provided by the data analysis tools. (The general differences between the results from functions as opposed to those from tools are discussed on the first page of Appendix B.) Excel's statistical function for computing covariance is COVAR. The value from this function for our example is shown in cell C24 of Figure 3.15 with a corresponding label added in cell A24. The entry in cell C24 may be directly keyed into the cell or the INSERT FUNCTION may be used to insert it **(Excel 2000-App. D)**. In either case the entry in the cell is **=COVAR(A6:A17,B6:B17)** and the result is the population covariance value.

3.5.2 The CORRELATION Analysis Tool

As a numerical measure of the association between two variables, covariance has a weakness. The value of covariance depends on the units of measurement of the two variables. As a result, it is difficult to judge the strength of the relationship from the covariance. A measure of the relationship between two variables that avoids this difficulty is the correlation coefficient, sometimes called the Pearson product moment correlation coefficient. Excel provides a data analysis tool, called CORRELATION, and two statistical functions, called CORREL and PEARSON, that compute this numerical measure.

The procedure for using the CORRELATION analysis tool is the same as that for the COVARIANCE tool with two changes. In particular for Step 4 of the procedure in Subsection 3.5.1, the substitution of the selection of **Correlation** from the pull-down menu instead of the selection of *Covariance* will result in a dialog box almost identical to that of Figure 3.16. For Step 5 the dialog box entries are the same except the *Output Range* entry is **E20** instead of A20. The results will be as shown in cells E20 through G22 of Figure 3.15. Note the label in cell E19 was added for clarification.

The value 0.85046 given in cell F22 is the value for the correlation coefficient for the two variables *No. of Stops* and *Maintenance Cost*. It is the **sample correlation coefficient** if the input data are from a sample such as our example. If the input data were for a population, then the result would have been the population value. The values given in cells F21 and G22 will always have the value 1. They indicate that each variable has perfect positive correlation with itself. Thus, these two values are not particularly useful.

Excel's two statistical functions for computing correlation are CORREL and PEARSON. Values for these two functions are shown in cells G24 and G25 respectively with appropriate labels in cells E24 and E25. The entry in cell G24 may be keyed directly into the cell or the INSERT FUNCTION may be used to insert it **(Excel 2000-App. D)**. In either case the entry in the cell is **=CORREL(A6:A17,B6:B17)** and that for cell G25 is **=PEARSON(A6:A17,B6:B17)**. These two results will always be the same.

This then completes our look at descriptive numerical measures. At this point you may wish to save your worksheet one last time and perhaps print out your results. Then you will need to close your worksheet and exit Excel.   If you need to review the process of these operations, you may review Subsection 1.2.3 of Chapter 1.

CHAPTER 4. PROBABILITY AND SAMPLING DISTRIBUTIONS

4.1 Discrete Probability Distributions
    4.1.1 Binomial Distribution
    4.1.2 Poisson Distribution
    4.1.3 Hypergeometric Distribution

4.2 Continuous Probability Distributions
    4.2.1 Normal Distribution
    4.2.2 Exponential Distribution
    4.2.3 Uniform Distribution

4.3 Sampling Distributions
    4.3.1 Sample Mean
    4.3.2 Sample Proportion

Twenty-four of the 80 statistical functions listed in Appendix B compute values for various probability distributions. These include many common probability distributions such as the binomial, Poisson and normal, and some less well-known distributions such as the beta, negative binomial and Weibull. **Section 4.1** presents three of the most common discrete probability distributions functions. These include the binomial, the Poisson and the hypergeometric probability distributions. **Section 4.2** presents three commonly used continuous probability distributions functions: the normal, the exponential and the uniform. Some of the other distribution functions given in Appendix B such as those for the chi-square distribution, the t distribution and the F distribution are discussed in the appropriate later chapters. The final section, **Section 4.3**, of this chapter demonstrates the Central Limit Theorem through the use of data analysis tool RANDOM NUMBER GENERATION. In this section we show that the sampling distribution for the two most used sample statistics, the sample mean and the sample proportion, become approximately normally distributed as sample size increases.

4.1 DISCRETE PROBABILITY DISTRIBUTIONS ———

The INSERT FUNCTION feature includes functions for four standard discrete probability distributions, the binomial, Poisson, hypergeometric and negative binomial **(Excel 2000-App. D)**. The functions for the binomial and the Poisson distributions can directly compute both an individual probability value (the probability an individual value for the variable will occur) and the cumulative probability (the probability an individual value or less will occur.). For these other two standard discrete distributions, Excel directly computes only individual probability values.

4.1.1 Binomial Distribution ————————————

As an example, consider the Small Tomato Café. Its specialty is a pasta dish called the Bean Scene. Over the years, Skippy, the owner, has determined that about 20 per cent of the customers who enter the café purchase a Bean Scene. In other words the probability that an individual customer purchases a Bean Scene is 0.20. Suppose 12 customers enter the café, what is the probability that no one purchases a Bean Scene; that three persons make a purchase; or that four or fewer persons make a purchase? Such values can be obtained from the binomial probability distribution.

The following procedure allows you to use Excel to compute all the individual probabilities and cumulative probabilities for this example. In addition, it uses the HISTOGRAM analysis tool to plot both the individual and cumulative probabilities.

1. Use the **Start-up Procedure** of Section 1.1 of Chapter 1 to start Excel.

2. Open a new Excel worksheet and enter the **Identification Material** as discussed in Section 1.5 of Chapter 1: the worksheet title in cell B1, your name in B2, the date in A3 and the file name you wish to use in D3 such as PROBS.xls.

3. Enter the label **No. Purchased** in Cell A5, and the values **0** through **12** in cells A6 through A18. Refer ahead to Figure 4.3 to see the results of these first three steps.

4. Enter the label **Prob.** in Cell B5.

5. Use the **Saving a Workbook** procedure given in Subsection 1.2.3 of Chapter 1 to save your worksheet using the file name PROBS.

6. Move the pointer to cell B6 and click the INSERT FUNCTION Icon, *fx*, with the left mouse button. The result should be as shown in Figure 4.1.

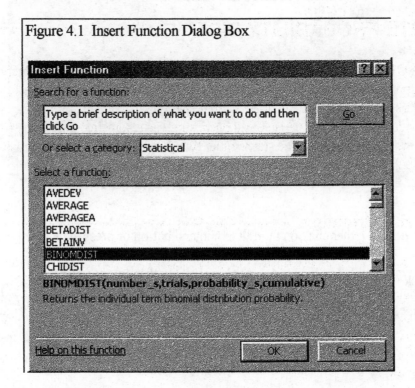

Figure 4.1 Insert Function Dialog Box

Insert Function

Search for a function:

Type a brief description of what you want to do and then click Go   Go

Or select a category: Statistical

Select a function:

AVEDEV
AVERAGE
AVERAGEA
BETADIST
BETAINV
BINOMDIST
CHIDIST

BINOMDIST(number_s,trials,probability_s,cumulative)
Returns the individual term binomial distribution probability.

Help on this function   OK   Cancel

7. Click on **Statistical** in the drop-down list box labeled *Or select a category*.

8. Click on **BINOMDIST** in the scrolling list box labeled *Select a function*. Click on **OK**.

9. In the first field of the subsequent dialog box as shown in Figure 4.2, enter the cell address for the cell containing the first value for No. Purchased. Enter **A6**.

10. Use the Tab key to move to the next field and enter **12** for the number of trials.

11. Tab to the next field and enter **0.2** for the probability value.

12. Tab to the last field and enter the word **FALSE** to indicate that the individual probability values are to be computed. (As a shortcut, you may enter the number **0** instead of the word FALSE.)

Figure 4.2 BINOMDIST Dialog Box

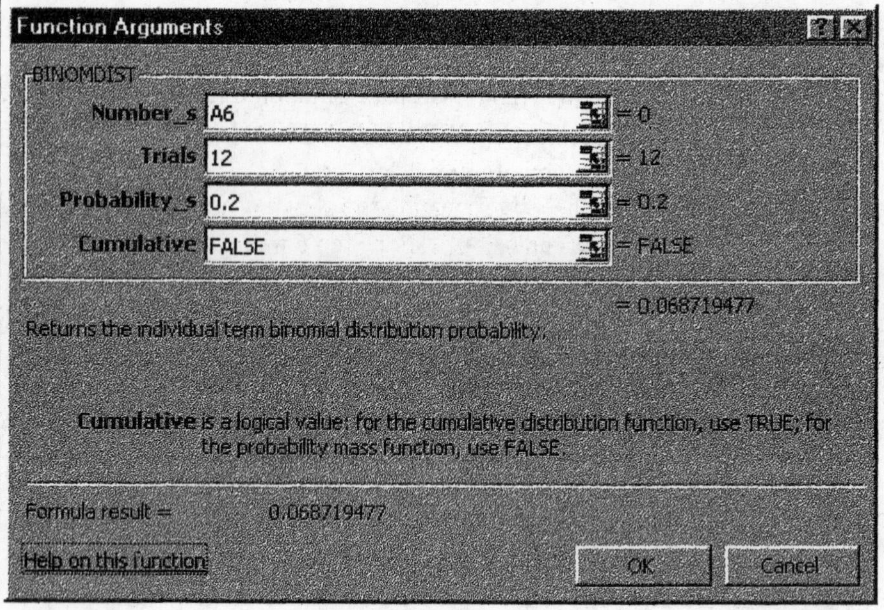

13. To end this operation, either click on the **OK** command button or press the **Enter** key.

14. The result shown in cell B6 of Figure 4.3 is the probability that no one will make a purchase.   Now copy the contents of cell B6 into cells B7 through B18 in order to compute the other 12 individual probability values for this binomial distribution. These are shown in Column B of Figure 4.3.

Figure 4.3 Binomial Distribution Results

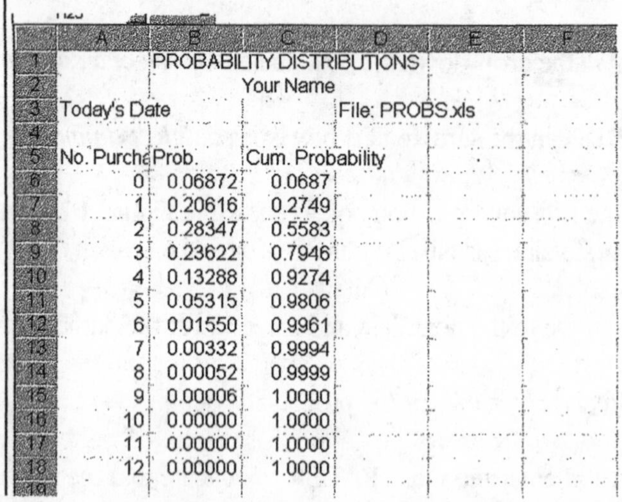

	A	B	C	D	E	F
1		PROBABILITY DISTRIBUTIONS				
2		Your Name				
3	Today's Date		File: PROBS.xls			
4						
5	No. Purcha	Prob.	Cum. Probability			
6	0	0.06872	0.0687			
7	1	0.20616	0.2749			
8	2	0.28347	0.5583			
9	3	0.23622	0.7946			
10	4	0.13288	0.9274			
11	5	0.05315	0.9806			
12	6	0.01550	0.9961			
13	7	0.00332	0.9994			
14	8	0.00052	0.9999			
15	9	0.00006	1.0000			
16	10	0.00000	1.0000			
17	11	0.00000	1.0000			
18	12	0.00000	1.0000			

15. To adjust the number of decimal values, click and drag over the 13 probability values. Then move the pointer to the **Decrease Decimal (or Increase Decimal)** icon on the formatting toolbar and click to get the number of decimal values you would like to view.

As a check, you may wish to compare the results you have computed to those values given in the table of binomial probabilities in your textbook.

We will continue to develop the worksheet by repeating the above procedure starting with Step 4. For Step 4, enter the label **Cum. Probability** in cell C5. For Step 6 move the pointer to Cell C6. For Step 12 enter **TRUE** (or the number 1 as a shortcut) in the fourth field (*Cumulative*) this time. Copy the equation in cell C6 into cells C7 through C18 to obtain all the values for the cumulative distribution. These values are shown in Column C of Figure 4.3.

Next we will develop a combination chart that graphs both the individual probability values and the cumulative probability values. The procedure is the following. (Note: If you have not used the Chart Wizard before you may wish to refer to the discussion for Figures 2.8 through 2.12 of Chapter 2.)

1. Highlight the range of cells from B5 through C18 by dragging through them.

2. Move the pointer to the CHART WIZARD icon on the standard toolbar and click once. The *Chart Wizard — Step 1 of 4—Chart Type* dialog box will appear (see prior Figure 2.8). Click on the **Custom Types** tab.

3. Use the mouse to select the **Line-Column on 2 Axes**. Click on the **Next** command button. The *Chart Wizard — Step 2 of 4—Chart Source Data* dialog box will be displayed.

4. If the **Data Range** tab is not in front, click it. Check to make sure the data range is given as **B5:C18**. Make sure **Columns** option button is selected for *Series in*. Click on the **Next** command button. The *Chart Wizard — Step 3 of 4—Chart Options* dialog box will be displayed.

5. Click on the **Titles** tab if it is not in front. Move the mouse pointer to the **Chart title** text box and click. Enter the title *BINOMIAL PROBABILITIES FOR N=12 & P=0.2.* Enter *Number Purchased* for the **Category (X) axis** and enter *Individual Probability* for **Value (Y) axis** and *Cumulative Probability* for **Second Value (Y) axis**.

6. Click on the **Axes** tab. Select the check boxes for both the **Category (X) axis** and **Value (Y) axis** under the *Primary axis* label and for **Value (Y) axis** under the *Secondary axis* label.

7. Click on the **Gridlines** tab. None of the four check boxes should be selected.

8. Click on the **Legend** tab. The check box *Show legend* should not be selected.

9. Click on the **Data Labels** tab. None of the boxes under the words **Label Contains** should be checked **(Excel 2000-App. D)**. Click on the **Next** button and the *Chart Wizard — Step 4 of 4—*

Chart Location dialog box will be presented.

10.　Click on the option **As object in.**　Click on the **Finish** command button.　Click and drag the chart to a position beside the data.　The result will be as shown in Figure 4.4.

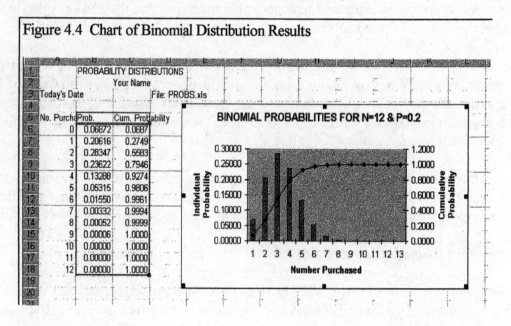

Figure 4.4　Chart of Binomial Distribution Results

4.1.2 Poisson Distribution

The procedure for producing Poisson probability distribution values is almost the same as that for the binomial distribution.　To demonstrate the process, consider the following example.

The historical records for the University Branch of the DD&V Bank indicate that the average number of customers arriving at the bank is four per hour.　Suppose the manager wishes to determine the probability that no customers arrive in an hour?　That three arrive in an hour? That four or fewer arrive in an hour?　Such values can be determined from the Poisson probability distribution.

We may proceed by continuing with the worksheet for the binomial distribution of the prior subsection as follows.

1.　Enter the label **No. of Arrivals** in Cell A25 and the values **0** through **16** in cells A26 through A42 as shown later in Figure 4.6.

2.　Enter the label **Probability** in Cell B25.

3. Use the **Saving a Workbook** procedure of Chapter 1 to save your worksheet with the name PROBS.

4. Move the pointer to cell B26 and click the INSERT FUNCTION icon, *fx*. The result should be as was previously shown in Figure 4.1 **(Excel 2000-App. D)**.

5. Select the function category **Statistical**. Scroll to and click on the function **POISSON** and click **OK.**

6. In the first field of the subsequent dialog box as shown in Figure 4.5, enter the cell address for the cell containing the first value for *No. of Arrivals*. Enter **A26**.

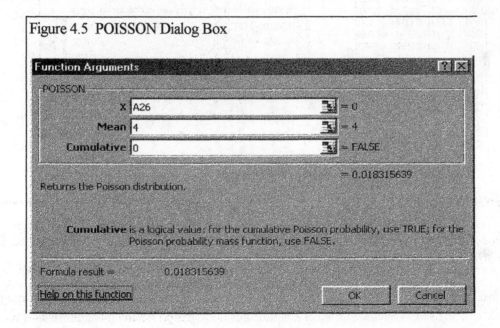

Figure 4.5 POISSON Dialog Box

7. Use the Tab key to move to the next field and enter **4** for the mean of the distribution.

8. Tab to the last field and enter the word **FALSE** to indicate the individual probability values are to be computed. (As a shortcut, you may enter the number 0 instead.)

9. To end this operation, either click on **OK** or press the **Enter** key.

10. The result in cell B26 as shown in Figure 4.6 is the probability that no customers arrive in an hour. Now copy the contents of cell B26 into cells B27 through B42 in order to compute the next 15 individual values for this Poisson probability distribution.

11. You may wish to select cells B26 through B42 and move the pointer to the **Decrease Decimal** icon on the formatting toolbar in order to adjust the number of decimal values.

How do the values given in Column B of Figure 4.6 compare to the probability values in the Poisson distribution table of your textbook?

To obtain the cumulative probability values, repeat the above procedure starting with Step 2. For Step 2, enter the label **Cum. Probability** in cell C25. For Step 4 move the pointer to Cell C26. For Step 8 enter **TRUE** (or the number 1 as a shortcut) in the third field (*cumulative*) this time. Copy the equation in cell C26 into cells C27 through C42 to obtain all the values for the cumulative distribution. These values are shown in Column C of Figure 4.6.

Figure 4.6 Poisson Distribution Results with Chart

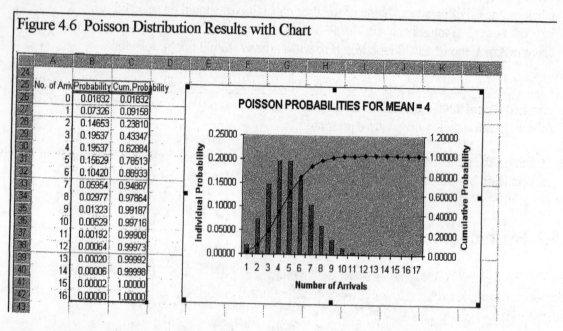

No. of Arriv	Probability	Cum. Probability
0	0.01832	0.01832
1	0.07326	0.09158
2	0.14653	0.23810
3	0.19537	0.43347
4	0.19537	0.62884
5	0.15629	0.78513
6	0.10420	0.88933
7	0.05954	0.94887
8	0.02977	0.97864
9	0.01323	0.99187
10	0.00529	0.99716
11	0.00192	0.99908
12	0.00064	0.99973
13	0.00020	0.99992
14	0.00006	0.99998
15	0.00002	1.00000
16	0.00000	1.00000

As with binomial distribution, you can develop a chart that shows both the individual probability values and the cumulative probability values. (Note: If you have not used the Chart Wizard before you may wish to refer to the discussion for Figures 2.8 through 2.12 given in Chapter 2.) The procedure is the following.

1. Highlight the range of cells from B25 through C42 by dragging through them.

2. Move the pointer to the CHART WIZARD icon on the standard toolbar and click once. The *Chart Wizard — Step 1 of 4—Chart Type* dialog box will appear (see prior Figure 2.8). Click on the **Custom Types** tab.

3. Use the mouse to select the **Line-Column on 2 Axes**. Click on the **Next** command button. The *Chart Wizard — Step 2 of 4—Chart Source Data* dialog box will be displayed.

4. If the **Data Range** tab is not in front, click it. Check to make sure the data range is given as B25:C42. Make sure **Columns** option button is selected for *Series in*. Click on the **Next** command button. The *Chart Wizard — Step 3 of 4—Chart Options* dialog box will be displayed.

5. Click on the **Titles** tab if it is not in front. Move the mouse pointer to the **Chart title** text box and click. Enter the title *POISSON PROBABILITIES FOR MEAN = 4*. Enter *Number of Arrivals* for the **Category (X) axis** and enter *Individual Probability* for **Value (Y) axis** and *Cumulative Probability* for **Second Value (Y) axis**.

6. Click on the **Axes** tab. Select the check boxes for both the **Category (X) axis** and **Value (Y) axis** under the *Primary axis* label and for **Value (Y) axis** under the *Secondary axis* label.

7. Click on the **Gridlines** tab. None of the four check boxes should be selected.

8. Click on the **Legend** tab. The check box *Show legend* should not be selected.

9. Click on the **Data Labels** tab. None of the boxes under the words **Label Contains** should be checked **(Excel 2000-App. D)**. Click on the **Next** button and the *Chart Wizard — Step 4 of 4 — Chart Location* dialog box will be presented.

10. Click on the option **As object in.** Click on the **Finish** command button. Click and drag the chart to a position beside the data. The result will be as shown in Figure 4.6.

4.1.3 Hypergeometric Distribution

The INSERT FUNCTION also includes the function HYPGEOMDIST **(Excel 2000-App. D)**. It computes individual probability values, but not cumulative probability values, for the hypergeometric distribution.

Consider the following example. Twenty-four people have applied for a position at Merry State University. Eight of the applicants are women. If five of the applicants are randomly selected from the 24, what is the probability that no women are in the sample? That three women are in the sample? That four or fewer are in the sample? The hypergeometric probability distribution can be used to compute such values.

As a demonstration of what you have learned from the two prior examples, use the INSERT FUNCTION to create the results of Figure 4.7. The following two suggestions may be of help.

1. Cell B46 will contain the HYPGEOMDIST function. The values for its dialog box are (a) the value for the random variable (the number of women in the sample), enter the cell address **A46**, (b) the sample size, **5**, (c) the number of women in the population, **8** and (d) the population size, **24**.

2. Since Excel's hypergeometric function does not directly return the cumulative probabilities, you must compute them. In particular, the cumulative probability for cell C46 should be set equal to the value in cell B46, that in cell C47 should be set equal to the value in B47 plus C46, that in C48 is equal to B48 plus C47, that in C49 is equal to B49 plus C48, and so on.

Figure 4.7 Hypergeometric Distribution Results with Chart

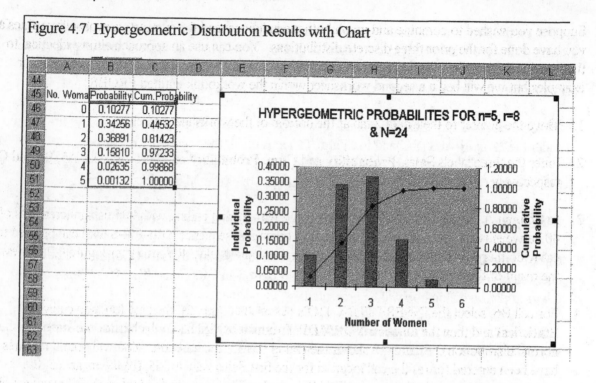

4.2 CONTINUOUS PROBABILITY DISTRIBUTIONS

Excel includes functions for nine standard continuous distributions: the beta, chi-square, exponential, F, gamma, lognormal, normal, t and Weibull. In addition Excel can be used to easily compute values for a tenth continuous distribution, the uniform. We present three of these in this section, the normal, the exponential and the uniform. The t is introduced later in Chapter 5, the F and chi-square in Chapter 7.

4.2.1 Normal Distribution

The normal distribution is the most important in business statistics. Excel includes functions for both the *standard normal distribution* (mean = 0 and standard deviation =1) and a *general normal distribution* (mean other than 0 and/or standard deviation other than 1). To obtain probability values for a standard normal distribution, the Excel function NORMSDIST is used. On the other hand, to obtain probability values for a general normal distribution the Excel function is named NORMDIST (note there is not an *S* between the *M* and *D*). We will use an example to demonstrate the use of NORMDIST. The use of NORMSDIST is identical except you do not have to specify the mean and standard deviation since they are specified to be zero and one respectively.

To demonstrate consider the following example. Cones Unlimited, known locally as the CU, sells an ice cream product known as the Schneesturm. They have determined that the number of Schneesturms sold each day can be described by a normal probability distribution with a mean of 485 and a standard deviation of 105.

Suppose you wished to compute and graph both the individual and the cumulative probability values as you have done for the prior three discrete distributions. You can use an approach almost identical to that previously described for the binomial distribution. We will continue with our work of the prior examples but we will begin a second worksheet within the workbook entitled PROBS.

1. Move the pointer to the **Sheet 2** tab at the bottom of the worksheet and click.

2. Enter the three labels **Sales**, **Probability** and **Cum. Probability** on Sheet 2 in cells A5, B5 and C5 respectively.

3. In Column A enter possible sales values starting with **65** and ending with **905** using increments of 40 between two successive numbers. Excel's command sequence **Edit-Fill-Series** can be used to easily do this or you can merely enter each number individually. Refer to later Figure 4.9 to view the result of these entries.

4. For cell B6, select the INSERT FUNCTION **(Excel 2000-App. D)**, then the function category **Statistical** and then the function **NORMDIST** (not NORMSDIST which is for the standard normal distribution). Figure 4.8 shows the dialog box for the function. You will note the values have been entered for (a) the cell location for the first Sales value of 65, (b) the mean, (c) the standard deviation and (d) the word **FALSE** which indicates *the individual probability value* will be computed and displayed.

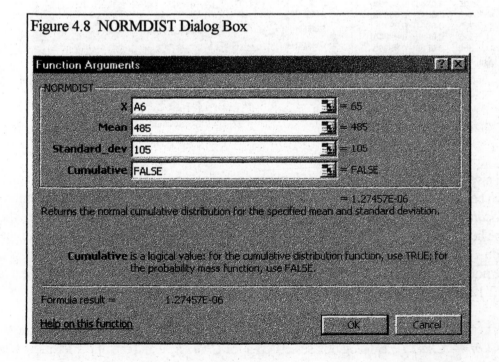

Figure 4.8 NORMDIST Dialog Box

5. Next we will use **NORMDIST** function a second time in cell C6 to compute and display *the cumulative probability value*. The entries for the dialog box are the values of Step 4 above except the word **TRUE** is entered instead of FALSE.

6. Finally, copy the functions in cells B6 and C6 into cells B7 through C27. The results will be as displayed in columns A, B and C of Figure 4.9.

Figure 4.9 Normal Distribution Results

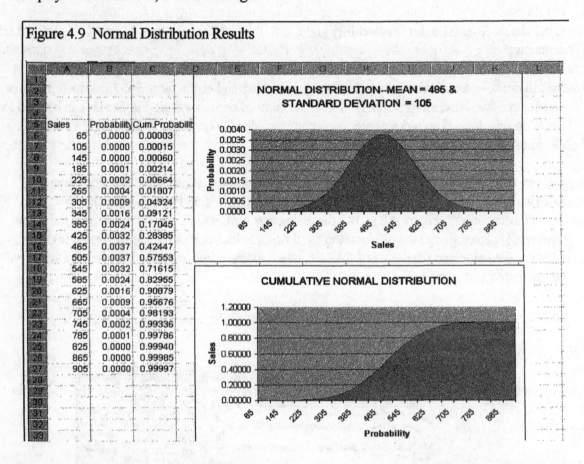

You will also note in Figure 4.9, graphs of both the individual and cumulative probability values. These can be graphed through either an *XY (Scatter)* chart or an *Area* chart. Since we demonstrated the *XY (Scatter)* chart type through two different Chapter 2 examples, we will demonstrate the *Area* chart type here. The *XY (Scatter)* chart type will be used for the exponential distribution in the next subsection. The steps required to graph the individual probability values are the following. (Note: If you have not used the Chart Wizard before you may wish to refer to the discussion for Figures 2.8 through 2.12 in Chapter 2.)

1. Select cells B6 through B27 and click on the CHART WIZARD. For the resulting *Chart Wizard – Step 1 of 4 – Chart Type* dialog box select **Area** for *Chart type* and the upper leftmost *Chart sub-type*. Click **Next**.

2. For Step 2 of the CHART WIZARD, click on the **Series** tab. Select the box labeled *Category (X) axis labels*, and fill the box by dragging through cells A6 through A27. Click on **Next**.

3. For Step 3, enter the chart title, the *Category (X) axis* title and the *Value (Y) axis* title. Select the **Legend** tab and uncheck the box for *Show Legend*. Click **Next**.

4. For the Step 4, click **Finish**. You may move the chart and resize it as you would like.

The cumulative graph shown at the bottom right of Figure 4.9 is developed using the same 4 steps with one change.   The change is that the range selected for Step 1 of the CHART WIZARD is **C6:C27** instead of **B6:B27**. You may now develop this second chart.

4.2.2 Exponential Distribution

Excel also has a function that computes values for the exponential distribution. It is EXPONDIST. To demonstrate the use of this function we will consider the following example.

> The average number of customers arriving at Boomes' Cleaners and Laundry is 15 per hour, that is, 0.25 per minute. Thus, the average time between customer arrivals is 4 minutes (=1/0.25). Furthermore the distribution of the time between arrivals appears to be exponentially distributed. The probability distribution can be used to answer questions such as, if a customer has just arrived, what is the probability that the next customer will arrive within 5 minutes or less?

The EXPONDIST function can be used to compute individual and cumulative probability values as was done above for the normal distribution using the NORMDIST function. The CHART WIZARD can then be used to graph the probability values. Again as for the normal distribution, we could use either an *XY(Scatter)* type or an *Area* type of chart. Here we will demonstrate the *XY(Scatter)* type. You should proceed as follows.

1. Begin by entering the labels in cells A35, A36, B36 and C36 as shown in later Figure 4.11. Also enter the possible values for time between arrivals as shown in cells A37 through A57.

2. INSERT FUNCTION provides the appropriate EXPONDIST functions for cells B37 through B57 and C37 through C57 **(Excel 2000-App. D)**. The steps needed are similar to steps 4, 5 and 6 in the above subsection for the NORMDIST function. For the formula for cell B37, Figure 4.10 shows the EXPONDIST Function dialog box. The formula for cell C37 is done in the same manner except the last entry in the dialog box is **True** instead of False. The contents of cells B37 and C37 are copied into cells B38 through C57.

3. Use the CHART WIZARD to graph the individual and cumulative probability values on one chart. Begin by selecting the range of values for the data and labels. Select the range **A36:C57**. For the Chart Wizard Step 1 dialog box select the **XY(Scatter)** chart type and the rightmost subtype in the

second row.   For Step 3 dialog box, enter the titles for the chart, the X axis and the Y axis. The resulting chart will be as shown in Figure 4.11.

Figure 4.10 EXPONDIST Dialog Box

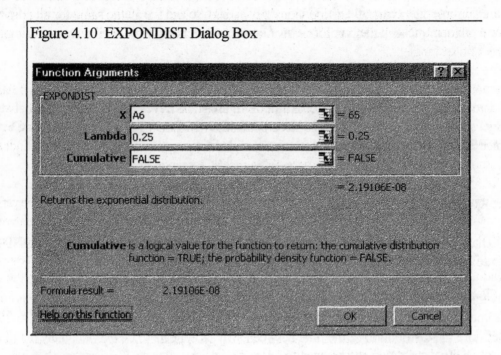

Figure 4.11 Exponential Distribution Results

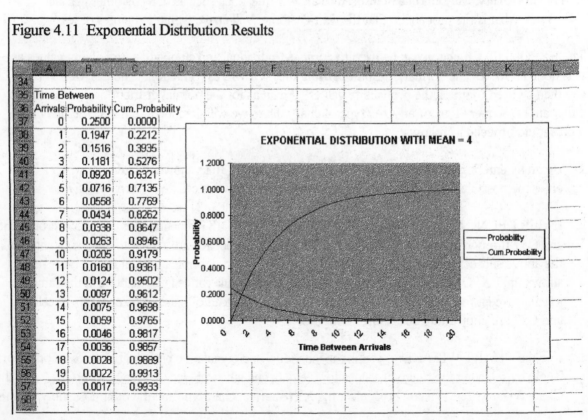

	A	B	C
34			
35	Time Between		
36	Arrivals	Probability	Cum.Probability
37	0	0.2500	0.0000
38	1	0.1947	0.2212
39	2	0.1516	0.3935
40	3	0.1181	0.5276
41	4	0.0920	0.6321
42	5	0.0716	0.7135
43	6	0.0558	0.7769
44	7	0.0434	0.8262
45	8	0.0338	0.8647
46	9	0.0263	0.8946
47	10	0.0205	0.9179
48	11	0.0160	0.9361
49	12	0.0124	0.9502
50	13	0.0097	0.9612
51	14	0.0075	0.9698
52	15	0.0059	0.9765
53	16	0.0046	0.9817
54	17	0.0036	0.9857
55	18	0.0028	0.9889
56	19	0.0022	0.9913
57	20	0.0017	0.9933
58			

4.2.3 Uniform Distribution

A special function is not needed to compute individual and cumulative probability values for the continuous uniform distribution. The individual probability values are all the same for all possible values for a uniformly distributed variable. Moreover, the cumulative probability value is simply equal to the area of a rectangle.

To demonstrate consider the situation for the Riggs and Bratton manufacturing plant. It has been determined that the amount of time it takes to assemble an engine module varies between 29 to 39 seconds. Moreover, suppose it has been determined that the assembly time can be represented by a uniform distribution. Suppose we wish to use Excel to determine the individual and cumulative probability values for assembly times at 1-second increments.

The individual probability value for each possible assembly time is equal to 1 divided by the range of possible values which is 39 - 29 = 10. This division results in the answer 0.10. The cumulative probability for a particular time value is that time value minus 29 times 0.10. For example, the cumulative probability for 32 seconds is (32 - 29) times 0.10 for an answer of 0.30. As a test of your understanding of the prior examples you should compute the probability values and create the chart given in Figure 4.12.

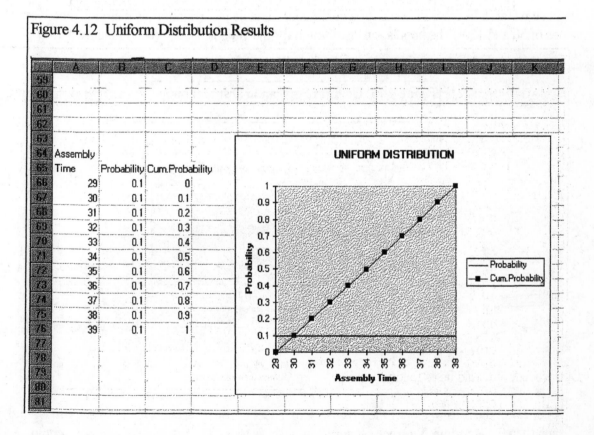

Figure 4.12 Uniform Distribution Results

4.3 SAMPLING DISTRIBUTIONS ──────────────

A sampling distribution is a probability distribution for a sample statistic such as the sample mean, sample variance, sample standard deviation or sample proportion. In this section we use the data analysis tool RANDOM NUMBER GENERATION to explore the form of the sampling distribution for two sample statistics, the sample mean and the sample proportion.

4.3.1 Sample Mean ──────────────────────

The Central Limit Theorem states that the sampling distribution of the sample mean is approximately normally distributed when the mean is computed from the values of a large sample. This is true regardless of the shape of the population distribution from which the sample is taken. This property is easily demonstrated with the use of Excel's RANDOM NUMBER GENERATION analysis tool.

The RANDOM NUMBER GENERATION tool fills a specified number of rows and columns within a worksheet with random values drawn from a specified probability distribution. The six distributions which may be specified include the uniform, normal, Bernoulli, binomial, Poisson and discrete. (It also includes a non-random selection called patterned.)

Suppose we wish to draw a sample for a continuous variable that is uniformly distributed between the values of 50 and 150. The population distribution for the variable is as shown in Figure 4.13.

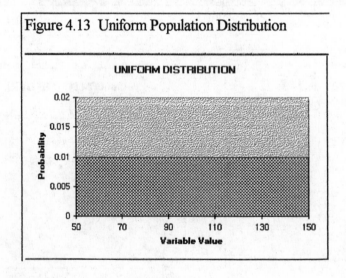

Figure 4.13 Uniform Population Distribution

Our procedure would be as follows.

1. First select the **Sheet3** tab for the PROBS worksheet. From the **Tools** menu select **Data Analysis** and then the **Random Number Generation** analysis tool. The resulting dialog box would be as

shown in Figure 4.14.

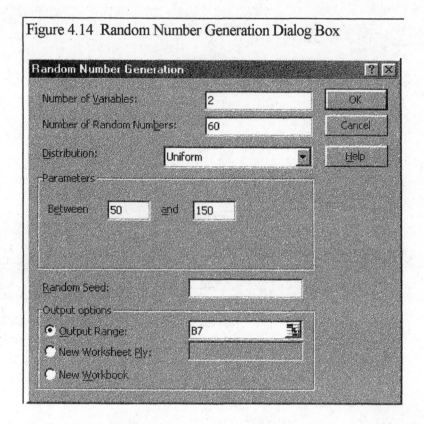

Figure 4.14 Random Number Generation Dialog Box

2. Figure 4.14 indicates you are to enter **2** for the *Number Of Variables* and **60** for the *Number of Random Samples*. The *Number Of Variables* corresponds to the *number of columns* to be filled with random values drawn from the uniform distribution of Figure 4.13. The *Number of Random Samples* corresponds to the *number of rows* to be filled with random values. Thus, this command will result in 120 random values arranged in 60 rows and 2 columns of random values. For our example, we will use these as 60 samples, one in each row and each with a sample size of 2.

3. The third input to be specified is the population distribution. The drop-down list box labeled with the word *Distribution* is used to specify a **Uniform** distribution. The lower limit of **50** and the upper limit of **150** are entered as the parameters for the distribution.

4. We can ignore the box labeled as **Random Seed** and use the mouse button to select **Output Range** as the *Output Option* and enter the output range as **B7**.

5. Select the **OK** button and the result will be 60 rows and 2 columns of numbers randomly selected from the specified uniform distribution. See Figure 4.15 but note that your random values will not be the same as those of Figure 4.15. After all they are random.

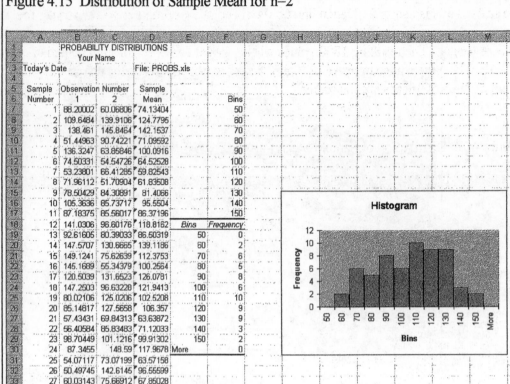

Figure 4.15 Distribution of Sample Mean for n=2

6. In cell D7, enter the formula **=AVERAGE(B7:C7)** in order to compute the mean of the first sample given in row 7. Copy the equation down in order to compute the remaining 59 sample means for rows 8 though 66.

7. Our last step is to use Excel's HISTOGRAM analysis tool to construct a histogram of the 60 sample means in cells D7 through D66. First we will determine the largest and smallest values for the means by entering at the bottom of Column D the expression **=MAX(D7:D66)** in cell D68, and the expression **=MIN(D7:D66)** in cell D69. These two values identify the range of mean values to be included in the histogram.

8. Based on the range of values and the number of bins to be used, the bin values are selected. As shown in cells F7 through F16 in Figure 4.15, we have selected 10 bins with an increment of 10 and starting with a lower limit of 50. The Histogram output range is specified as E18. (Refer to Section 2.1 of Chapter 2 for a more thorough discussion of the HISTOGRAM data analysis tool.)

As you will note from the histogram in Figure 4.15, the distribution of these means with a sample size of 2 appears peaked or triangular in shape, not shaped as a normal distribution. Since your random sample values differ from those used in Figure 4.15, your histogram will not be exactly like that of Figure 4.15. However, it should have the same general appearance.

This process is repeated in Figure 4.16 for 60 samples of size 30 instead of 60 samples of size 2. Thus the only change necessary to the dialog box shown in Figure 4.14 is to set the *Number of variables* (sample size) to 30 instead of 2. Depending on the speed of the computer you are using, the generation of 60 times 30 (= 1800) random observations from the uniform distribution may take a few moments or longer. The resulting 1800 values will be shown in rows 7 through 66 and in columns B through AE. The entries in column AF of Figure 4.16 compute the means for the 60 samples. The histogram of these 60 means is constructed.

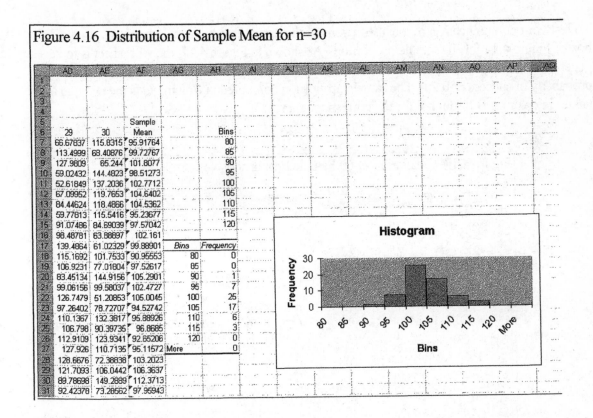

Figure 4.16 Distribution of Sample Mean for n=30

The results of Figure 4.16 show two significant changes from those of Figure 4.15. First, the range of values for the sample means is much reduced. Second, the histogram of the sample means appears more normal shaped than that of Figure 4.15. Thus, this example demonstrates that the distribution of the means of samples taken from a non-normal population becomes more normal shaped as the sample size is increased. You may wish to repeat the example for a sample size of 100 to make the demonstration more emphatic.

4.3.2 Sample Proportion

The sample proportion is second only to the sample mean as the most well used sample statistic in business and industry. The sampling distribution for the sample proportion is the binomial distribution.

However, the Central Limit Theorem applies to it also.   That is for large sample sizes, the sampling distribution for the sample proportion also can be approximated by the normal distribution.

To demonstrate this fact, we can use the RANDOM NUMBER GENERATION analysis tool to generate samples from a **Bernoulli** distribution. The two possible values for the Bernoulli distribution are *0* and *1*. Accordingly, the proportion or percent of times the value *1* occurs in a sample is equal to the average value for the sample. The histogram of these proportions can be plotted in order to see the shape of the distribution.

To test your comprehension of the instructions of the prior subsection, you should set up the dialog box of Figure 4.14 for the sample proportion. As shown in Figure 4.17, the worksheet is to be setup to generate 60 samples *(rows)* with a sample size of 5 *(columns)* from a Bernoulli distribution with a probability of success of 0.20. The sample proportion computed in Column G is the average of the values in columns B through F for the corresponding row.

Figure 4.17 Generation of 60 Sample Proportions with n=5

	A	B	C	D	E	F	G	H
75	Sample		Observation Number				Sample	
76	Number	1	2	3	4	5	Proportion	
77	1	0	0	1	0	1	0.4	
78	2	0	1	1	0	1	0.6	
79	3	0	0	0	0	1	0.2	
80	4	0	0	0	0	1	0.2	
81	5	1	0	0	0	0	0.2	
82	6	1	1	0	0	0	0.4	
83	7	0	0	0	0	0	0	
84	8	0	0	0	1	1	0.4	
85	9	0	1	1	1	1	0.8	
86	10	0	1	0	0	0	0.2	
87	11	0	0	0	0	0	0	
88	12	0	0	0	1	0	0.2	
89	13	0	1	0	0	0	0.2	
90	14	0	0	1	0	1	0.4	
91	15	1	0	0	0	0	0.2	
92	16	0	0	0	0	0	0	
93	17	1	0	0	0	0	0.2	
94	18	1	1	0	0	0	0.4	
95	19	1	0	1	0	0	0.4	
96	20	0	0	0	0	0	0	
97	21	0	0	0	0	0	0	
98	22	0	0	1	0	0	0.2	
99	23	0	0	0	0	0	0	
100	24	1	0	0	0	1	0.4	
101	25	0	0	1	0	0	0.2	
102	26	0	0	0	1	0	0.2	
103	27	0	0	0	0	0	0	
104	28	0	0	0	0	0	0	

The histogram for these 60 sample proportions is shown in Figure 4.18. As you will note, the form of the histogram suggests a binomial distribution as would be expected. Because the outcomes are random, your results may differ slightly from those we have presented.

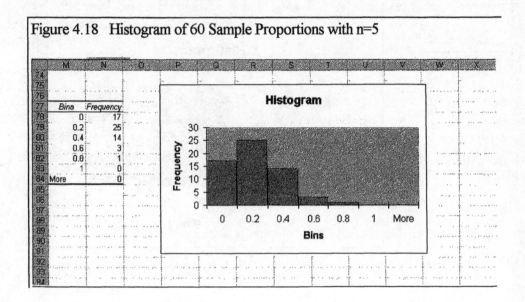

Figure 4.18   Histogram of 60 Sample Proportions with n=5

When this process is repeated using 60 samples of size 50 the resulting distribution of the 60 sample proportions is much more normally distributed in its shape as is shown in Figure 4.19 on the next page. This is as we would expect based on the Central Limit Theorem.

At this time you may wish to save your Excel workbook one last time and perhaps print the results. You will then need to close your workbook and exit Excel.

Figure 4.19 Histogram of 60 Sample Proportion with n=50

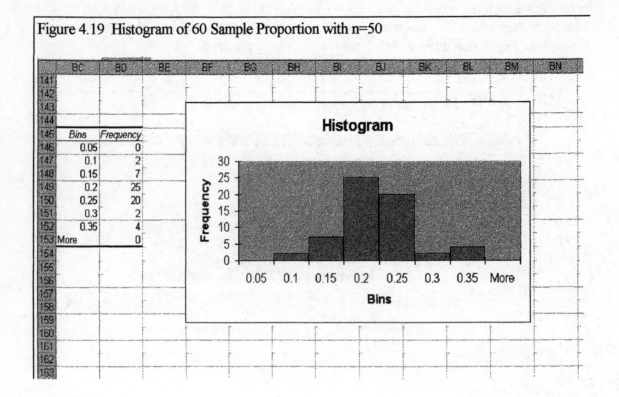

	Bins	Frequency
146	0.05	0
147	0.1	2
148	0.15	7
149	0.2	25
150	0.25	20
151	0.3	2
152	0.35	4
153 More		0

CHAPTER 5. STATISTICAL INFERENCE FOR POPULATION MEANS

5.1 One Population Mean
    5.1.1 Point Estimate and Confidence Interval—Normal Distribution
    5.1.2 Hypothesis Test—Normal Distribution
    5.1.3 Point Estimate and Confidence Interval—t Distribution
    5.1.4 Hypothesis Test—t Distribution
    5.1.5 Determining the Necessary Sample Size

5.2 The t-TEST: TWO-SAMPLE ASSUMING UNEQUAL VARIANCE Analysis Tool
    5.2.1 Hypothesis Test for Two Population Means with Independent Samples
    5.2.2 Point Estimate and Confidence Interval for Two Population Means
    5.2.3 Statistical Inference for One Population Mean

5.3 Two Additional Analysis Tools for Two Independent Samples
    5.3.1 The t-TEST: TWO-SAMPLE ASSUMING EQUAL VARIANCE Tool
    5.3.2 The z-TEST: TWO SAMPLE FOR MEANS Analysis Tool

5.4 The t-TEST: PAIRED TWO SAMPLE FOR MEANS Analysis Tool
    5.4.1 Hypothesis Test for Two Population Means with Dependent Samples
    5.4.2 Point Estimate and Confidence Interval for Two Population Means
    5.4.3 Statistical Inference for One Population Mean

At this point in this manual we have used Excel to support our study of the **descriptive use of sample statistics**, commonly called **descriptive statistics**. In Chapter 2 we constructed descriptive graphs and charts and in Chapter 3 we computed descriptive numerical measures. In Chapter 4 we computed values for probability distributions and examined sampling distributions. The study of these distributions provides background needed for understanding the material of the current chapter. In this chapter we use Excel to support our study of the **inferential use of sample statistics**, commonly called **inferential statistics** or **statistical inference**.

The term statistical inference refers to the process of acquiring information and drawing conclusions about **populations** based on **samples** taken from the populations. The two main thrusts of statistical inference are the *statistical estimation* and the *statistical testing* of an unknown **population parameter** through the use of a value for the corresponding **sample statistic**.

In business and industry, three of the most important population parameters are the population mean, the population proportion and the population variance (or standard deviation). For each one of these three, we can use Excel to (1) compute a **point estimate** with its corresponding **confidence interval** (also called **interval estimate**), and (2) conduct a **hypothesis test** for a single population. Moreover many times, it is necessary to estimate and/or test a comparison of parameters for two populations. For example, we may want to compare two population means, two population proportions or two population variances. Again for these situations, Excel provides the capability to easily compute a point estimate with its corresponding confidence interval and to conduct a hypothesis test.

This current chapter presents statistical inference for population means. The chapter treats both statistical estimation and testing for one population mean and also for two population means. Chapter 6 provides similar coverage of statistical inference for population proportions and Chapter 7 for population variances.

Section 5.1 of the current chapter covers statistical inference for one population mean. In it we demonstrate the use of formulas and statistical functions to compute values for the point estimate with its corresponding confidence interval and values for the hypothesis test. (Alternate approaches using two different Excel two-population data analysis tools are presented in subsections 5.2.3 and 5.4.3.)

Sections 5.2 and 5.3 cover statistical inference for two population means using independent samples. These two sections present the three approaches commonly given in statistics textbooks for estimating and testing the difference between two population means using independent samples. Usually the first approach given in a textbook is that based on the normal (or z) distribution. This approach is valid if the population variances are known. It is also used when the sample sizes of both samples are large enough that the normal distribution can be used to approximate the t distribution. The second and third approaches given in most statistics textbooks are based on the t distribution (*note some textbooks only present one or the other of these two*). These two approaches are applicable if the population variances are not known and if the z distribution is not to be used to approximate the t distribution. One of these two approaches requires the condition that the unknown variances of the two populations are known to be equal to each other. The other does not require this limiting condition.

Some statisticians feel the most general of these three approaches is that which uses the t distribution and does not require the condition that the population variances are known to be equal. Accordingly, **Section 5.2** presents this approach in detail. In it we use Excel's t-TEST: TWO-SAMPLE ASSUMING UNEQUAL VARIANCE analysis tool. We compute values for the point estimate with its corresponding confidence interval, and compute values for the hypothesis test for two population means using independent samples. Also in this section we show how to use this two-population analysis tool to compute the same values for the one population situation. **Section 5.3** then discusses the other two approaches. These are based on the t-TEST: TWO-SAMPLE ASSUMING EQUAL VARIANCE analysis tool and z-TEST: TWO SAMPLE FOR MEANS analysis tool. Section 5.3 highlights the differences between the use of these two analysis tools and the tool presented in Section 5.2.

Finally **Section 5.4** covers statistical inference for two population means using dependent samples. Your textbook may call dependent samples paired samples, matched samples, related samples or matched pairs. The approach of this section uses the t distribution and is based on the t-TEST: PAIRED TWO SAMPLE FOR MEANS analysis tool. Section 5.4 also indicates how to use this two population analysis tools to compute the same values for the one population situation.

5.1 ONE POPULATION MEAN

As previously mentioned the two main thrusts of statistical inference are estimation and testing. **Estimation** involves using the value for a sample statistic, such as the sample mean, to provide a **point estimate** for an unknown corresponding population parameter, such as the population mean. In order to quantify the precision or accuracy of the point estimate, a corresponding **confidence interval** (or interval estimate) is computed. The confidence interval is of the form

Point Estimate ± (Confidence Level Critical Value) * (Standard Error for the Point Estimate).

The confidence level critical value is found from an appropriate probability distribution such as the normal, the t, the F and so on.

On the other hand, **testing** involves using the value for a sample statistic, such as the sample mean, to test a tentative assumption regarding an unknown value for a corresponding population parameter. The result of the **hypothesis test** is either the rejection or not of the tentative hypothesis which is called the null hypothesis. The test is conducted using a test statistic that generally is of the form

Test Statistic = (Point Estimate-Null Hypothesis Value) / (Standard Error for the Point Estimate).

The value computed by this equation is compared to critical value from an appropriate probability distribution such as the normal, the t, the F and so on. Based on this comparison, the null hypothesis is either rejected or not.

In order to demonstrate the use of the above formulas in Excel we will consider the following example in this section.

Ms. Lizabert Humperdinck, the general manager of the Read and Feed chain of restaurants, is investigating promotional ideas for the *Country Basket* dinners. She has proposed using spot advertisements on local TV to promote the product. Furthermore, she feels the spot ads will increase average sales to 215 per store. The advertising program is pursued in the service area of eight randomly selected restaurants and the resulting sales from the eight are as given in Table 5.1.

Table 5.1 Number of Country Basket Dinners Sold after TV Promotion								
Number Sold	240	220	190	175	220	215	219	195

We will use this example to demonstrate the computations for both (1) the point estimate and confidence interval, and (2) the hypothesis test for one population mean. If you wish to compute these using the **normal (or z) distribution** proceed through subsections **5.1.1** and **5.1.2**. If you wish to use the **t distribution** you should proceed through subsections **5.1.3** and **5.1.4**. These parts of the manual are written assuming you will be studying either 5.1.1 and 5.1.2, or 5.1.3 and 5.1.4. In particular, 5.1.3 and 5.1.4 do not refer to any material in 5.1.1 and 5.1.2. Instead they repeat some material from these prior subsections. If you proceed through all four sections, there will be some duplicated material in subsections 5.1.3 and 5.1.4. We use *Sheet1* of our workbook for the normal distribution computations and *Sheet2* for the t distribution. The last subsection, 5.1.5, shows how to compute the sample size required to attain a specified width and confidence level for a confidence interval. These computations are included on *Sheet3* of the workbook. They follow either the normal distribution computations of *Sheet1* or the t distribution computations of *Sheet2*.

5.1.1 Point Estimate and Confidence Interval—Normal Distribution——

The point estimate and confidence interval can be computed easily for the data set of Table 5.1. For example, we can proceed in the following manner in order to compute the point estimate and 95% confidence interval.

1. Start Excel and enter the **Identification Material** shown in rows 1 and 2 of later Figure 5.2. Then enter the labels of rows 3 through 17. (Note some of the column widths have been adjusted for readability. You may also wish to do this.) Enter the data values in cells A5 through A12 and the input value in cell E4. (Note the labels in rows 18 through 25 and the input values given in cells E6 and E7 will be entered later when the hypothesis test computations are added.) Save the workbook with the name MEANS-1.

2. Compute the value for the sample mean, sample standard deviation and sample size by entering the functions **AVERAGE**, **STDEV** and **COUNT** in cells L5, L6 and L7 as shown in Figure 5.1. As you will note from the figure, we have set the range for these functions as A5 through A104. Thus, the worksheet will compute these sample statistics for data sets with up to 100 data values.

3. To compute the point estimate for the population mean, enter the formula =L5 in cell L9.

4. Cell L13 uses the Excel function NORMSINV to find the critical z-value for the specified confidence level given in cell E4. The confidence level is converted from percentage to decimal form by first dividing by 100, and then it is converted to the two-tailed value by dividing by 2. Finally 0.5 is added to the result in order to find the z-value on the right-hand of the distribution. The resulting formula for cell L13 is **=NORMSINV(E4/100/2+0.5)** as shown in Figure 5.1.

Figure 5.1 Statistical Inference Formulas for One Population Mean—Normal Distribution

		J	K	L	
1	OR ONE MEAN WITH NORMAL DISTRIBUTION				
2			Fil		
3					
4	*Sample Statistics*				
5		Sample Mean			=AVERAGE(A5:A104)	
6		Sample Standard Deviation			=STDEV(A5:A104)	
7		Sample Size			=COUNT(A5:A104)	
8						
9	*Point Estimate*				=L5	
10						
11	*Confidence Interv*					
12						
13		Confidence Level Critical z-value			=NORMSINV(E4/100/2+0.5)	
14		Standard Error of the Point Estimate			=L6/SQRT(L7)	
15		Confidence Interval–Half Width			=L13*L14	
16		--Lower Limit			=L9-L15	
17		--Upper Limit			=L9+L15	
18	*Hypothesis Test*					
19		Test Statistic			=(L9-E6)/L14	
20		z critical value–Two-Tailed			=-1*NORMSINV($E$7/2)	
21		--Upper-Tailed			=-1*NORMSINV($E$7)	
22		--Lower-Tailed			=NORMSINV($E$7)	
23		p-value–Two-Tailed			=IF($L$19<0,2*NORMSDIST($L$19),2*(1-NORMSDIST($L$19)))	
24		--Upper-Tailed			=1-NORMSDIST($L$19)	
25		--Lower-Tailed			=NORMSDIST($L$19)	
26						

5. The formula in cell L14 computes the standard error of the point estimate from the values for the sample standard deviation and the sample size computed in cells L6 and L7 respectively. The formula in cell L14 is **=L6/SQRT(L7)**.

6. Half the width of the confidence interval is found by multiplying the critical z-value times the standard error of the point estimate as shown in cell L15.

7. The half width is subtracted from the point estimate to compute the confidence interval lower limit as shown in cell L16. It is added to the point estimate to compute the upper limit in L17.

Figure 5.2 shows the results of these computations. Cell L9 presents the best estimate of Read and Feed's sales after the spot advertisement campaign. Its value is 209.25. The precision of this estimate is quantified by the 95% confidence interval given in cells L16 and L17. It is from 194.782 to 223.718. Since this 95% confidence interval includes Lizabert's postulated sales value of 215, she can conclude her sales expectation have been attained.

Figure 5.2 Statistical Inference for One Population Mean—Normal Distribution

	A	B	C	D	E	F	G	H	I	J	K	L	M
1	STATISTICAL INFERENCE FOR ONE MEAN WITH NORMAL DISTRIBUTION												
2	Today's Date				Your Name						File: MEANS-1.xls		
3	*INPUT DATA*						*STATISTICAL OUTPUTS*						
4	*Data Values*		Confidence Level		95	%	*Sample Statistics*						
5	240						Sample Mean					209.250	
6	220		Hypothesized Mean =		215		Sample Standard Deviation					20.879	
7	190		Significance Level of Test=		0.05		Sample Size					8	
8	175												
9	220						*Point Estimate*					209.250	
10	215												
11	219						*Confidence Interval*						
12	195												
13							Confidence Level Critical z-value					1.95996	
14							Standard Error of the Point Estimate					7.382	
15							Confidence Interval--Half Width					14.468	
16							--Lower Limit					194.782	
17							--Upper Limit					223.718	
18							*Hypothesis Test*						
19							Test Statistic					-0.779	
20							z critical value--Two-Tailed					1.960	
21							--Upper-Tailed					1.645	
22							--Lower-Tailed					-1.645	
23							p-value--Two-Tailed					0.436	
24							--Upper-Tailed					0.782	
25							--Lower-Tailed					0.218	
26													
27													

5.1.2 Hypothesis Test—Normal Distribution

The values needed for conducting a hypothesis test can also be computed easily with Excel. To demonstrate we will use the data set of Table 5.1 to compute the values needed to conduct a hypothesis test both for the **critical z-value approach** and for the **p-value approach**. We will compute the values needed for these two testing approaches for all three of the possible forms of the hypothesis test as shown in Table 5.2. We will refer to the three forms as Two-Tailed, Upper-Tailed and Lower-Tailed hypothesis tests.

Table 5.2 Possible Hypothesis Forms for Testing One Population Mean

Two-Tailed	**Upper-Tailed**	**Lower-Tailed**
H_0: $\mu = 215$	H_0: $\mu \leq 215$	H_0: $\mu \geq 215$
H_a: $\mu \neq 215$	H_a: $\mu > 215$	H_a: $\mu < 215$

We can proceed in the following manner in order to conduct a hypothesis test to determine if the sales level is 215 after the advertising campaign. We will conduct the test using a significance level of 0.05 and continue with the worksheet presented in Figure 5.2.

1. Enter the labels in rows 18 through 25 and the input values in cells E6 and E7 as shown in Figure 5.2.

2. Enter the formula **=(L9-E6)/L14** into cell L19 to compute the z-statistic value for the sample (Figure 5.1 shows the formula in the worksheet.)

3. In cell L20 the function NORMSINV is used to determine the critical value for the z-statistic for the **Two-Tailed** form of the test. The function is multiplied by a minus one to obtain the needed positive value. Thus, the entry for cell L20 is **= - 1*NORMSINV($E$7/2)**. (Note it is not necessary for E7 to have the absolute address, $E$7.)

4. The NORMSINV function is also used in cells L21 and L22 to determine the critical value for the z-statistic for the **Upper-Tailed** and **Lower-Tailed** test forms. For cell L21 the formula is **= -1*NORMSINV($E$7)** and for cell L22 **=NORMSINV($E$7)**.

5. Move the cell pointer to cell L25 and enter the formula **=NORMSDIST($L$19)** to compute the p value for the **Lower-Tailed** test.

6. Cell L24 computes the p value for the **Upper-Tailed** test by the formula **=1-NORMSDIST($L$19)**.

7. Finally in cell L23 an IF function is used to determine the p value for the **Two-Tailed** test form. If the value for the test statistic, cell L19, is less than zero, the p value is computed as two times the computation of cell L25. Otherwise it is computed as two times the computation of L24. You may feel the resulting formula appears somewhat intimidating. However, it is merely made up of three parts separated by commas: (1) a test for negativity, (2) a

computation similar to cell L25 and (3) a computation similar to cell L24. The resulting formula is **=IF($L$19<0,2*NORMSDIST($L$19),2*(1-NORMSDIST($L$19)))**.

The results of these steps are as shown in previous Figure 5.2. Your worksheet provides the statistics necessary to conduct the single sample hypothesis test for both the critical z-value and the p-value approaches. For both of these two approaches, it provides the values for testing all three of the possible forms of the hypotheses given in Table 5.2.

For the **CRITICAL z-VALUE APPROACH,** the value for the test statistic in cell L19 of Figure 5.2 is -0.779. For the **Two-Tailed** test, cell L20 indicates the critical values for the test statistic are -1.960 and +1.960. Since the value of -0.779 does not fall outside these limits, the null hypothesis is not rejected. The sample evidence does not support rejecting the hypothesis that *Read and Feed* sales level is 215 after the advertising campaign. In other words, in light of the sample evidence the assumption of a sales level of 215 seems reasonable.

For the **Upper-Tailed** test, the test value of -0.779 is not greater than the critical value of +1.645 given in cell L21 of Figure 5.2. Thus, we cannot reject the null hypothesis. The sample data supports the contention that the market share is less than or equal to 215.

Finally for the **Lower-Tailed** test, the test value of -0.779 is not less than the critical value of -1.645 given in cell L22 so the hypothesis of a sales level of greater than or equal to 215 is not rejected. Thus, all three forms of the test indicate an acceptance of the null hypothesis, and for all three forms the null hypothesis includes the possibility of a sales level of 215. Lizabert's hypothesis (conjecture, hunch, estimate, guess, etc.) that the spot TV advertisements boost sales of the *Country Dinners* to 215 per store, is supported by the sample evidence.

The results of Figure 5.2 also let us consider the **p-VALUE APPROACH** to this test. Conventional usage of p-values classifies test results according to the categories given in Table 5.3 (see for example Siegel, *Practical Business Statistics*, 5th ed., McGraw-Hill, 2003, p.393).

Table 5.3 p-Value Classification Categories

If the P-Value is	Then the Difference is
Greater than 0.05	Not Significant
Greater than 0.01 but less than or equal to 0.05	Significant
Greater than 0.001 but less than or equal to 0.01	Highly Significant
Less than or equal to 0.001	Very Highly Significant

Utilizing the classification categories of this table, we would classify the results as *not significant* for all three forms of the hypotheses. That is, the p values of 0.436, 0.782 and 0.218 are all greater than 0.05. The conclusion is not to reject the null hypothesis regardless of what hypotheses form we were testing. This is the same conclusion drawn using the critical z-value approach.

You should save your completed worksheet of Figure 5.2 for future use. Although you developed it for a particular test situation, it is completely general. Thus, you can use it for estimating and testing a population mean based on a sample from that population. The sample size can be 100 or less. To use the worksheet, you only need to enter

1. The data values for the sample beginning in cell A5. As previously indicated the formulas you entered allow for up to 100 data values. This limit could be increased by simply expanding the range used in the formulas of cells L5, L6 and L7,

2. The confidence level you desire for the confidence interval in cell E4, and

3. The hypothesized value for the mean in cell E6 and the significance level for the test in cell E7.

After entering these input values, your worksheet will provide you with the point estimate and its confidence interval based on the normal distribution. In addition, it will return all the necessary values for conducting all three forms of the hypothesis test for both the critical z-value and the p-value approaches.

5.1.3 Point Estimate and Confidence Interval—t Distribution

The point estimate and confidence interval can easily be computed for the data set of Table 5.1. For example, we can proceed in the following manner in order to compute the point estimate and 95% confidence interval. To begin, click on **Sheet2** at the bottom of the worksheet window.

1. Start Excel and enter the **Identification Material** shown in rows 1 and 2 of later Figure 5.4. Then enter the labels of rows 3 through 17. (Note some of the column widths have been adjusted for readability. You may also wish to do this.) Enter the data values in cells A5 through A12 and the input value in cell E4. (Note the labels in rows 18 through 25 and the input values given in cells E6 and E7 will be entered later when the hypothesis test computations are added.) Save the workbook with the name MEANS-1.

2. Compute the value for the sample mean, sample standard deviation and sample size by entering the functions **AVERAGE**, **STDEV** and **COUNT** in cells L5, L6 and L7 as shown in Figure 5.3. As you will note from the figure, we have set the range for these functions as A5 through A104. Thus, the worksheet will compute these sample statistics for data sets with up to 100 data values.

3. To compute the point estimate for the population mean, enter the formula =**L5** in cell L9.

4. Cell L12 computes the degrees of freedom as equal to the sample size minus one, and cell L13 uses the Excel function TINV to find the critical t value for the specified confidence level given in cell E4. The confidence level is converted from percentage to decimal form by first dividing by 100, and the resulting value is subtracted from one to obtain the probability in the tail of the distribution. It is not necessary to divide by 2 because the TINV function returns a two-tailed value. The resulting formula for cell L13 is =**TINV(1-E4/100,L12)** where cell L12 refers to the degrees of freedom.

5. The formula in cell L14 computes the standard error of the point estimate from the values for the sample standard deviation and the sample size computed in cells L6 and L7 respectively. The formula in cell L14 is =**L6/SQRT(L7)**.

Figure 5.3 Statistical Inference Formulas for One Population Mean—t Distribution

	H	I	J	K	L	M
1						
2				File: ME		
3						
4	*Sample Statistics*					
5		Sample Mean			=AVERAGE(A5:A104)	
6		Sample Standard Deviation			=STDEV(A5:A104)	
7		Sample Size			=COUNT(A5:A104)	
8						
9	*Point Estimate*				=L5	
10						
11	*Confidence Interval*					
12		Degrees of Freedom			=L7-1	
13		Confidence Level Critical t-va			=TINV(1-E4/100,L12)	
14		Standard Error of the Point E			=L6/SQRT(L7)	
15		Confidence Interval--Half Wic			=L13*L14	
16		--Low			=L9-L15	
17		--Upp			=L9+L15	
18	*Hypothesis Test*					
19		Test Statistic			=(L9-E6)/L14	
20		t critical value--Two-Tailed			=TINV($E$7,L12)	
21		--Upper-Tailed			=TINV(2*$E$7,L12)	
22		--Lower-Tailed			=-1*TINV(2*$E$7,L12)	
23		p-value--Two-Tailed			=TDIST(ABS(L19),L12,2)	
24		--Upper-Tailed			=IF(L19<0,1-TDIST(ABS(L19),L12,1),TDIST(ABS(L19),L12,1))	
25		--Lower-Tailed			=1-L24	

6. Half the width of the confidence interval is found by multiplying the critical t value times the standard error of the point estimate as shown in cell L15.

7. The half width is subtracted from the point estimate to compute the confidence interval lower limit as shown in cell L16. It is added to the point estimate to compute the upper limit in cell L17.

Figure 5.4 shows the results of these computations. As given in cell L9 the best estimate of Read and Feed's sales after the spot advertisement campaign is 209.25. The precision of this estimate is quantified by the 95% confidence interval given in cells L16 and L17. Based on the t distribution it is 191.795 to 226.705. Since this 95% confidence interval includes Lizabert's postulated sales value of 215, she can conclude her sales expectation has been attained.

Figure 5.4 Statistical Inference for One Population Mean—t Distribution

	A	B	C	D	E F G	H	I	J	K	L	M
1			STATISTICAL INFERENCE FOR ONE MEAN WITH t DISTRIBUTION								
2	Today's Date				Your Name				File: MEANS-1.xls		
3	INPUT DATA					STATISTICAL OUTPUTS					
4	Data Values		Confidence Level		95 %	Sample Statistics					
5	240						Sample Mean			209.250	
6	220		Hypothesized Mean =		215		Sample Standard Deviation			20.879	
7	190		Significance Level of Test=		0.05		Sample Size			8	
8	175										
9	220					Point Estimate				209.250	
10	215										
11	219					Confidence Interval					
12	195						Degrees of Freedom			7	
13							Confidence Level Critical t-value			2.365	
14							Standard Error of the Point Estimate			7.382	
15							Confidence Interval--Half Width			17.455	
16								--Lower Limit		191.795	
17								--Upper Limit		226.705	
18						Hypothesis Test					
19							Test Statistic			-0.779	
20							t critical value--Two-Tailed			2.365	
21								--Upper-Tailed		1.895	
22								--Lower-Tailed		-1.895	
23							p-value--Two-Tailed			0.462	
24								--Upper-Tailed		0.769	
25								--Lower-Tailed		0.231	
26											

5.1.4 Hypothesis Test—t Distribution

The values needed for conducting a hypothesis test can also easily be computed with Excel. To demonstrate we will use the data set of Table 5.1 to compute the values needed to conduct a hypothesis test both for the **critical t-value approach** and for the **p-value approach**.   We will compute the values needed for these two testing approaches for all three possible forms for the hypothesis test as shown in Table 5.4. We will refer to these as the Two-Tailed, Upper-Tailed and Lower-Tailed hypothesis tests.

We can proceed in the following manner in order to conduct a hypothesis test to determine if the sales level is 215 after the advertising campaign. We will conduct the test using a significance level of 0.05 and continue with the worksheet presented in Figure 5.4.

Table 5.4 Possible Hypothesis Forms for Testing One Population Mean

Two-Tailed	Upper-Tailed	Lower-Tailed
$H_0: \mu = 215$	$H_0: \mu \leq 215$	$H_0: \mu \geq 215$
$H_a: \mu \neq 215$	$H_a: \mu > 215$	$H_a: \mu < 215$

---

1. Enter the labels in rows 18 through 25 and the input values in cells E6 and E7 as shown in Figure 5.4.

2. Enter the formula **=(L9-E6)/L14** into cell L19 to compute the t-statistic value for the sample (Figure 5.3 shows the formula in the worksheet.)

3. In cell L20 the function TINV is used to determine the critical value for the t-statistic for a **Two-Tailed** test. The function refers to the significance level of the test and to the degrees of freedom. Thus, the entry for cell L20 is **=TINV($E$7,L12)**. (Note it is not necessary that the E7 address be the absolute form $E$7.)

4. The TINV function is also used in cells L21 and L22 to determine the critical value for the t-statistic for the **Upper-Tailed** and **Lower-Tailed** test forms. For cell L21 the formula is **=TINV(2*$E$7,L12)** and for cell L22 it is **= -1*TINV(2*$E$7,l12)**.

5. Move the cell pointer to cell L23 and enter the formula **=TDIST(ABS(L19),L12,2)** to compute the p value for a **Two-Tailed** test.

6. In cell L24 the p value is computed for the **Upper-Tailed** test. This computation is performed by one of two ways depending on the value of the t-statistic value computed in cell L19. We use an IF function to determine the value of L19 and then compute the p-value using one of two formulas. The entry for cell L24 is
    =IF(L19<0,1-TDIST(ABS(L19),L12,1),TDIST(ABS(L19),L12,1)).

7. Finally in cell L25 the p value for **Lower-Tailed** test is computed. The entry for this cell is **=1-L24**.

The results of these steps are as previously shown in Figure 5.4. Your worksheet provides the statistics necessary to conduct the single sample hypothesis test for both the critical t-value and the p-value approaches. For both of these two approaches, it provides for testing all three of the possible forms of the hypotheses as given in Table 5.4.

For the **CRITICAL t-VALUE APPROACH,** the value for the test statistic in cell L19 of Figure 5.4 is -0.779. For the **Two-Tailed** test, cell L20 indicates the critical values for the test statistic are -2.365 and +2.365. Since the value of -0.779 does not fall outside these limits, the null hypothesis is not rejected. The sample evidence does not support rejecting the hypothesis that Read and Feed sales level is 215 after the advertising campaign. Thus, Lizabert's hypothesis (conjecture, hunch, estimate, guess, etc.) that the spot TV advertisements would boost sales of the *Country Dinners* to 215 per store, is supported by the sample evidence.

For the **Upper-Tailed** test value of -0.779 is not greater than the critical value of +1.895 given in cell L21 of Figure 5.4. Thus, we cannot reject the null hypothesis. The sample data supports the contention that the market share is less than or equal to 215.

Finally for the **Lower-Tailed** test form, the value of -0.779 is not less than the critical value of -1.895 given in cell L22 so the hypothesis of a sales level of greater than or equal to 215 is not rejected. Thus, all three forms of the test indicate an acceptance of the null hypothesis that includes the possibility of equality to 215 for the sales level.

The results of Figure 5.4 also let us consider the **p-VALUE APPROACH** to this test. Conventional usage of p-values classifies test results according to the categories given in Table 5.5 (see for example Siegel, *Practical Business Statistics*, 5th ed., McGraw-Hill, 2003, p.393).

Table 5.5 p-Value Classification Categories

If the P-Value is	Then the Difference is
Greater than 0.05	Not Significant
Greater than 0.01 but less than or equal to 0.05	Significant
Greater than 0.001 but less than or equal to 0.01	Highly Significant
Less than or equal to 0.001	Very Highly Significant

Utilizing the classification categories of this table, we would classify the results as *not significant* for all three forms of the hypotheses. That is, the p values of 0.462, 0.769 and 0.231 are all greater than 0.05. The conclusion is not to reject the null hypothesis regardless of what hypotheses form we were testing. This is the same conclusion drawn using the critical t-value approach.

You should save your completed worksheet of Figure 5.4 for future use. Although you developed it for a particular test situation, it is completely general. Thus, you can use it for estimating and testing a population mean based on a sample from that population. The sample size can be 100 or less. To use the worksheet, you only need to enter

1. The data values for the sample beginning in cell A5. As previously indicated the formulas you entered allow for up to 100 data values. This limit could be increased by

simply expanding the range used in the formulas of cells L5, L6 and L7.

2. The confidence level you desire for the confidence interval in cell E4, and

3. The hypothesized value for the mean in cell E6 and the significance level in cell E7.

After entering these input values, your worksheet will provide you with the point estimate and its confidence interval. In addition, it will return all the necessary values for conducting any three forms of the hypothesis test for both the critical t-value and the p-value approaches.

5.1.5 Determining the Necessary Sample Size

The precision of a point estimate is measured by the width of the corresponding confidence interval. The confidence interval width is inversely related to the sample size. If the sample size is increased, the width of the confidence interval is decreased, and vice versa. Consequently, if sample size is increased sufficiently, we can obtain a confidence interval small enough to satisfy any desired level of precision for the point estimate of a population mean. In this subsection, we use Excel to compute the sample size that is necessary for a specified interval width and specified confidence level for a confidence interval. We will continue with the workbook of this chapter but we will use the worksheet *Sheet3*.

Let us continue with the example of this section. As you will recall we began with the *Read and Feed* sales data of Table 5.1. The confidence interval was computed for these data in Figure 5.2 using the normal distribution and in Figure 5.4 using the t distribution. The 95% confidence interval width was ±14.468 with the normal distribution and ±17.455 with the t distribution. Suppose we wish to have a 95% confidence interval width of ±10. How many additional observations would be required to attain this specified confidence interval?

We can proceed in the following manner

1. Enter the **Identification Material** shown in rows 1, 2 and 3 of later Figure 5.6. Then enter the labels of rows 5 through 20. Enter the desired confidence level in cell D8 and the desired half width in cell D9. Also enter the sample standard deviation and the sample size for our initial sample in cells D12 and D13.

2. Cell E18 uses the Excel function NORMSINV to find the critical z-value for the specified confidence level given in cell D8. The confidence level is converted from percentage to decimal form by first dividing by 100, and then it is converted to the two-tailed value by dividing by 2. Finally 0.5 is added to the result in order to find the z-value on the right-hand of the distribution. The resulting formula for cell E18 is **=NORMSINV(D8/100/2+0.5)** as shown in Figure 5.5.

Figure 5.5 Formulas for Necessary Sample Size

	A	B	C	D	E
1			DETERMINING THE NECESSARY SAMPLE SIZE		
2			Your Name		
3	Today's Date				File: MEANS-1.xls
4					
5	INPUT DATA				
6					
7		Specified Confidenc			
8			Confidence Level =	95	%
9			Half Width =	10	
10					
11		Preliminary Sample			
12			Standard Deviation =	20.879	
13			Sample Size =	8	
14					
15					
16	STATISTICAL OUTP				
17					
18		Confidence Level Criti			=NORMSINV(D8/100/2+0.5)
19		Required			=ROUNDUP((E18*D12/D9)^2,0)
20		Additional Observatior			=IF(E19<D13,0,E19-D13)
21					
22					
23					

3. The formula in cell E19 computes the number of observations required to attain the specified confidence interval. Next the function ROUNDUP is used to round the result up to the next higher integer. The formula in cell E19 is **=ROUNDUP((E18*D12/D9)^2,0)**.

4. Finally, an IF function is used to determine how many additional observations are required. If the initial sample was sufficient, the result will be zero. The formula in cell E20 is **=IF(E19<D13,0,E19-D13)**.

Figure 5.6 shows the results of these computations. As indicated in cell E19, approximately 17 observations are required to attain the specified confidence interval. As shown in cell E20, nine additional observations are required.

After obtaining nine additional observations, these nine sales values would be combined with the original eight sales values of Table 5.1. This combined data set of 17 observations would be entered into the worksheet of Figure 5.2 (normal distribution) or of Figure 5.4 (t distribution). The worksheet would compute the new confidence interval. The width of the confidence interval should be near ±10. Since the process of Figure 5.6 is an approximation, it is possible the width may be slightly larger than ±10. If that is true, the new sample standard deviation computed for sample of size 17 should be entered into cell D12 and the sample size of 17 entered into cell D13 of Figure 5.6. The worksheet will then provide an estimate of the number of observations needed in a third sample in order to attain the specified confidence interval.

You should now save and close your workbook. The next section will start a new workbook.

Figure 5.6 Necessary Sample Size Results

	A	B	C	D	E	F
1	DETERMINING THE NECESSARY SAMPLE SIZE					
2			Your Name			
3	Today's Date				File: MEANS-1.xls	
4						
5	INPUT DATA					
6						
7			Specified Confidence Interval Values			
8			Confidence Level =	95	%	
9			Half Width =	10		
10						
11			Preliminary Sample Values			
12			Standard Deviation =	20.879		
13			Sample Size =	8		
14						
15						
16	STATISTICAL OUTPUTS					
17						
18			Confidence Level Critical z-value =		1.960	
19			Required Sample Size		17	
20			Additional Observations Needed =		9	
21						
22						
23						

5.2 THE t-TEST: TWO-SAMPLE ASSUMING UNEQUAL VARIANCE ANALYSIS TOOL

This section presents hypothesis tests, point estimates and confidence intervals for population means utilizing Excel's data analysis tool t-TEST: TWO-SAMPLE ASSUMING UNEQUAL VARIANCES. This tool is designed to test the difference between two population means under the following conditions.

1. The samples from the two populations are independent
2. The appropriate sampling distribution is the t distribution
3. The unknown variances of the two populations are not known to be equal

Subsection 5.2.1 presents the hypothesis test and **Subsection 5.2.2** presents the point estimate and confidence interval for comparing two population means. **Subsection 5.2.3** shows how this tool can also be used for the one population situation. We will see that the one-population results obtained from this two-population tool duplicate those of subsections 5.1.3 and 5.1.4.

In order to demonstrate the two independent samples, unequal variance t-test tool consider the following example situation.

Ms. Lizabert Humperdinck, the general manager of the *Read and Feed* chain of restaurants, is continuing her investigation of promotional ideas for the *Country Basket* dinners. One of her ideas is to hang posters that picture the item in the restaurant. To test the effectiveness of this idea she randomly selected eight restaurants to feature the poster and she randomly selected another eight to not display the poster. Table 5.1 shows the number of Country Basket dinners that were sold in these 16 restaurants.

Table 5.6 Number of Country Basket Dinners Sold

Without Posters	With Posters
215	240
180	220
150	190
180	175
201	220
207	215
195	219
180	195

We will use this example to demonstrate both (1) the hypothesis test, and (2) the point estimate and confidence interval for the comparison of the two population means using independent samples. We will begin a new workbook entitled *MEANS-2.xls* for these computations.

5.2.1 Hypothesis Test for Two Population Means
with Independent Samples

Suppose we wish to use the data of the two samples to see if the difference in the two population means appears to be significantly different from zero. Furthermore, suppose we wish to use a significance level of 0.05 for the test. We would proceed as follows after opening a new workbook.

1. Enter the **Identification Material** shown in rows 1, 2 and 3 of later Figure 5.8. Then enter the labels and data in columns B and C. Save the workbook with the title MEANS-2.

2. From the menu bar select **Tools**, **Data Analysis** and **t-Test: Two-Sample Assuming Unequal Variances** and the dialog box shown in Figure 5.7 will appear.

3. Enter the ranges for the two variables by keying the cell locations or by dragging the mouse pointer over the data (Excel will show the cell locations as absolute addresses if you drag).

Figure 5.7 t-Test Two-Sample, Unequal Variances Dialog Box

4. The hypothesized difference between the two means is entered as **0**, the alpha or significance level of the test as **0.05** and the upper left cell of the output range as **E5**. Click on **OK** and the result will be the screen shown in Figure 5.8. Note that the width of column E has been increased.

Figure 5.8 t-Test: Two-Sample Assuming Unequal Variances Results

	A	B	C	D	E	F	G
1	**STATISTICAL INFERENCE FOR TWO MEANS WITH t DISTRIBUTION**						
2				Your Name			
3	Today's Date					File: MEANS-2.xls	
4							
5		Stores	Stores		t-Test: Two-Sample Assuming Unequal Variances		
6		without	with				
7		Poster	Poster			Variable 1	Variable 2
8		215	240		Mean	188.5	209.25
9		180	220		Variance	420.286	435.929
10		150	190		Observations	8	8
11		180	175		Hypothesized Mean Difference	0	
12		201	220		df	14	
13		207	215		t Stat	-2.00573	
14		195	219		P(T<=t) one-tail	0.0323	
15		180	195		t Critical one-tail	1.76131	
16					P(T<=t) two-tail	0.06461	
17					t Critical two-tail	2.14479	
18							

As you will note Excel has computed three sample statistic values for the two individual samples: the means, variances and sample sizes. In addition, the bottom of the results table displays values for conducting a *t test* to determine if the two population means are equal or not. These values allow you to conduct the test either using the critical t-value approach or the p-value approach. For both of these approaches the null and the alternative hypothesis can be one of the three forms shown in Table 5.7.

Table 5.7 Possible Hypothesis Forms for Test of Two Population Means

Two-Tailed	**Upper-Tailed**	**Lower-Tailed**
$H_0: \mu_1 - \mu_2 = 0$	$H_0: \mu_1 - \mu_2 \leq 0$	$H_0: \mu_1 - \mu_2 \geq 0$
$H_a: \mu_1 - \mu_2 \neq 0$	$H_a: \mu_1 - \mu_2 > 0$	$H_a: \mu_1 - \mu_2 < 0$

Let us first consider the **CRITICAL t-VALUE APPROACH**. For a **Two-Tailed** test, the testing rule is that the null hypothesis is rejected when the absolute value of the number labeled *t Stat* is greater than the value of the number labeled *t Critical two-tail*. Otherwise the null hypothesis is not rejected. For the example of Figure 5.8, we note the **absolute value** of *t Stat* is 2.00573 and the value for *t Critical two-tail* is 2.144789. Thus, we would not reject the null hypothesis. We would conclude that from a statistical standpoint the difference between the two means is not significantly different from zero.

Suppose the hypotheses are those for an **Upper-Tailed** test. For these hypotheses the testing rule is that the null hypothesis is rejected if *t Stat* is greater than *t Critical one-tail* and otherwise it is not rejected. From Figure 5.8 we note the *t Stat* value of -2.00573 is less than the *t Critical one-tail* value of 1.761309. Thus, we would not reject the null hypothesis and would conclude the difference between the mean of the first population and the second population is less than or equal to zero.

Finally, suppose the hypotheses are those for a **Lower-Tailed** test. For this situation, the testing rule is that the null hypothesis is rejected if *t Stat* is less than minus one times the value for *t Critical one-tail*. From Figure 5.8 we note the *t Stat* value of -2.00573 is less than -1.761309, minus one times *t Critical one-tail* value. Thus for this form of the hypotheses, we would reject the null hypothesis but again conclude the difference in the two means is not greater than or equal to zero.

For your future use, Table 5.8 summarizes the decision rules presented in the three preceding paragraphs. Refer to it when you are using the critical t-value approach for hypothesis testing with the t-TEST: TWO-SAMPLE ASSUMING UNEQUAL VARIANCES analysis tool. It shows the conditions under which the null hypothesis is rejected for each of the three possible forms of the hypotheses. To interpret the results of this data analysis tool, **first** refer to Table 5.7 and identify the form of your hypotheses. **Second** select the appropriate decision rule from Table

5.8. **Third**, use the value for *t Stat* and the appropriate *t Critical* value to determine if the null hypothesis is rejected or not.

Table 5.8 Conditions for Rejecting the Null Hypothesis

Hypotheses	Reject Null Hypothesis If
Two-Tailed	$\lvert t\ Stat \rvert$ > t Critical two-tail
Upper-Tailed	*t Stat* > t Critical one-tail
Lower-Tailed	*t Stat* < - t Critical one-tail

The results of Figure 5.8 also let us perform the **p-VALUE APPROACH** to this test. If our hypotheses are for a **Two-Tailed** test, the p-value for the test is equal to the value given for *P(T<=t) two tail*. For the example of Figure 5.8, this value is 0.06461. Using the p-value categories of Table 5.3 (or 5.5), we would conclude that the difference in the population means is not statistically significant.

For the **Upper-Tailed** and **Lower-Tailed** test, the p-value depends upon two items from the results of Figure 5.8. One is the *P(T<=t) one tail* and other is the algebraic sign of *t Stat*. The p-value is either equal to (*P(T<=t) one tail*) or equal to (1 - *P(T<=t) one tail*). There are four possibilities. Table 5.9 summarizes these.

Table 5.9 Computation of p-Values for Upper-Tailed and Lower-Tailed Tests

	FORM OF HYPOTHESES	
Sign of *t Stat*	Upper-Tailed	Lower-Tailed
Negative	1 - *P(T<=t) one tail*	*P(T<=t) one tail*
Positive	*P(T<=t) one tail*	1 - *P(T<=t) one tail*

To demonstrate the use of this table, suppose we are performing an **Upper-Tailed** test for the example of Figure 5.8. We note that the sign of *t Stat* is negative so the p-value for this test is equal to *1 - P(T<=t) one tail* or 0.96795. Referring to the p-value categories of Tables 5.3 (or 5.5), we would classify the results as not significant. As for the critical t-value approach, we would conclude the difference between the mean of the first population and the second population is less than or equal to zero.

On the other hand, suppose we were conducting a **Lower-Tailed** test. For this situation Table 5.9 indicates the p-value is equal to *P(T<=t) one tail*, that is, 0.0323205. Table 5.3 (or 5.5) suggests these results are *significant*. Thus for this form of the hypotheses, we would reject the null hypothesis but again conclude the difference in the two means is not greater than or equal to zero.

5.2.2 Point Estimate and Confidence Interval for
Two Population Means ———

As shown in your textbook, the point estimate of the difference between the two population means is equal to the difference in the two corresponding sample means. The precision of this estimate is measured by a confidence interval. The computation of both of these statistics, the point estimate and the confidence interval, can continue from the results we have obtained above for the hypothesis test.

Continuing with the worksheet represented in Figure 5.8, we can proceed as follows.

1. Enter the labels in cells I7 through I17 as shown in Figure 5.9.

Figure 5.9 Point Estimate and Confidence Interval
Formulas for Two Populations

	H	I	J	K
5				
6				
7		*Point Estimate & Confidence Interval*		
8		Confidence Level	95	
9				
10		Point Estimate	=F8-G8	
11				
12		Confidence Interval		
13		Confidence Critical t-value	=TINV((100-J8)/100,F12)	
14		Std. Error of Point Estimate	=(J10-F11)/F13	
15		Conf. Int. Half Width	=J14*J13	
16		Lower Conf. Int. Limit	=J10-J15	
17		Upper Conf. Int. Limit	=J10+J15	
18				

2. Enter the confidence level in cell J8. We are using 95%.

3. Enter the formula **=F8-G8** in cell J10 to compute the point estimate of the difference between the two population means.

4. Cell J13 uses the Excel function TINV to find the critical t-value for a specified confidence level. The first argument for TINV equals 100 minus the confidence level in J8 and the result divided by 100. The second argument for TINV is equal to the degrees of freedom as given in cell F12 from the prior hypothesis test results. Thus, the entry for cell J13 is **=TINV((100-J8)/100,F12)**.

5. The standard error of the point estimate can be found through the use of the value for *t Stat* given with the hypothesis test results. The computation involves subtracting the hypothesized difference from the point estimate and then dividing the *t Stat* value into the result. This computation is shown in cell J14 as **=(J10-F11)/F13**.

6. The half width of the confidence interval is found by multiplying the critical t-value times the standard error of the point estimate. Cell J15 contains the formula **=J14*J13**.

7. The half width is subtracted from the point estimate to yield the lower confidence limit in cell J16, and the half width is added to the point estimate to yield the upper limit in cell J17. Thus, cell J16 contains the formula **=J10-J15** and cell J17 contains **=J10+J15**. Figure 5.10 shows the numerical results for this example.

Figure 5.10 Point Estimate and Confidence Interval Results for Two Populations

	D	E	F	G	H	I	J	K
1	E FOR TWO MEANS WITH t DISTRIBUTION							
2	Your Name							
3			File: MEANS-2.xls					
4								
5		t-Test: Two-Sample Assuming Unequal Variances						
6								
7			Variable 1	Variable 2		Point Estimate & Confidence Interval		
8		Mean	188.5	209.25		Confidence Level	95	
9		Variance	420.2857	435.9286				
10		Observations	8	8		Point Estimate	-20.75	
11		Hypothesized Mean Difference	0					
12		df	14			Confidence Interval		
13		t Stat	-2.00573			Confidence Critical t-value	2.14479	
14		P(T<=t) one-tail	0.032305			Std. Error of Point Estimate	10.3454	
15		t Critical one-tail	1.761309			Conf. Int. Half Width	22.1886	
16		P(T<=t) two-tail	0.06461			Lower Conf. Int. Limit	-42.9386	
17		t Critical two-tail	2.144789			Upper Conf. Int. Limit	1.43864	
18								
19								
20								

In conclusion the point estimate of the difference between mean sales for stores without the posters minus mean sales for stores with the posters is -20.75. That is those with posters are estimated to have a greater number of sales. In addition, the precision of this estimate is provided by the 95% confidence interval. It is -42.9386 to 1.438643.

5.2.3 Statistical Inference for One Population Mean————————

The hypothesis tests, point estimates and confidence intervals presented in subsections 5.2.1 and 5.2.2 are for comparing two populations. Such a comparison is oftentimes of interest in the use of statistics for business and industry. However at other times, interest may be in only one population. As discussed in subsections 5.1.2 and 5.1.4, the test of concern might be to determine if a population mean is equal to some specific value or not. Thus, you would proceed by drawing a sample from the single population and using the sample mean to determine if there is sufficient evidence to conclude that the population mean is equal to the specified value. The test often used in this situation is a one-population t-test. This was previously presented in Subsection 5.1.4 through a user-developed worksheet. However, it is also possible to use Excel's data analysis tool for a **t-test for two populations** to perform the computations for the one population situation.

The validity of this approach is based on the fact that the formulas for the two-population t-test and those for the one population t-test are equivalent under one condition. The condition is that the second sample is not a sample at all but instead all the values are some constant value. Thus, the mean for this second sample is equal to the constant value and the variance of this second sample is zero. If these values are put into the two-population t-statistic formula and the corresponding degrees of freedom equation, these two equations reduce to that for the one-population test. Although we spare you the details of this proof here, you may wish to explore it on your own. The conclusion is that the test Excel calls *the t-TEST: TWO SAMPLE ASSUMING UNEQUAL VARIANCES as represented by the dialog box of Figure 5.7 can also be used for single sample hypothesis tests, point estimates and confidence intervals.*

Let us pursue this approach by again visiting the Read and Feed chain of restaurants example given in Section 5.1. For this example, Lizabert the manager had obtained the data in Table 5.1 and wished to determine if the average sales was 215 per store.

So that you may more easily compare the one-population results to those of the prior two-population example, these sample values have been made the same as the second column in Table 5.6. We will use this example to demonstrate both (1) the hypothesis test, and (2) the point estimate and confidence interval for one population mean.

A one population **HYPOTHESIS TEST** using the two-population data analysis tool can be done in one of two ways. Referring to The dialog box of Figure 5.11, the most obvious approach would be to set the *Hypothesized Mean Difference* equal to specified value for the mean. That is for this example, equal to 215. In addition, the *Variable 2 Range* could be set equal to an empty column. However, this approach results in an error in the data analysis tool. It will not perform the computations if one of the two ranges refers to an empty column. Consequently, a second approach is used. This second approach enters values for the second sample equal to the specified value, 215. The number of values entered for this second sample can be two or more. However, we feel it might be clearer if the number of values for this second sample is equal to the number of values for the first sample. This is not necessary but perhaps more appealing from the standpoint of understanding. Our approach then for this example is the following.

1. Begin by entering the values shown in Table 5.1 into column B starting with cell B28. Enter the number 215 in column C beginning in cell C28. As you will note in later Figure 5.12, labels for these columns have also been entered.

2. Select **Tools/Data Analysis/t-Test: Two-Sample Unequal Variances** to obtain the dialog box of Figure 5.11.

3. Make the appropriate entries as shown in Figure 5.11 to obtain the results of Figure 5.12.

Figure 5.11 t-Test Dialog Box for One Population Test

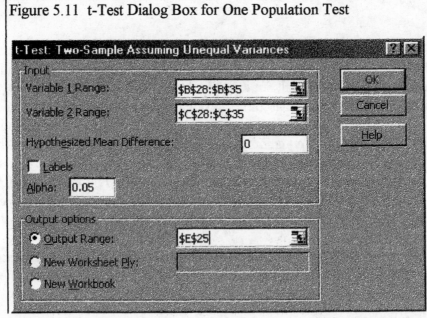

The results given in Figure 5.12 are quite similar to the two-sample results of Figure 5.8. You will note that the values for the sample mean, sample variance and number observations for Variable 1 are the same as those given for Variable 2 in Figure 5.8. This is as it should be since we used the same sample observations for both of these two variables. The mean for Variable 2 in Figure 5.12 is 215, that is, the specified value for the test, and the variance is zero. Both of these values are as expected.   The remaining values in Figure 5.12 differ from those of Figure 5.8, as they should. These values are used for conducting the hypothesis tests for both the both the critical t-value and the p-value approaches. There are three possible forms to the hypotheses. These are shown in Table 5.2 (or 5.4).

For the **Critical t-Value Approach,** Table 5.8 summarizes the conditions under which the null hypothesis is rejected.   For the example represented in Figure 5.12, we would not reject the null hypothesis for any of the three forms of the hypotheses. For **Two-Tailed** test 0.77894 is not greater than 2.364623, for **Upper-Tailed** test, -0.77894 is not greater than 1.894578 and for

Lower-Tailed test, -0.77894 is not less than -1.894578. The manager's hypothesis (conjecture, hunch, estimate, guess, etc.) that the spot TV advertisements would boost sales of the *Country Dinners* to 215 per store, is supported by the sample evidence. This is the same conclusion as found in Subsection 5.1.3.

Figure 5.12 t-Test Results for One Population Test

	A	B	C	D	E	F	G	H
23								
24		Sales						
25		After	Expected		t-Test: Two-Sample Assuming Unequal Variances			
26		TV	Average					
27		Promotion	Sales			Variable 1	Variable 2	
28		240	215		Mean	209.25	215	
29		220	215		Variance	435.92857	0	
30		190	215		Observations	8	8	
31		175	215		Hypothesized Mean Difference	0		
32		220	215		df	7		
33		215	215		t Stat	-0.7789421		
34		219	215		P(T<=t) one-tail	0.2307649		
35		195	215		t Critical one-tail	1.8945775		
36					P(T<=t) two-tail	0.4615299		
37					t Critical two-tail	2.3646226		
38								

The data of Figure 5.12 can be used to establish the p-value for the **p-Value Approach.** For a **Two-Tailed** test, the p-value is equal to *P(T<=t) two tail*, 0.46153. Using the categories from Table 5.3 (or 5.5), we would conclude the results are *not significant*. That is we would not reject the null hypothesis.   For the other two forms of the hypotheses, Table 5.9 can be used to determine the p-values. Since the sign of *t-stat* as given in Figure 5.12 is negative, the p-value is equal to 1 - 0.230765 = 0.769235 for an **Upper-Tailed** test. In this instance we would not reject the null hypothesis. For a **Lower-Tailed** test, the p-value is equal to 0.230765 and again we would not reject the null hypothesis. Our final conclusion is a sales level of 215 *Country Dinners* per store is supported by the sample evidence.

A one population **POINT ESTIMATE AND CONFIDENCE INTERVAL** can also be obtained from the data of this two-population data analysis tool. The point estimate of the sales level with the spot TV advertisements is equal to the sample mean for the eight stores. From the results of Figure 5.12 we note it is equal to 209.25. The precision of this estimate is measured by a confidence interval and the computation of it can continue from the results we have already obtained for the hypothesis test. We proceed as follows.

1.   Enter the labels in cells I27 through I37 as shown in Figure 5.13.

2.   Enter the confidence level in cell J27. We are using 95%.

3.   Enter the formula **=F28** in cell J29 to compute the point estimate.

Figure 5.13 Point Estimate and Confidence Interval Formulas for One Population

	I	J	K
26			
27	Confidence Level	95	
28			
29	Point Estimate	=F28	
30	Point Estimate-Null Hyp. Value	=F28-G28	
31			
32	Confidence Interval		
33	Confidence Critical t-value	=TINV((100-J27)/100,F32)	
34	Std. Error of Point Estimate	=J30/F33	
35	Conf. Int. Half Width	=J33*J34	
36	Lower Conf. Int. Limit	=J29-J35	
37	Upper Conf. Int. Limit	=J29+J35	
38			

4. Enter the formula =F28-G28 in cell J30 to compute the difference between the point estimate and the value from the null hypothesis.

5. Cell J33 uses the Excel function TINV to find the critical t-value for a specified confidence level. The first argument for TINV equals 100 minus the confidence level with this result divided by 100. The second argument for TINV is equal to the degrees of freedom as given in cell F32 from the prior hypothesis test results. Thus, the entry for cell J33 is =TINV((100-J27)/100,F32).

6. The standard error of the point estimate can be found through the use of the value for *t Stat* given with the hypothesis test results. The computation involves subtracting the hypothesized difference in cell F31 from the point estimate in cell J30 and then dividing by the *t Stat* value in cell F33. For this use of the data analysis tool the hypothesized difference will always be zero, so the computation for cell J34 can be =J30/F33.

7. Half the width of the confidence interval is found by multiplying the critical t-value times the standard error of the point estimate as shown in cell J35. Cell J35 contains the formula =J33*J34.

8. The half width is subtracted from the point estimate to yield the lower confidence limit in cell J36, and the half width is added to the point estimate to yield the upper limit in cell J37. Thus, J36 contains the formula =J29-J34, and cell J37 contains =J29+J34. Figure 5.14 shows the results for this example.

In conclusion the point estimate of the number of sales for stores after the TV promotions is 209.25. The accuracy of this estimate is provided by the 95% confidence interval that is 191.7948 to 226.7052. These results are the same as those of Figure 5.4 as they should be.

Figure 5.14 Point Estimate and Confidence Interval Results for One Population

	D	E	F	G	H	I	J	K
24								
25		t-Test: Two-Sample Assuming Unequal Variances						
26								
27			Variable 1	Variable 2		Confidence Level	95	
28		Mean	209.25	215				
29		Variance	435.9286	0		Point Estimate	209.25	
30		Observations	8	8		Point Estimate-Null Hyp. Value	-5.75	
31		Hypothesized Mean Difference	0					
32		df	7			Confidence Interval		
33		t Stat	-0.77894			Confidence Critical t-value	2.3646	
34		P(T<=t) one-tail	0.230765			Std. Error of Point Estimate	7.3818	
35		t Critical one-tail	1.894578			Conf. Int. Half Width	17.4552	
36		P(T<=t) two-tail	0.46153			Lower Conf. Int. Limit	191.7948	
37		t Critical two-tail	2.364623			Upper Conf. Int. Limit	226.7052	
38								

5.3 TWO ADDITIONAL ANALYSIS TOOLS
FOR TWO INDEPENDENT SAMPLES ———

Excel includes three data analysis tools that compute statistics for testing two population means based on data from two independent samples. Section 5.2 presented the t-TEST: TWO-SAMPLE ASSUMING UNEQUAL VARIANCE analysis tool in great detail. It applies when the following conditions exist.

1. The samples from the two populations are independent
2. The appropriate sampling distribution is the *t distribution*
3. The unknown variances of the two populations *are **not** known to be equal*

On the other hand, a second tool, the t-TEST: TWO-SAMPLE ASSUMING EQUAL VARIANCE, discussed in Subsection 5.3.1 below is applicable for the following situation.

1. The samples from the two populations are independent
2. The appropriate sampling distribution is the *t distribution*
3. The unknown variances of the two populations *are **known** to be equal*

Third, the z-TEST: TWO SAMPLE FOR MEANS analysis tool of subsection 5.3.2 applies to the following situation.

1. The samples from the two populations are independent
2. The appropriate sampling distribution is the *normal (z) distribution*

As you will note from these conditions, the last two analysis tools can be used in special situations, whereas that given in Section 5.2 is more generally applicable. The inputs and outputs for these two special purpose analysis tools are almost identical to analysis tool of Section 5.2. Thus, the detailed instructions of that section are equally applicable to these two additional tools. The following two subsections highlight the small differences that do exist.

5.3.1 The t-TEST: TWO-SAMPLE ASSUMING EQUAL VARIANCE Analysis Tool

The t-TEST: TWO-SAMPLE ASSUMING EQUAL VARIANCES analysis tool is appropriate if it is known, or if a hypothesis test has shown, the variance for the first population and that for the second population to be equal. The use of this test is quite similar to that for unequal variances. For example, its dialog box is exactly as given in Figure 5.7 except for the box's title. Moreover, the output for this test is the same as that given in Figure 5.8 except it presents one additional output. The extra output is the value for the **Pooled Variance**. Under the condition of equal variances for the two populations, it is appropriate to combine the two samples in order to estimate the common population variance value. The interpretation of the test results for both the critical t-value approach and the p-value approach is exactly as has been explained is Section 5.2.

5.3.2 The z-TEST: TWO SAMPLE FOR MEANS Analysis Tool

The z-TEST: TWO-SAMPLE FOR MEANS analysis tool is appropriate if the variances of the two populations are known. They do not have to be equal but the values must be known. This approach is also used for test situations when both of the samples are large (usually specified to be greater than 30). For such a situation the two sample variances are used as estimates for the two corresponding population variances. The dialog box for the two-sample z-test is again as given in Figure 5.7 with the addition of input space for each of the known values for the two population variances. The output is as given in Figure 5.8 except there is no value for degrees of freedom and the statistical values are based on the normal distribution not the t distribution.

5.4 THE t-TEST: PAIRED TWO SAMPLE FOR MEANS ANALYSIS TOOL

This final section of the chapter considers the situation in which two samples are not independent. This condition occurs when each individual observation within a sample is related (matched or paired) to an individual observation in the second sample. The relatedness may be the result of the individual observations in the two samples

1. Representing before and after results,

2. Having matching characteristics,
3. Being matched by location or
4. Being matched by time.

If there are definite reasons for pairing (or matching) the individual observations in the two samples, the two samples are dependent not independent samples. Generally, the precision from an analysis of dependent samples is greater than that from the analysis of independent samples. Thus, if a paired analysis is appropriate, it is the preferred approach.

In the first two subsections below we utilize Excel's t-TEST: PAIRED TWO-SAMPLE FOR MEANS analysis tool to conduct a hypothesis test and to make a point estimate with a confidence interval. The final subsection shows how to also use the tool for the one population situation.

The Read and Feed restaurant example will again be used.

Lizabert is continuing her investigation of hanging posters in the restaurants as a means of promoting the sales of their *Country Basket* dinners. To test the idea, this time she randomly selects eight restaurants. First, she gathers sales values for the eight restaurants without the posters. Then the posters are placed in the restaurants and she again gathers comparable sales values. The data are as given in Table 5.10. The two samples are related since the same stores are used for both samples. Recall that for the prior Read and Feed two-sample example, eight randomly selected restaurants did not have the posters and a second randomly selected sample of eight restaurants did have the posters.

Table 5.10 Number of Dinners Sold Before and After Posters

Store Number	Sales Before	Sales After
218	215	240
224	180	220
236	150	190
252	180	175
270	201	220
282	207	215
292	195	219
304	180	195

5.4.1 Hypothesis Test for Two Population Means
with Dependent Samples ————

Suppose we wish to use the data of the two samples to determine if the population mean of the change in sales is significantly different from zero at a significance level of 0.05. Continuing with the MEANS-2 worksheet of Section 5.2, we would proceed in the following manner.

1. Enter the data in cells A48 through C55 and labels in cells A45 through C47 as shown in later Figure 5.16.

2. From the menu bar select **Tools/Data Analysis/t-Test: Paired Two-Sample for Means** and the dialog box shown in Figure 5.15 will appear.

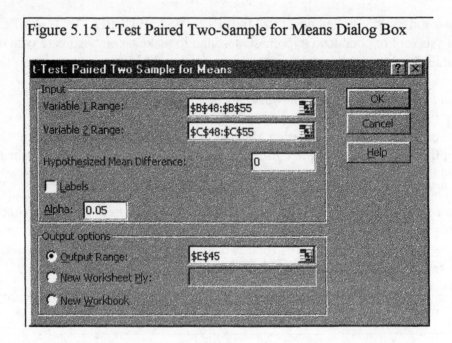

Figure 5.15 t-Test Paired Two-Sample for Means Dialog Box

3. Enter the ranges for the two variables.

4. The hypothesized mean of the differences is entered as **0**, the alpha or significance level of the test as **0.05** and the upper left cell of the output range as **E45**. The results are the outputs given in Figure 5.16.

As you will note the sample statistic values for the individual samples, the means, variances and number of observations, are the same as for the independent sample results of Figure 5.8. The next output item in Figure 5.16 is the Pearson Correlation coefficient value. This value is a measure of how well two variables vary together as was discussed earlier in Subsection 3.5.2. The remaining output values given in Figure 5.16 are used for conducting the hypothesis tests. As with the two prior hypothesis test examples, statistical values are provided for conducting both a critical t-value approach and the p-value approach.

Figure 5.16 t-Test: Paired Two-Sample for Means Results

	A	B	C	D	E	F	G	H
45		Sales without Promotion	Sales with Promotion		t-Test: Paired Two Sample for Means			
46	Store							
47	Number					Variable 1	Variable 2	
48	218	215	240		Mean	188.5	209.25	
49	224	180	220		Variance	420.286	435.929	
50	236	150	190		Observations	8	8	
51	252	180	175		Pearson Correlation	0.72791		
52	270	201	220		Hypothesized Mean Difference	0		
53	282	207	215		df	7		
54	292	195	219		t Stat	-3.84431		
55	304	180	195		P(T<=t) one-tail	0.00317		
56					t Critical one-tail	1.89458		
57					P(T<=t) two-tail	0.00634		
58					t Critical two-tail	2.36462		
59								

Again there are three possible forms for the hypotheses. Those for this test are shown in Table 5.11.

Table 5.11 Possible Hypothesis Forms for Test of Two Paired Population Means

Two-Tailed	Upper-Tailed	Lower-Tailed
H_0: $\mu_d = 0$	H_0: $\mu_d \leq 0$	H_0: $\mu_d \geq 0$
H_a: $\mu_d \neq 0$	H_a: $\mu_d > 0$	H_a: $\mu_d < 0$

For the **CRITICAL t-VALUE APPROACH,** the conditions under which the null hypothesis is rejected are summarized in the previous Table 5.8. For the example represented in Figure 5.16, we would reject the null hypothesis for a **Two-Tailed** test since 3.84431 is greater than 2.364623. For an **Upper-Tailed** test -3.84431 is not greater than 1.894578 so we would not reject the null hypothesis, and for a **Lower-Tailed** test -3.84431 is less than -1.894578 so we would reject the null hypothesis. Thus, the manager's hypothesis that the poster advertisements boost the sales of the *Country Dinners*, is supported by the sample evidence.

For the **p-VALUE APPROACH,** the data of Figure 5.16 can be used to establish the p-values. For a **Two-Tailed** test, the p-value is equal to *P(T<=t) two tail*, 0.006339. Using the categories from Table 5.3 (or 5.5), we would conclude the results are *highly significant*. That is, we would strongly reject the null hypothesis. For the other two forms of the hypotheses, Table 5.9 can be used to convert the value from Figure 5.16 for *P(T<=t) one tail* to the corresponding p-value.

Since *t-stat* has a negative sign, the p-value is equal to 1 - 0.00317 = 0.99683 for an **Upper-Tailed** test. For it, we would not reject the null hypothesis. For a **Lower-Tailed** test, the p-value is 0.00317 and again we would reject the null hypothesis. Thus the p-value approach also leads to the conclusion that the sales level after the posters were used is significantly higher than the sales level before the posters were used.

5.4.2 Point Estimate and Confidence Interval
for Two Population Means ——————

The point estimate of the difference in the sales level before and after the poster campaign is equal to the difference in the two sample means. From the results of Figure 5.16 we note the point estimate is -20.75 (= 188.5 - 209.25). The precision of this estimate is measured by a confidence interval. The computation of the confidence interval can continue from the results we have already obtained for the hypothesis test.

Continuing with the worksheet represented in Figure 5.16, we can proceed as follows.

1. Enter the labels in cells I47 through I57 as shown in Figure 5.17.

Figure 5.17 Paired Samples Point Estimate and Confidence Interval Formulas

	I	J	K
46			
47	*Point Estimate & Confidence Interval*		
48	Confidence Level	95	
49			
50	Point Estimate	=F48-G48	
51			
52	Confidence Interval		
53	Confidence Critical t-value	=TINV((100-J48)/100,F53)	
54	Std. Error of Point Estimate	=(J50-F52)/F54	
55	Conf. Int. Half Width	=J53*J54	
56	Lower Conf. Int. Limit	=J50-J55	
57	Upper Conf. Int. Limit	=J50+J55	
58			

2. Enter the confidence level in cell J48. We are using 95%.

3. Enter the formula **=F48-G48** in cell J50 to compute the point estimate of the mean of differences in the number sold.

4. Cell J53 uses the Excel function TINV to find the critical t-value for a specified confidence level. The first argument for TINV equals 100 minus the confidence level in J48 and the

result divided by 100. The second argument is equal to the degrees of freedom as given in cell F53 of Figure 5.16. The entry for cell J53 is **=TINV((100-J48)/100,F53)**.

5. The standard error of the point estimate is found by first subtracting the hypothesized difference from the point estimate. Then that value of the difference is divided by the *t Stat* value. This computation is shown in cell J54 as **=(J50-F52)/F54**.

6. Half the width of the confidence interval is found by multiplying the critical t-value times the standard error of the point estimate as shown in cell J55. The formula is **=J53*J54**.

7. The half width is subtracted from the point estimate to yield the lower confidence limit in cell J56, and the half width is added to the point estimate to yield the upper limit in cell J57. Thus, the cell J56 contains the formula **=J50-J55**, and the cell J57 contains **=J50+J55**. Figure 5.18 shows the results for this example.

Figure 5.18 Paired Samples Point Estimate and Confidence Interval Results

	E	F	G	H	I	J	K
44							
45	t-Test: Paired Two Sample for Means						
46							
47		Variable 1	Variable 2		Point Estimate & Confidence Interval		
48	Mean	188.5	209.25		Confidence Level	95	
49	Variance	420.2857	435.9286				
50	Observations	8	8		Point Estimate	-20.75	
51	Pearson Correlation	0.72791					
52	Hypothesized Mean Difference	0			Confidence Interval		
53	df	7			Confidence Critical t-value	2.3646	
54	t Stat	-3.84431			Std. Error of Point Estimate	5.3976	
55	P(T<=t) one-tail	0.00317			Conf. Int. Half Width	12.7633	
56	t Critical one-tail	1.894578			Lower Conf. Int. Limit	-33.5133	
57	P(T<=t) two-tail	0.006339			Upper Conf. Int. Limit	-7.9867	
58	t Critical two-tail	2.364623					
59							

In conclusion, the point estimate of the difference in the sales before and after the poster campaign is -20.75. The accuracy of this estimate is provided by the 95% confidence interval that is from -33.5133 to -7.98675. We could also note that since the confidence interval does not contain zero, there is a significant difference in sales after the posters were used.

5.4.3 Statistical Inference for One Population Mean

The hypothesis tests, point estimates and confidence intervals presented above are for comparing two populations using paired samples. The data analysis tool t-TEST: PAIRED TWO-SAMPLE MEANS also can be used to provide hypothesis test statistics, point estimates and confidence intervals for the one population situation. This is just as the data analysis tool t-TEST: TWO-SAMPLE UNEQUAL VARIANCES was used in subsection 5.2.3 for the one population situation. In fact, both these tools for a one-population situation provide the same results.

The validity of this approach is based on the fact that the equations for the two population t-test and those for the one population t-test are equivalent under the condition the second sample is not a sample but instead all the values are some constant value.   Again we spare you the details of this proof here but demonstrate it with the previous one population Read and Feed example of Subsection 5.1.3.

As previously stated, the manager of the chain is investigating the use of spot TV advertisements to promote *Country Basket* dinners. She believes the resulting average sales will increase to 215 per store. The sales values were previously presented in Table 5.1.

Figure 5.19 presents the dialog box and Figure 5.20 the results for the data analysis tool.

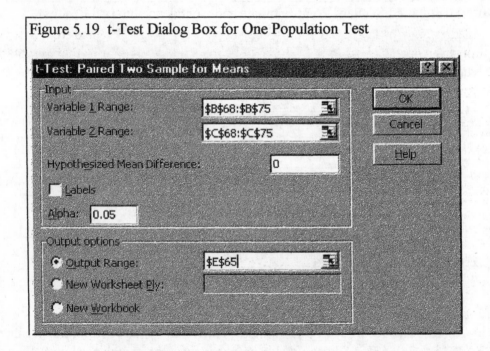

Figure 5.19 t-Test Dialog Box for One Population Test

The results shown in Figure 5.20 are the same as the prior one population results shown in Figure 5.12. Figure 5.20 has one addition entry. It is the value for the Pearson's Correlation coefficient which has no meaning for a one-population situation.

The conclusions drawn from these results for the hypothesis test are exactly the same as those discussed earlier for the results of Figure 5.12.

Figure 5.20 t-Test Results for One Population Test

	B	C	D	E	F	G
64	Sales			t-Test: Paired Two Sample for Means		
65	After	Expected				
66	TV	Average				
67	Promotion	Sales			Variable 1	Variable 2
68	240	215		Mean	209.25	215
69	220	215		Variance	435.929	0
70	190	215		Observations	8	8
71	175	215		Pearson Correlation	#DIV/0!	
72	220	215		Hypothesized Mean Difference	0	
73	215	215		df	7	
74	219	215		t Stat	-0.77894	
75	195	215		P(T<=t) one-tail	0.23076	
76				t Critical one-tail	1.89458	
77				P(T<=t) two-tail	0.46153	
78				t Critical two-tail	2.36462	
79						

A one-population point estimate and confidence interval can also be obtained from these data with the two-population data analysis tool. Figure 5.21 shows the computations that provide these results. Figure 5.22 presents the results. The discussion of these two figures would be that previously given for Figures 5.13 and 5.14 since the results are identical.

Figure 5.21 Point Estimate and Confidence Interval Formulas for One Population

	I	J	K
66			
67	Confidence Level	95	
68			
69	Point Estimate	=F68	
70	Point Estimate-Null Hyp. Value	=F68-G68	
71			
72	Confidence Interval		
73	Confidence Critical t-value	=TINV((100-J67)/100,F73)	
74	Std. Error of Point Estimate	=J70/F74	
75	Conf. Int. Half Width	=J73*J74	
76	Lower Conf. Int. Limit	=J69-J75	
77	Upper Conf. Int. Limit	=J69+J75	
78			

Figure 5.22 Point Estimate and Confidence Interval Results for One Population

	E	F	G	H	I	J	K
64							
65	t-Test: Paired Two Sample for Means						
66							
67		Variable 1	Variable 2		Confidence Level	95	
68	Mean	209.25	215				
69	Variance	435.9286	0		Point Estimate	209.25	
70	Observations	8	8		Point Estimate-Null Hyp. Value	-5.75	
71	Pearson Correlation	#DIV/0!					
72	Hypothesized Mean Difference	0			Confidence Interval		
73	df	7			Confidence Critical t-value	2.364623	
74	t Stat	-0.77894			Std. Error of Point Estimate	7.381807	
75	P(T<=t) one-tail	0.230765			Conf. Int. Half Width	17.45519	
76	t Critical one-tail	1.894578			Lower Conf. Int. Limit	191.7948	
77	P(T<=t) two-tail	0.46153			Upper Conf. Int. Limit	226.7052	
78	t Critical two-tail	2.364623					
79							
80							

The conclusion from these results is that *either of the two data analysis tools t-TEST: PAIRED TWO-SAMPLE MEANS or t-TEST: TWO-SAMPLE UNEQUAL VARIANCES may be used to provide the hypothesis test statistics, point estimate and confidence intervals for the one population situation.*

This completes our discussion of statistical estimation and hypothesis testing for population means. In the next chapter, we will consider estimation and testing for population proportions.

CHAPTER 6. STATISTICAL INFERENCE FOR POPULATION PROPORTIONS

Many times for business and industry, there is a need to estimate or test the proportion of a population that has a specified attribute. For example, the proportion of the output of a production process that meets quality control specifications, the proportion of income tax returns that have a computation error, or the proportion of potential customers who prefer a particular product. In order to estimate or test proportions, a sample(s) is taken, and the proportion of the sample(s) that have the specified attribute provides the measure for making the estimate or performing the hypothesis test.

This chapter presents statistical estimation and testing for population proportions. As we stated in Chapter 5, estimation involves using the value of a sample statistic, such as the sample proportion, to provide a **point estimate** for the unknown corresponding population parameter, such as the population proportion. As before, we can quantify the precision or accuracy of the point estimate by computing the **confidence interval** (also called **interval estimate**). As in the last chapter, a **hypothesis test** uses the value for a **sample statistic**, such as the sample proportion, to test a tentative assumption regarding the unknown value for a corresponding **population parameter**.

The computations for the confidence interval and hypothesis test are based on the sampling distribution for the sample proportion.   The form of its sampling distribution is the binomial. However, most statistics textbooks use the normal approximation to the binomial distribution for these computations. They take this approach for a number of reasons. First, discrete distributions such as the binomial are awkward to use for statistical inference. Second, a relatively large sample size is usually required to attain a reasonable amount of precision in the estimation or testing of a proportion. Third, the binomial distribution can be approximated by the normal distribution for large sample sizes. Accordingly, the normal approximation provides the basis for the statistical inference for proportions presented in this chapter.

Section 6.1 presents statistical inference for one population proportion. In it, we use formulas and statistical functions to compute values for the point estimate with its corresponding confidence interval and values for the hypothesis test. This section closes with a demonstration of the computations for determining the sample size that is necessary to attain a specified width and confidence level for a confidence interval.

Point estimates, confidence intervals and hypothesis tests for the two-population proportion situation are presented in **Section 6.2**.

6.1 ONE POPULATION PROPORTION ———————————

We will consider the following example to demonstrate both the point estimate with confidence interval and the hypothesis test for a single proportion.

Ms. Lizabert Humperdinck, the general manager of the *Read and Feed* chain of restaurants, wishes to estimate Read and Feed's share of the Sunday morning breakfast market in Buffalo City. She engages *Numbers Unlimited, Inc.*, a marketing research company, to conduct a survey to determine the proportion of Sunday morning breakfast customers who prefer to dine at a Read and Feed restaurant. After a period of time and a few thousand dollars, Numbers Unlimited reports that out of a survey of 1215 Sunday morning breakfast customers 373 preferred Read and Feed.

The tabulation necessary to determine that 373 of 1215 respondents prefer Read and Feed can be done by hand. However, if the individual customer responses are in an Excel worksheet, Excel has a feature that can easily perform this tabulation. The feature is the PIVOT TABLE WIZARD. The use of it to perform a tabulation is presented in Subsection 9.3.1 of Chapter 9.

6.1.1 Point Estimate and Confidence Interval

The point estimate and confidence interval for these sample results can be easily computed with Excel. For example, we may proceed in the following manner in order to compute the point estimate and 95% confidence interval.

1. Start Excel and enter the **Identification Material** shown in rows 1, and 2 of later Figure 6.2. Then enter the labels of rows 3 through 7 and rows 11 through 19. (Note the labels in rows 9, 10 and 20 through 27 will be entered later.) Also, enter the data in cells F4, F5 and F7. (Note the other numerical values given in column F will be entered later.) Save the workbook with the file name PROPOR-1.

2. To compute the point estimate for the population proportion, move the cell pointer to cell F12 and enter the formula =**F5/F4** as shown in Figure 6.1.

Figure 6.1 Statistical Inference Formulas for One Population Proportion

	A	B	C	D	E	F	G
8							
9				Hypc	0.333		
10				Sign	0.05		
11		STATI					
12			Poin			=F5/F4	
13							
14			Conf				
15				Confic	=NORMSINV(F7/100/2+0.5)		
16				Stand	=SQRT(F12*(1-F12)/F4)		
17				Confic	=F15*F16		
18					=IF(F12-F17<0,0,F12-F17)		
19					=IF(F12+F17>1,1,F12+F17)		
20			Hypc				
21				Test S	=(F12-F9)/SQRT(F9*(1-F9)/F4)		
22				z critic	=-1*NORMSINV($F$10/2)		
23					=-1*NORMSINV($F$10)		
24					=NORMSINV($F$10)		
25				p-valu	=IF($F$21<0,2*NORMSDIST($F$21),2*(1-NORMSDIST($F$21)))		
26					=1-NORMSDIST($F$21)		
27					=NORMSDIST($F$21)		
28							

---

3. Cell F15 uses the Excel function NORMSINV to find the critical z-value for the specified confidence level given in cell F7. The confidence level is converted to the form necessary for the function by first dividing by 100, then by 2 and finally by adding 0.5 to the result. The resulting formula for cell F15 is =**NORMSINV(F7/100/2+0.5)** as shown in Figure 6.1.

4. The formula in cell F16 computes the standard error of the point estimate from the value of the point estimate in cell F12. The formula is **=SQRT(F12*(1-F12)/F4)**.

5. Half the width of the confidence interval is found by multiplying the critical z-value times the standard error of the point estimate. Cell F17 contains the formula **=F15*F16**.

6. The half width is subtracted from the point estimate to compute the lower confidence limit. However, the lower limit cannot be less than zero for a proportion. Consequently, an IF function is used to set the value equal to zero when the computation results in a negative number. The formula for cell F18 is **=IF(F12-F17<0,0,F12-F17)**.

7. The half width is added to the point estimate to compute the upper limit. However here, the upper limit cannot be more than 1.0 for a proportion. Consequently, an IF function is used to set the value equal to 1.0 when the computation results in a value greater than 1.0. The formula for cell F18 is **=IF(F12+F17>1,1,F12+F17)**.

Figure 6.2 presents the results of these computations. As shown in cell F12 the best estimate of *Read and Feed's* share of the Sunday morning breakfast market is 0.307. The precision of this estimate is quantified by the 95% confidence interval in cells F18 and F19 as 0.281 to 0.333.

Figure 6.2 Point Estimate and Confidence Interval
for One Population Proportion

	A	B	C	D	E	F	G	H
1			STATISTICAL INFERENCE FOR ONE PROPORTION					
2	Today's Date			Your Name		File: PROPOR-1.xls		
3	INPUT DATA							
4					Sample Size =	1215		
5			Number of Successes in Sample =			373		
6								
7					Confidence Level =	95 %		
8								
9					Hypothesized Proportion =	0.333		
10					Significance Level of Test=	0.05		
11	STATISTICAL OUTPUTS							
12		*Point Estimate*				0.307		
13								
14		*Confidence Interval*						
15			Confidence Level Crititcal z-value			1.960		
16			Standard Error of the Point Estimate			0.013		
17			Confidence Interval--Half Width			0.026		
18				--Lower Limit		0.281		
19				--Upper Limit		0.333		

6.1.2 Hypothesis Test

Continuing with our example above, suppose Lizabert wishes to use the sample data to test her feeling that they have a one-third share of the Sunday morning breakfast market. We will enhance our current worksheet to compute the necessary values to perform a hypothesis test using either the critical z-value approach or the p-value approach. In addition, our worksheet will allow the test to be conducted for all three possible forms of the null and alternative hypotheses as shown in Table 6.1.

Table 6.1 Hypothesis Forms for the Test of One Population Proportion

Two-Tailed	**Upper-Tailed**	**Lower-Tailed**
H_0: p = 0.333	H_0: p ≤ 0.333	H_0: p ≥ 0.333
H_a: p ≠ 0.333	H_a: p > 0.333	H_a: p < 0.333

We will continue with the current worksheet to develop the necessary critical values and p values for all three hypotheses forms in the following manner.

1. Enter the labels in rows 9, 10 and 20 through 27 as shown in Figure 6.3. Enter the data in cells F9 and F10.

2. Move the cell pointer to cell F21 and enter the formula **=(F12-F9)/SQRT(F9*(1-F9)/F4)** to compute the z-statistic value for the sample (Figure 6.1 shows the formula in the worksheet).

3. In cell F22 the function NORMSINV is used to determine the critical value for the z-statistic for a **Two-Tailed** test. The function is multiplied by a minus one in order to obtain a positive value as is needed. The entry is **= - 1*NORMSINV($F$10/2)**. (Note it is not necessary that the F10 address be the absolute form, $F$10.)

4. The NORMSINV function is also used in cells F23 and F24 to determine the critical value for the z-statistic for the **Upper-Tailed** and **Lower-Tailed** tests. For cell F23 the formula is **= -1*NORMSINV($F$10)** and for cell F24 **=NORMSINV($F$10)**.

5. Move the cell pointer to cell F27 and enter the formula **=NORMSDIST($F$21)** to compute the p value for a **Lower-Tailed** test.

6. Cell F26 computes the p value for **Upper-Tailed** test through the formula **=1-NORMSDIST($F$21)**.

7. Finally in cell F25 an IF function is used to determine the p value for a **Two-Tailed** test. If the value for the z-statistic, cell F21, is less than zero, the p value is computed as two times the computation of cell F27. Otherwise it is computed as two times the computation of F26. The resulting somewhat intimidating formula is **=IF($F$21<0,2*NORMSDIST($F$21),2*(1-NORMSDIST($F$21)))**.

The results of these steps are as shown in Figure 6.3. Your worksheet provides the statistics necessary to conduct the single sample hypothesis test for both the critical z-value and the p-value approaches. For both of these two approaches, it provides for testing all three of the possible forms of the hypotheses as given in Table 6.1.

Figure 6.3 Hypothesis Test for One Population Proportion

	A	B	C	D	E	F	G	H
10					Significance Level of Test=	0.05		
11	STATISTICAL OUTPUTS							
12		Point Estimate				0.307		
13								
14		Confidence Interval						
15			Confidence Level Crititcal z-value			1.960		
16			Standard Error of the Point Estimate			0.013		
17			Confidence Interval--Half Width			0.026		
18			--Lower Limit			0.281		
19			--Upper Limit			0.333		
20		Hypothesis Test						
21			Test Statistic			-1.923		
22			z critical value--Two-Tailed			1.960		
23			--Upper-Tailed			1.645		
24			--Lower-Tailed			-1.645		
25			p-value--Two-Tailed			0.054		
26			--Upper-Tailed			0.973		
27			--Lower-Tailedl			0.027		
28								

For the **CRITICAL z-VALUE APPROACH,** the value for the test statistic in cell F21 of Figure 6.3 is -1.923. For a **Two-Tailed** test, cell F22 shows the critical values for the test statistic are -1.960 and +1.960. Since the value of -1.923 just falls within these limits the null hypothesis is not rejected. The sample evidence does not support rejecting the hypothesis that *Read and Feed* has a one-third share of the Sunday morning breakfast market. In other words, in light of the sample evidence the assumption of a one-third share does seem reasonable.

For an **Upper-Tailed** test, the test value of -1.923 is not greater than the critical value of +1.645 given in cell F23 of Figure 6.3. Thus, we cannot reject the null hypothesis. The sample supports the contention that the market share is less than or equal to 0.333.

Finally for a **Lower-Tailed** test, the test value of -1.923 is less than the critical value of -1.645 given in cell F24. Thus, the hypothesis of a market share of greater than or equal to 0.333 is rejected. The results for all three forms of the test indicate the market share is less than or equal to 0.333.

The results of Figure 6.3 also let us consider the **p-VALUE APPROACH** for this test. Utilizing the p-value classification categories previously given in Table 5.3 (or 5.5), we would classify the results as *significant* for a **Lower-Tailed** test, and *not significant* for a **Two-Tailed** or an **Upper-**

Tailed test. As for the critical z-value approach, the conclusion is that the results for all three forms of the test indicate the market share is less than or equal to 0.333.

You should save your completed worksheet for future use. Although you developed it for a particular test situation, it is completely general. Thus, you can use it for estimating and testing for any one-proportion situation in which the normal approximation to the binomial distribution is a reasonable approach. To use the worksheet, you only need to enter values for

1. The two inputs from the sample, the sample size and number of successes, in cells F4 and F5,

2. The confidence level you desire for the confidence interval in cell F7, and

3. The hypothesized value for the proportion in cell F9 and the significance level for the test in cell F10.

After entering these five input values, your worksheet will provide you with the point estimate and its confidence interval. In addition, it will return all the necessary values for conducting any three forms of the hypothesis test by the critical z-value approach and by the p-value approach.

6.1.3 Determining the Necessary Sample Size

The precision of a point estimate is measured by the width of the corresponding confidence interval. The confidence interval width is inversely related to the sample size. If the sample size is increased, the width of the confidence interval is decreased, and vice versa. Consequently, if sample size is increased sufficiently, we can obtain a confidence interval small enough to satisfy any desired level of precision for the point estimate of a population proportion. In this subsection, we use Excel to compute the sample size that is necessary for a specified width and specified confidence level for a confidence interval. We will continue with the prior workbook of this chapter but we will use the worksheet *Sheet2*.

Let us continue with the example of this section. As you will recall 373 respondents out of a sample of 1215 persons preferred the Read and Feed restaurants for Sunday morning breakfast. The confidence interval was computed for these data in Figure 6.2. The 95% confidence interval width was ±0.026. Suppose we wish to have a 95% confidence interval width of ±0.020. How many additional observations would be required to attain this specified confidence interval?

We can proceed in the following manner

1. Enter the **Identification Material** shown in rows 1, 2 and 3 of later Figure 6.5. Then enter the labels of rows 5 through 20. Enter the desired confidence level in cell D8 and the desired

half width in cell D9. Also enter the sample proportion and the sample size for our initial sample in cells D12 and D13.

2. Cell E18 uses the Excel function NORMSINV to find the critical z-value for the specified confidence level given in cell D8. The confidence level is converted from percentage to decimal form by first dividing by 100, and then it is converted to the two-tailed value by dividing by 2. Finally 0.5 is added to the result in order to find the z-value on the right-hand of the distribution. The resulting formula for cell E18 is **=NORMSINV(D8/100/2+0.5)** as shown in Figure 6.4.

3. The formula in cell E19 computes the number of observations required to attain the specified confidence interval. Then the function ROUNDUP is used to round the result up to the next higher integer. The formula in cell E19 is **=ROUNDUP(E18^2*D12*(1-D12)/D9^2,0)**.

4. Finally, an IF function is used to determine how many additional observations are required. If the initial sample was sufficient, the result will be zero. The formula in cell E20 is **=IF(E19<D13,0,E19-D13)**.

Figure 6.5 shows the results of these computations. As indicated in cell E19, approximately 2044 observations are required to attain the specified confidence interval. Accordingly, cell E20 shows that 829 additional observations are required.

Figure 6.4 Formulas for Necessary Sample Size

	A	B	C	D	E	F
1	DETERMIN					
2			Your Name			
3	Today's Date				File: PROPOR-1.xls	
4						
5	INPUT DATA					
6						
7		Specified				
8			Confidence Level =	95	%	
9			Half Width =	0.02		
10						
11		Prelimina				
12			Sample Proportion =	0.307		
13			Sample Size =	1215		
14						
15						
16	STATISTICA					
17						
18		Confidenc			=NORMSINV(D8/100/2+0.5)	
19					=ROUNDUP(E18^2*D12*(1-D12)/D9^2,0)	
20		Additional			=IF(E19<D13,0,E19-D13)	
21						
22						

Figure 6.5 Necessary Sample Size Results

	A	B	C	D	E	F
1	DETERMINING THE NECESSARY SAMPLE SIZE					
2			Your Name			
3	Today's Date				File: PROPOR-1.xls	
4						
5	INPUT DATA					
6						
7		Specified Confidence Interval Values				
8		Confidence Level =		95	%	
9		Half Width =		0.02		
10						
11		Preliminary Sample Values				
12		Sample Proportion =		0.307		
13		Sample Size =		1215		
14						
15						
16	STATISTICAL OUTPUTS					
17						
18		Confidence Level Critical z-value			1.960	
19		Required Sample Siz			2044	
20		Additional Observations Needed			829	
21						
22						

After obtaining 829 additional observations, those results would be combined with the original 1215 results. The sample size and number of successes for the combined data set of 2044 observations would be entered into the worksheet of Figure 6.2. The worksheet would compute the new confidence interval. The width of the confidence interval should be near ±0.020. Since the process of Figure 6.5 is an approximation, it is possible the width may be larger than ±0.020. For that situation, the new sample proportion computed for sample of size 2044 should be entered into cell D12 and the sample size of 2044 entered into cell D13 of Figure 6.5. The worksheet will then provide an estimate of the number of observations needed in a third sample in order to attain the specified confidence interval.

6.2 TWO POPULATION PROPORTIONS

Frequently for business and industry problems and decisions, an analyst wishes to compare two population proportions. In this section we show how to compute point estimates with confidence intervals, and the values needed to conduct a hypothesis test for the difference between two population proportions.   Consider the following example.

Lizabert's next project for the *Read and Feed* restaurant chain is concerned with customers' complaints. Two months ago the number of complaints was 137, and last month the number was 196. She is concerned about this drastic increase in the number of complaints.

She feels somewhat better when she learns that the number of total customers for the two months increased from 1401 and to 2313, but she still feels the firm has a problem with increasing customer complaints. To investigate the problem further, she first computes a point estimate with a confidence interval for the difference in the proportion of complaints for the two months. Next she conducts a hypothesis test to determine if there is an increase in the proportion of customer complaints from the first month to the second.

6.2.1 Point Estimate and Confidence Interval————————————

We will again develop an Excel worksheet to perform the statistical computations required by Lizabert. The worksheet will be completely general so you may keep it to perform such computations for any situation involving the difference between two population proportions. This worksheet will be an enhanced version of the one you did for one population proportion. Whereas Figure 6.6 provides the formulas for this new worksheet, Figure 6.7 shows the computational results. Proceed as follows by initiating a new Excel workbook.

1. Start Excel and enter the **Identification Material** shown in rows 1 and 2 of Figure 6.7. Enter the labels of rows 3 through 8 and rows 12 through 21. Also, enter the data of cells F4 through F8. Save the workbook with the title PROPOR-2. (The additional information shown in Figure 6.7 will be entered for the hypothesis test later.)

2. To compute the point estimates for the two population proportions and their difference, successively move the cell pointer to cells F13, F14 and F15, and enter the formulas shown in Figure 6.6 for those cells.

Figure 6.6 Statistical Inference Formulas for Two Population Proportions

	A	B	C	D	E	F	G
12	STA						
13		Point				=F5/F4	
14				Se		=F7/F6	
15			Difference			=F13-F14	
16		Conf					
17			Confidence Le			=NORMSINV(F8/100/2+0.5)	
18			Standard Erro			=SQRT(F13*(1-F13)/F4+F14*(1-F14)/F6)	
19			Confidence Int			=F17*F18	
20						=IF(F15-F19<0,0,F15-F19)	
21						=IF(F15+F19>1,1,F15+F19)	
22		Hypo					
23			Proportion–C			=(F5+F7)/(F4+F6)	
24			Pooled Stand			=SQRT(F23*(1-F23)*(1/F4+1/F6))	
25			Test Statistic			=(F15-F10)/F24	
26			z critical value			=-1*NORMSINV($F$11/2)	
27						=-1*NORMSINV($F$11)	
28						=NORMSINV($F$11)	
29			p-value–Two–			=IF($F$25<0,2*NORMSDIST($F$25),2*(1-NORMSDIST($F$25)))	
30			–Uppe			=1-NORMSDIST($F$25)	
31			–Lowe			=NORMSDIST($F$25)	
32							

3. Cell F17 uses the Excel function NORMSINV to find the critical z-value for the specified confidence level given in cell F8. The confidence level is converted to the form necessary for the function by first dividing by 100, then by 2 and finally by adding 0.5 to the result. The formula is **=NORMSINV(F8/100/2+0.5)**.

4. The formula in cell F18 computes the standard error of the point estimate of the difference in the two population proportions using the individual point estimates of cells F13 and F14. The formula for the standard error is **=SQRT(F13*(1-F13)/F4+F14*(1-F14)/F6)**.

5. Half the width of the confidence interval is found in cell F19 as **=F17*F18**.

6. The half width is subtracted from the point estimate to compute the lower confidence limit. However, the lower limit cannot be less than zero for a proportion. Consequently, the IF function is used in cell F20 to set the value equal to zero when the computation results in a negative number. The formula is **=IF(F15-F19<0,0,F15-F19)**.

7. The half width is added to the point estimate to compute the upper limit. However here, the upper limit cannot be more than one for a proportion. Consequently, an IF function is used to set the value equal to one when the computation results in a value greater than one. The formula is **=IF(F15+F19>1,1,F15+F19)**.

Figure 6.7 Point Estimate and Confidence Interval for Two Population Proportions

	A	B	C	D	E	F	G
1	**STATISTICAL INFERENCE FOR TWO PROPORTIONS**						
2	Today's Date			Your Name		File: PROPOR-2.xls	
3	INPUT DATA						
4		First Sample			Sample Size =	1401	
5				Number of Successes in Sample		137	
6		Second Sample			Sample Size =	2313	
7				Number of Successes in Sample		196	
8					Confidence Level	95	%
9							
10				Hypothesized Proportion Difference		0	
11					Significance Level of Test	0.05	
12	STATISTICAL OUTPUTS						
13		Point Estimates			First Population	0.098	
14					Second Population	0.085	
15				Difference Between 2 Population		0.013	
16		Confidence Interval					
17			Confidence Level Crititcal z-value			1.960	
18			Standard Error of the Point Estimate			0.010	
19			Confidence Interval--Half Width			0.019	
20				--Lower Limit		0.000	
21				--Upper Limit		0.032	

As shown in Figure 6.7, the best estimate of the difference in the two proportions (first month minus the second month) is 0.013 with a confidence interval of 0.000 to 0.032. Accordingly, the proportion of complaints is actually less for the second month so Lizabert should not be concerned there has been an increase in the complaint rate.

6.2.2 Hypothesis Test

Suppose Lizabert wishes to use the sample data for complaints for the two prior months to test whether there is a statistically significant difference in the two population proportions. As for the previous one population situation, we can enhance our current worksheet to compute the necessary values to perform the hypothesis test for both the critical z-value and the p-value approaches. We will compute the statistics for all three of the possible forms of the null and alternative hypotheses as specified in Table 6.2.

Table 6.2 Hypothesis Forms for the Test of Two Population Proportions

Two-Tailed	**Upper-Tailed**	**Lower-Tailed**
H_0: $p_1-p_2 = 0$	H_0: $p_1-p_2 \leq 0$	H_0: $p_1-p_2 \geq 0$
H_a: $p_1-p_2 \neq 0$	H_a: $p_1-p_2 > 0$	H_a: $p_1-p_2 < 0$

We will proceed with the following steps.

1. Enter the labels in rows 10, 11 and 22 through 31 as shown in Figure 6.6. Enter the data shown in cells F10 and F11.

2. Move the cell pointer to cell F23 and enter the formula **=(F5+F7)/(F4+F6)** to compute the pooled sample proportion.

3. In cell F24 the square root function is used to compute the standard error for the point estimate based on the pooled sample proportion. The formula for it is **=SQRT(F23*(1-F23)*(1/F4+1/F6))**.

4. Move the cell pointer to cell F25 and enter the formula **=(F15-F10)/F24** to compute the z-statistic value for the sample.

5. In cell F26 the function NORMSINV is used to determine the critical value for the z-statistic for a **Two-Tailed** test. The function is multiplied by minus one in order to obtain a positive

value. The formula is = -1*NORMSINV($F$11/2).

6. The NORMSINV function is also used in cells F27 and F28 to determine the critical value for the z-statistic for the two possible one-tailed tests. For F27 enter = -1*NORMSINV($F$11) and for F28 enter =NORMSINV($F$11).

7. Move the cell pointer to cell F31 and enter the function =NORMSDIST($F$25) to compute the p value for a **Lower-Tailed** test.

8. Cell F30 determines the p value for an **Upper-Tailed** test as = 1-NORMSDIST($F$25).

9. Finally in cell F29 an IF function is used to determine the p value for a **Two-Tailed** test. If the value for the z-statistic, cell F25, is less than zero, the p value is computed as two times the computation of cell F31. Otherwise it is computed as two times the computation of F30. The formula for cell F29 is
=IF($F$25<0,2*NORMSDIST($F$25),2*(1-NORMSDIST($F$25))).

The results of these steps are shown in Figure 6.8. Your worksheet provides the statistics necessary to conduct the two-sample hypothesis test for both the critical z-value and the p-value approaches. For both of these two approaches, it provides for testing all three of the possible forms of the hypotheses as given in Table 6.2.

Figure 6.8 Hypothesis Test for 2 Population Proportions

	A	B	C	D	E	F	G
12	STATISTICAL OUTPUTS						
13		Point Estimates			First Population	0.098	
14					Second Population	0.085	
15				Difference Between 2 Population		0.013	
16		Confidence Interval					
17				Confidence Level Crititcal z-value		1.960	
18				Standard Error of the Point Estimate		0.010	
19				Confidence Interval--Half Width		0.019	
20					--Lower Limit	0.000	
21					--Upper Limit	0.032	
22		Hypothesis Test					
23				Proportion--Combined Samples		0.090	
24				Pooled Standard Error of the Point E		0.010	
25				Test Statistic		1.349	
26				z critical value--Two-Tailed		1.960	
27					--Upper-Tailed	1.645	
28					--Lower-Tailed	-1.645	
29				p-value--Two-Tailed		0.177	
30					--Upper-Tailed	0.089	
31					--Lower-Tailed	0.911	
32							

For the **CRITICAL z-VALUE APPROACH,** Figure 6.8 shows the value for the test statistic in cell F25 as 1.349. For a **Two-Tailed** test, cell F26 indicates the critical values for the test statistic are -1.960 and +1.960. Since the value of 1.349 does not fall outside these limits, the null hypothesis is not rejected. The sample evidence does not support rejecting the hypothesis that the two proportions of customer complaints differ significantly.   Similarly, the test statistic value is not greater than the **Upper-Tailed** critical value. Also, it is not less than the **Lower-Tailed** critical value. Thus for all three forms of the hypotheses, the conclusion is the acceptance of the null hypothesis which includes the possibility of the equality of the two population proportions.

The results of Figure 6.8 also support the **p-VALUE APPROACH** for this test.   Utilizing the p-value classification categories previously given in Table 5.3 (or 5.5), we would classify the results as *not significant* for all three forms of the hypotheses. That is, the p values of 0.177, 0.089 and 0.911 are all greater than 0.05. As for the critical z-value approach, the conclusion is not to reject the null hypothesis regardless of what form of the hypotheses we are testing.

You should save your completed worksheet for future use. Although you developed it for a particular test situation, it is completely general. Thus, you can use it for estimating and testing for any two proportions situation in which the normal approximation to the binomial distribution is a reasonable approach. To use the worksheet, you only need to enter values for

1. The four inputs from the two samples, the sample sizes and numbers of successes, in cells F4 through F7.

2. The confidence level you desire for the confidence interval in cell F8, and

3. The hypothesized value for the difference in the two proportions in cell F10 and the significance level for the test in cell F11.

After entering these seven input values, your worksheet will provide you with the point estimate and its confidence interval, and the necessary values for conducting any three forms of the hypothesis test by both the critical z-value and the p-value approaches.

This completes our discussion of statistical estimation and hypothesis testing for population proportions. In the next chapter, we will consider estimation and testing for population variances.

CHAPTER 7. STATISTICAL INFERENCE FOR POPULATION VARIANCES

7.1 One Population Variance
     7.1.1 Point Estimate and Confidence Interval
     7.1.2 Hypothesis Test

7.2 The F-TEST: TWO-SAMPLE VARIANCES Analysis Tool
     7.2.1 Hypothesis Test for Two Population Variances
     7.2.2 Point Estimate and Confidence Interval

In the preceding two chapters we presented statistical inference methods for population means and population proportions. In this chapter we extend our discussion to statistical inference for variances (and standard deviations). Statistical inference for variances can be used to make decisions in a number of problems in business and industry. This is particularly true for the area of quality control for which the central issue is to control the variability of a production or service process. It is also true for the area of finance for which the variability of an investment or portfolio of investments is used as a measure of risk.

The statistical inference procedures of this chapter utilize either the chi-square distribution or the F distribution. In both instances, it is assumed that the samples are taken from normally distributed populations. This was also assumed for the t distribution statistical inference procedures for means of Chapter 5. Unlike the t distribution procedures, however, the chi-square and F distribution procedures are highly sensitive to departures from the normal population condition.

Section 7.1 uses Excel for the statistical inference computations for the one population situation. In it we demonstrate the use of formulas and statistical functions to determine the values for the point estimate with its corresponding confidence interval, and values for the hypothesis test. In **Section 7.2**, we demonstrate the use of the F-TEST: TWO-SAMPLE FOR VARIANCES analysis tool for determining the same values for the two-population situation.

7.1 ONE POPULATION VARIANCE

Statistical inference for the variance of one population utilizes the chi-square distribution. Although Excel does not provide an analysis tool for this situation, it does have two statistical functions, CHIDIST and CHIINV, for developing confidence intervals and conducting hypothesis tests. We will use the following example to demonstrate the use of these functions.

Ms. Kay T. Bodatie is the manager of Mr. Green Gene's restaurant. She needs to estimate the variance in daily sales of the menu specialty item *Liver and Biscuit Dinner*. She has gathered sales for eight randomly selected restaurants as given in Table 7.1.

Table 7.1 Number of Liver and Biscuit Dinners Sold								
Number Sold	240	220	190	175	220	215	219	195

7.1.1 Point Estimate and Confidence Interval

The point estimate and confidence interval for these sample results can be computed very easily with Excel. For example, we can proceed in the following manner in order to compute the point estimate and 90% confidence interval.

1. Start Excel, enter the **Identification Material** shown in rows 1, and 2 of later Figure 7.2, and enter the labels of rows 3 and 4 on the left-hand side of the worksheet and in rows 3 through 16 on the right-hand side of the worksheet. Also, enter the data of cells A5 through A12 and cell E4. Save the workbook with the name VARIAN-1. (The information given in rows 6 and 7 on the left and rows 17 through 26 on the right will be entered later. Also note the width of some columns, and the number of decimal places shown has been changed to

accommodate the presentation of the worksheet here.)

2. The sample statistics are computed in cells L5, L6 and L7 using the functions **AVERAGE,**
    VAR and **COUNT** as shown in Figure 7.1. The ranges shown allow for the inclusion of
    samples of size up to 100.

Figure 7.1 Statistical Inference Formulas for One Population Variance

	H	I	J	K	L
3					
4	*Sample Statistics*				
5		Sample Mean			=AVERAGE(A5:A104)
6		Sample Variance			=VAR(A5:A104)
7		Sample Size			=COUNT(A5:A104)
8					
9	*Point Estimate*				=L6
10					
11	*Confidence Interval*				
12		Degrees of Freedom			=L7-1
13		Chi-square--Lower Va			=CHIINV((1+E4/100)/2,L12)
14		--Upper V			=CHIINV((1-E4/100)/2,L12)
15		Confidence Interval--L			=L6*$L$12/L14
16		--L			=L6*$L$12/L13
17	*Hypothesis Test*				
18		Test Statistic			=L12*L6/E6
19		Chi-square critical val			
20		--Two-Tailed			=CHIINV(1-E7/2,$L$12)
21		--Two-Tailed			=CHIINV(E7/2,$L$12)
22		--Upper-Tail			=CHIINV(E7,$L$12)
23		--Lower-Tail			=CHIINV(1-E7,$L$12)
24		p-value--Two-Tailed			=IF(L25<0.5,2*L25,2*L26)
25		--Upper-Tailed			=CHIDIST($L$18,$L$12)
26		--Lower-Tailed			=1-CHIDIST($L$18,$L$12)
27					

---

3. The point estimate computed in cell L9 is equal to the sample variance and the degrees of
    freedom in cell L12 is equal to the sample size minus 1.

4. Cell L13 uses the Excel function CHINV to find the lower chi-square value for the specified
    confidence level given in cell E4. The confidence level is converted to the form necessary for
    the function by first dividing by 100, then adding 1 and finally by dividing the result by 2. As
    shown in Figure 7.1, the formula in cell L13 is **=CHIINV((1+E4/100)/2,L12)**.

5. The upper chi-square value is found in cell L14 in the same manner except the plus sign is
    changed to a negative sign.

6. As shown in Figure 7.1, the formula in cell L15 computes the lower confidence limit and that
    in cell L16 the upper confidence limit.

Figure 7.2 presents the results for the Liver and Biscuit Dinner example. As shown, the best estimate of the variance in the sales of the dinners is 435.9 with a 90% confidence interval from 216.9 to 1407.9. The range of the confidence interval is quite large. It suggests the need for a larger sample size to provide a more precise estimate.

Figure 7.2 Point Estimate & Confidence Interval for One Population Variance

STATISTICAL INFERENCE FOR ONE VARIANCE		
Today's Date	Your Name	File: VARIAN-1.xls
INPUT DATA	**STATISTICAL OUTPUTS**	
Data Values Confidence Level : 90 %	**Sample Statistics**	
240	Sample Mean	209.250
220 Hypothesized Variance = 150	Sample Variance	435.929
190 Significance Level of Test 0.1	Sample Size	8
175		
220	**Point Estimate**	435.929
215		
219	**Confidence Interval**	
195	Degrees of Freedom	7
	Chi-square—Lower Value	2.167
	—Upper Value	14.067
	Confidence Interval—Lower Limit	216.924
	—Upper Limit	1407.941
	Hypothesis Test	
	Test Statistic	20.343
	Chi-square critical values	
	—Two-Tailed (lower limit)	1.690
	—Two-Tailed (upper limit)	16.013
	—Upper-Tailed	14.067
	—Lower-Tailed	2.167
	p-value—Two-Tailed	0.010
	—Upper-Tailed	0.005
	—Lower-Tailed	0.995

7.1.2 Hypothesis Test

Suppose Kay T. Bodatie wishes to use the sample data to test her feeling that the variance in sales is equal to 150. We will enhance our current worksheet to compute the necessary values to perform a hypothesis test either using the critical χ^2-value approach or the p-value approach. In addition, our worksheet will allow the test to be conducted for all three of the possible forms of the null and alternative hypotheses shown in Table 7.2.

Table 7.2 Possible Hypothesis Forms for Test of One Population Variance

Two-Tailed	Upper-Tailed	Lower-Tailed
$H_0: \sigma^2 = 150$	$H_0: \sigma^2 \leq 150$	$H_0: \sigma^2 \geq 150$
$H_a: \sigma^2 \neq 150$	$H_a: \sigma^2 > 150$	$H_a: \sigma^2 < 150$

We will continue with the current worksheet to develop the necessary critical values and p values.

1. Enter the labels in rows 6 and 7 on the left-hand side of the worksheet and rows 17 through 26 of the right-hand side as shown in Figure 7.3. Enter the data in cells E6 and E7.

2. Move the cell pointer to cell L18 and enter the formula =**L12*L6/E6** to compute the chi-square test statistic value for the sample (see Figure 7.1).

Figure 7.3 Hypothesis Test for One Population Variance

	A	B	C	D	E	F	G	H	I	J	K	L	M
6	220		Hypothesized Variance =		150				Sample Variance			435.929	
7	190		Significance Level of Test=		0.05				Sample Size			8	
8	175												
9	220								*Point Estimate*			435.929	
10	215												
11	219								*Confidence Interval*				
12	195								Degrees of Freedom			7	
13									Chi-square--Lower Value			2.167	
14									--Upper Value			14.067	
15									Confidence Interval--Lower Limit			216.924	
16									--Upper Lim			1407.941	
17									*Hypothesis Test*				
18									Test Statistic			20.343	
19									Chi-square critical values				
20									--Two-Tailed (lower limit			1.690	
21									--Two-Tailed (upper limi			16.013	
22									--Upper-Tailed			14.067	
23									--Lower-Tailed			2.167	
24									p-value--Two-Tailed			0.010	
25									--Upper-Tailed			0.005	
26									--Lower-Tailed			0.995	
27													

3. In cell L20 the function CHIINV is used to determine the lower critical value for the chi-square statistic for the **Two-Tailed** test of Table 7.2. The formula for cell L20 is =**CHIINV(1-E7/2,$L$12)**.

4. The upper critical value is computed in cell L21 as =**CHIINV(E7/2,$L$12)**.

5. As shown in Figure 7.1, the CHIINV function is also used in cells L22 and L23 to determine the critical value for the chi-square statistic for the two possible one-tailed tests. The formulas are =**CHIINV(E7,$L$12)** and =**CHIINV(1-E7,$L$12)**.

6. Next move the cell pointer to cell L25 and enter the function =**CHIDIST($L$18,$L$12)** to compute the p value for an **Upper-Tailed** test.

7. Cell L26 determines the p value for a **Lower-Tailed** test as   =**1-CHIDIST($L$18,$L$12)**.

8. Finally in cell L24 an IF function is used to determine the p value for a **Two-Tailed** test. If the value as computed in cell L25 is less than 0.5, the p value is computed as two times the computation of cell L25. Otherwise it is computed as two times the computation of cell L26.

The formula is =IF(L25<0.5,2*L25, 2*L26).

The results allow us to test all three forms of the hypotheses for both the critical χ^2-value and the p-value approaches.

For the **CRITICAL χ^2-VALUE APPROACH,** the value for the test statistic in cell L18 of Figure 7.3 is 20.343. For a **Two-Tailed** test, cells L20 and L21 show the critical values for the test statistic are 1.690 and 16.013. Since the value of 20.343 falls outside these limits, the null hypothesis is rejected. The sample evidence does support rejecting the hypothesis that the population variance is 150. For an **Upper-Tailed** test, the test value of 20.343 is greater than the critical value of 14.067 given in cell L22 of Figure 7.3. Thus, we can reject the null hypothesis. The sample does not support the contention that the variance is less than or equal to 150. Finally for a **Lower-Tailed** test, the test value of 20.343 is not less than the critical value of 2.167 given in cell L23 so the hypothesis of a variance greater than or equal to 150 is not rejected. All three forms of the test would lead us to believe the population variance is greater than 150.

The results of Figure 7.3 also let us consider the **p-VALUE APPROACH** for this test.   Utilizing the p-value classification categories previously given in Table 5.3 (or 5.5), we would classify the results as *highly significant* both for a **Two-Tailed** and for an **Upper-Tailed** test, and *not significant* for a **Lower-Tailed** test. As for the critical value approach, the conclusion for all three forms of the hypotheses is that the variance is greater than 150.

You should save your completed worksheet for future use. Although you developed it for a particular test situation, it is completely general. Thus, you can use it for estimating and testing for a population variance based on a sample from that population. To use the worksheet, you only need to enter

1. The data values for the sample beginning in cell A5. As previously indicated the formulas you entered allow for up to 100 data values. This limit could be increased by simply expanding the range used in the formulas of cells L5, L6 and L7,

2. The confidence level you desire for the confidence interval in cell E4, and

3. The hypothesized value for the variance in cell E6 and the significance level for the test in cell E7.

Your worksheet will provide you with the point estimate and its confidence interval, and the necessary values for conducting any three forms of the hypothesis test by both the critical χ^2-value and the p-value approaches.

7.2 The F-TEST: TWO-SAMPLE
FOR VARIANCES ANALYSIS TOOL

Excel provides a data analysis tool for testing the equivalence of the variances of two populations. It is the F-TEST: TWO-SAMPLE FOR VARIANCES tool. We will first demonstrate its use for the equivalence of variances test. We will then extend the results from the data analysis tool to provide a point estimate and confidence interval for the ratio of the two population variances.

In order to demonstrate, consider the following example.

Kay T. Bodatie, the manager of Mr. Green Gene's restaurant, wishes to investigate promotional ideas for the *Liver and Biscuit* dinners. One of her ideas is to hang posters that picture the item in the restaurant. To test the effectiveness of this idea she randomly selected eight restaurants to feature the poster and she randomly selected another eight that did not use the poster. Table 7.3 shows the number of Liver and Biscuit dinners that were sold in these 16 restaurants.

Table 7.3 Number of Liver and Biscuit Dinners Sold

Without Posters	With Posters
215	240
180	220
150	190
180	175
201	220
207	215
195	219
180	195

7.2.1 Hypothesis Test for Two Population Variances

Suppose we wish to use the data of Table 7.3 to determine if the variances of populations are equal or not at a significance level of 0.05. We would proceed as follows with a new workbook.

1. Start Excel and enter the **Identification Information** in rows 1 and 2 of later Figure 7.5. Also enter the labels and data in columns B and C. Save the workbook with an appropriate title. We have used VARIAN-2.

2. From the menu bar select **Tools/Data Analysis/F-test: Two-Sample for Variances**. The dialog box of Figure 7.4 will appear on the screen.

Figure 7.4 F-test: Two-Sample for Variances Dialog Box

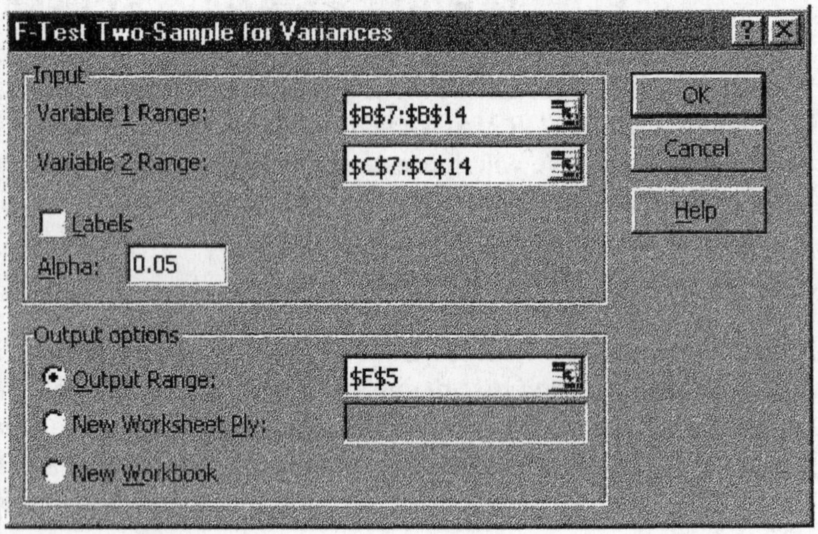

3. Within the dialog box, enter (a) the two ranges for the sample values, (b) the significance level for alpha ***(for a Two-Tailed test, enter one-half the significance level for alpha—see Table 7.5 for further explanation)***, and (c) the upper right hand cell for the output range as shown in the Figure 7.4.

4. Click **OK** and the output as shown in Figure 7.5 will be displayed on your screen.

Figure 7.5 F-test: Two-Sample for Variances Results

	A	B	C	D	E	F	G	H
1		STATISTICAL INFERENCE FOR TWO VARIANCES						
2	Today's Date				Your Name	File: VARIAN-2.xls		
3								
4		Stores	Stores		F-Test Two-Sample for Variances			
5		without	with					
6		Poster	Poster			*Variable 1*	*Variable 2*	
7		215	240		Mean	188.5	209.25	
8		180	220		Variance	420.286	435.9286	
9		150	190		Observations	8	8	
10		180	175		df	7	7	
11		201	220		F	0.96412		
12		207	215		P(F<=f) one-tail	0.5186		
13		195	219		F Critical one-tail	0.26406		
14		180	195					

You will note the results are similar to those of the hypothesis testing data analysis tools discussed in Chapter 5. For example, the values for the means, standard deviations and number of observations are just as they were in the first three rows of results in Figure 5.8 for a similar example. The fourth row of output in Figure 7.5 presents the two values for the degrees of freedom associated with the F statistic. These are followed in the next three rows by (1) the computed value of the F statistic, (2) the value for conducting the test using p values and (3) and the critical value for the F statistic.

As with the previous tests of this chapter, the necessary information is provided for conducting the hypothesis test for either the critical F-value or the p-value approach. All three forms of the null and alternative hypotheses given in Table 7.4 can be pursued for both approaches.

Table 7.4 Possible Hypothesis Forms for Test of Two Population Variances

Two-Tailed	**Upper-Tailed**	**Lower-Tailed**
$H_0: \sigma_1^2 = \sigma_2^2$	$H_0: \sigma_1^2 \leq \sigma_2^2$	$H_0: \sigma_1^2 \geq \sigma_2$
$H_a: \sigma_1^2 \neq \sigma_2^2$	$H_a: \sigma_1^2 > \sigma_2^2$	$H_a: \sigma_1^2 < \sigma_2^2$

Consider the **CRITICAL F-VALUE APPROACH** first. This approach for the test can be made both when the sample variance of the first sample is greater than that for the second sample, and when it is less than that for the second sample. In other words, both when value for F is greater than 1.0, and vice versa.

Some Excel statistical analysis books suggest the test is valid only if variance of the first sample is greater than the variance for the second sample. However the results of the tool can be used for both situations. The key is that the tool only provides results for the relevant critical value for the F-test. If the value for the F-statistic is greater than 1.0, it provides only the right-hand critical value. If the value for the F-statistic is less than 1.0, it provides only the left-hand critical value.

In order to clarify the interpretation of the results of this tool we present Table 7.5. It provides the interpretation for the six possible combinations of the three forms of the hypotheses and the two ranges of the value for F.

To demonstrate the interpretation provided by Table 7.5, consider our example given in Figure 7.5. For it we note the value for F is less than 1.0. Thus, if we were conducting a **Two-Tailed** test the F value of 0.96412 is not less than the *F Critical one-tail* value of 0.26406 so we would not reject the null hypothesis. We would conclude the variances of the two populations are equal at a significance level of 0.10 (two times the alpha specified in Figure 7.4).

On the other hand, if we were conducting the test using an **Upper-Tailed** test, we would note from Table 7.5 that we always fail to reject the null hypothesis. Thus, we would conclude the variance of the first population is less than or equal to that of the second population.

Table 7.5 Interpretation of Variance Test: Critical F-Value Approach

FORM OF HYPOTHESES

VALUE for F	Two-Tailed Test	Upper-Tailed Test	Lower-Tailed Test
≥ 1.0	Reject null if F > F Critical one-tail	Reject null if F > F Critical one-tail	Always fail to reject null since F ≥ 1.0
	Sig. Level = 2*Alpha	Sig. Level = Alpha	Sig. Level = Alpha
< 1.0	Reject null if F < F Critical one-tail	Always fail to reject null since F < 1.0	Reject null if F < F Critical one-tail
	Sig. Level = 2*Alpha	Sig. Level = Alpha	Sig. Level = Alpha

Finally, if we were conducting a **Lower-Tailed** test, we also would not reject the null hypothesis. Since the F value of 0.96412 is not less than the *F Critical one-tail* value of 0.26406, we would conclude the variance for population one is greater than or equal to that for the second population. The significance level in this situation would be 0.05, that is, the alpha value specified in Figure 7.4.

The results of Figure 7.5 also provide the means for conducting the **p-VALUE APPROACH** to this test. The interpretation of the results again depends on the form of the hypotheses and whether the sample value for the F-statistic is greater than 1.0 or not. Table 7.6 presents the formulas for computing the p value for the six possible situations.

Table 7.6 Computation of p-Values for F-Test

FORM OF HYPOTHESES

VALUE for F	Two-Tailed Test	Upper-Tailed Test	Lower-Tailed Test
≥ 1.0	2 * P(F<=f) one-tail	P(F<=f) one-tail	1 - P(F<=f) one tail
< 1.0	2 * (1 - P(F<=f) one-tail)	P(F<=f) one-tail	1 - P(F<=f) one tail

For our example results of Figure 7.5, the F-statistic is less than 1.0. Thus the p value for the three forms of the hypotheses would be computed for **Two-Tailed** as 0.9628 [=2*(1-0.5186)], for **Upper-Tailed** as 0.5186, and for **Lower-Tailed** as 0.4814 (=1-0.5186).

Utilizing the p-value categories of Table 5.3 (or 5.5) from chapter 5, we would classify the results as *not significant* for all three forms of the hypotheses. So as for the critical value approach to this test, we would not reject the null hypothesis for all three forms.

7.2.2 Point Estimate and Confidence Interval

As shown in your textbook, the point estimate of the ratio of two population variances is equal to the ratio of the two corresponding sample variances. As always, the precision of the point estimate is measured by a confidence interval. The necessary computations can continue from the results we have obtained in Figure 7.5 for the hypothesis test. We proceed as follows.

1. Enter the labels in cells I6 through I13 as shown in Figure 7.6.

2. Enter the confidence level in cell J7. We are using 95%.

3. Enter the formula **=F11** in cell J8 to obtain the value for the point estimate of the ratio of the two population variances.

Table 7.6 Point Estimate and Confidence Interval Formulas for Two Variances

	I	J	K
1			
2			
3			
4			
5			
6	Point Estimate & Confidence Interval		
7	Confidence Level	95	%
8	Point Estimate	=F11	
9	F Distribution Values		
10	Lower Value	=1/FINV((100-J7)/100/2,G10,F10)	
11	Upper Value	=FINV((100-J7)/100/2,F10,G10)	
12	Lower Conf.Int.Limit	=J8/J11	
13	Upper Conf.Int.Limit	=J8/J10	
14			

4. Cell J10 uses the function FINV to find the lower or left-tailed critical F-value for a specified confidence level. The function's first argument equals 100 minus the confidence level with this result divided by 100 and then divided by two. The second argument for FINV is equal to the degrees of freedom as given in cell G10 and the third is the degrees of freedom given in

cell F10. Finally, the value from this function is divided into one. Thus, the entry for cell J10 is =1/FINV((100-J5/100/2,G10,F10).

5. Cell J11 also uses the function FINV to find the upper or right-tailed critical F-value for a specified confidence level. The first argument is the same as that for cell J10. The second and third arguments are reversed from those of cell J10. Also, the value of the function is not divided into one. Thus, the entry for cell J11 is =FINV((100-J5/100/2,F10,G10).

6. The lower confidence limit is computed in cell J12 by the formula =J7/J11.

7. The upper confidence limit is computed in cell J13 by the formula =J7/J10.

Figure 7.7 shows the numerical results for this example.

Table 7.7 Point Estimate and Confidence Interval
for Two Variances

	H	I	J	K	L
1					
2					
3					
4					
5					
6		*Point Estimate & Confidence Interval*			
7		Confidence Level	95 %		
8		Point Estimate	0.964116		
9		F Distribution Values			
10		Lower Value	0.200205		
11		Upper Value	4.994888		
12		Lower Conf.Int.Limit	0.193021		
13		Upper Conf.Int.Limit	4.815652		
14					

In conclusion the point estimate of the ratio of the variance of the number of sales for stores without the posters to the variance of the number of sales for stores with the posters is 0.964116. The precision of this estimate is provided by the 95% confidence interval, 0.193021 to 4.815652. In passing we would note that the interval includes the value 1.0 so we would conclude the variances do not differ significantly.

CHAPTER 8. ANALYSIS OF VARIANCE

8.1   The ANOVA: SINGLE FACTOR Analysis Tool

8.2   The ANOVA: TWO-FACTOR WITHOUT REPLICATION Analysis Tool

8.3   The ANOVA: TWO-FACTOR WITH REPLICATION Analysis Tool

This chapter continues our use of Excel for inferential statistics. In particular, the statistical procedure referred to as the **analysis of variance** (commonly called **ANOVA**) allows you to test for the equivalence of the population means of two or more populations with independent samples. You may recall that the procedure of Section 5.2 of Chapter 5 was used to test for the equivalence of the population means of only two populations with independent samples. It utilized a t-test for the analysis. On the other hand, ANOVA utilizes a F-test and can be used if you have two populations or more than two. For the two-population situation, the results of the two-tailed t-test and that for the F-test are exactly alike. This is true both for the critical value approach and the p-value approach to hypothesis testing.

Excel provides three separate ANOVA analysis tools. These correspond to the three test situations, or experimental designs, usually discussed in business statistics textbooks. The first tool is the ANOVA: SINGLE FACTOR analysis tool presented in **Section 8.1** below. Single factor ANOVA is also called a one-way ANOVA. It is used to analyze the equivalence of the means for two or more **values** (sometimes called **levels**) for one **variable** (sometimes called **factor**). It requires that there be more than one observation for each of the values for the variable.

For example, you might wish to test the effectiveness of a number employee training programs by randomly assigning two or more employees to each program. For this situation, the variable (or factor) corresponds to the training programs and the values (or levels) are the different types of training programs. The result for an individual employee is an observation. The experimental structure of one variable with multiple levels and two or more observations per level is called a **completely randomized design**.

The second tool is the ANOVA: TWO-FACTOR WITHOUT REPLICATION analysis tool as discussed in **Section 8.2**. This is also called a two-way ANOVA without interaction. Again we have a single variable of interest but to test the effect of this variable, the sample observations are organized into **blocks**. Instead of obtaining independent observations for different levels as is done for the single factor situation of section 8.1, the observations are obtained from the same block. For example, the block might correspond to the same city, the same person or the same point in time. The experimental structure of this situation is called a **randomized block design**.

Section 8.3 presents the third tool the ANOVA: TWO-FACTOR WITH REPLICATION analysis tool. This is called a two-way ANOVA with interaction. It is used to analyze the equivalence of means for two or more values (levels) for two variables (factors). It requires that there be more than one observation for each combination of values of the two variables. For example, suppose the first variable is the training program for which there are five possible values, and the second variable is the gender of the employee for which there are two values. There are a total of ten (= 5 times 2) combinations of levels for the two variables. For each of the ten combinations, two or more observations would be required to analyze it as a two-way ANOVA with interaction. This experimental structure is called a **two-way factorial design**.

The test situations for all three of these ANOVA tools are based on three key assumptions. They are that (1) the observations are obtained randomly and independently from the populations, (2) the observations are drawn from normally distributed populations and (3) the populations have a common variance.

8.1 THE ANOVA: SINGLE FACTOR ANALYSIS TOOL ———

We will consider the use of the ANOVA: SINGLE FACTOR tool through the following example.

Ms. Bearferd Lynn is the sales manager for Eves Valves, Inc. The firm markets their valves throughout the United States through sales representatives. Currently, Bearferd is considering three new compensation plans for the sales representatives. One includes only a salary, one includes both a salary component and a commission component and the third includes only a commission. In order to compare the effectiveness of the three plans, Bearferd randomly selects

24 sales representatives and randomly assigns eight to each compensation plan. The sales levels for the 24 representatives for the next 6 months are recorded.

To analyze the results using Excel you would proceed as follows.

1. Start Excel, enter the **Identification Material**, and then enter the labels and data in columns B through D as shown in Figure 8.1. Save the workbook file with the name ANOVA.

Figure 8.1 One-way ANOVA Example Data

	A	B	C	D	E
1		Analysis of Variance Examples			
2		Your Name			
3	Today's Date			File: ANOVA.xls	
4					
5		COMPENSATION PLAN INCLUDES			
6		Salary	Sal.&Com.	Commissn	
7		4500	4430	5810	
8		4580	4740	5420	
9		4200	4530	4800	
10		4860	4830	5100	
11		5040	5100	5460	
12		4740	4920	6180	
13		4320	4140	4680	
14		4410	4320	4620	
15					

---

2. From the menu bar select **Tools**, from the subsequent pull-down menu select **Data Analysis** and from the Data Analysis dialog box select **ANOVA: Single Factor**.

3. Fill in the entries of the ANOVA: Single Factor dialog box as shown in Figure 8.2. Notice that the input range includes the labels in the cells B6, C6 and D6.

4. The output will appear as shown in Figure 8.3. In this figure column B has been widened to allow the display of the full labels.

As you will note Excel provides the means and variances for each of the three compensation plans. In addition, it presents an analysis of variance table with the sample statistics for conducting an F-test with the following hypotheses.

$$H_0: \mu_1 = \mu_2 = \mu_3$$
$$H_a: \text{not all } \mu\text{'s are equal}$$

The **CRITICAL F-VALUE APPROACH** for the test requires you to compare the computed value for the F-statistic to the critical value for F. If the computed F is greater than the critical value of F, the null hypothesis is rejected. Otherwise the null hypothesis is not rejected. The critical value is the value from the F distribution corresponding to the alpha value specified in Figure 8.2 and the degrees of freedom for the numerator and the denominator of the F statistic.

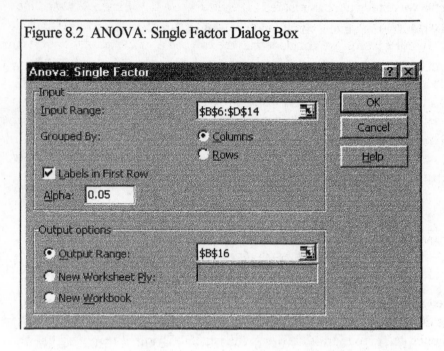

Figure 8.2 ANOVA: Single Factor Dialog Box

Figure 8.3 Results for One-way ANOVA

Anova: Single Factor

SUMMARY

Groups	Count	Sum	Average	Variance
Salary	8	36650	4581.25	80412.5
Sal.&Com.	8	37010	4626.25	106169.6
Commissn	8	42070	5258.75	313955.4

ANOVA

Source of Variation	SS	df	MS	F	P-value	F crit
Between Groups	2296233	2	1148117	6.881303	0.005031	3.466795
Within Groups	3503763	21	166845.8			
Total	5799996	23				

For this example we note that the computed value for F is 6.881303 in cell F27 and the critical value is 3.466795 in cell H27 so we would reject the null hypothesis. Thus, we would conclude that the means are not equal. In other words, we conclude that the compensation plans have had an effect on the sales levels.

For the **p-VALUE APPROACH** to the test, you will need to refer to Table 5.3 (or 5.5) of Chapter 5 to categorize the results. For our current example the p-value is given in cell G27 of Figure 8.3 as 0.005031. The categories of Table 5.3 (or 5.5) would classify the results as *highly significant*. Accordingly, we would again reject the null hypothesis that the means are equal. We would conclude that the compensation plans did have a statistically significant effect on the sales results.

8.2 THE ANOVA: TWO-FACTOR WITHOUT REPLICATION ANALYSIS TOOL

The experimental design of Section 8.1, a single factor completely randomized design, sometimes may not detect the difference in means. This result may occur because the variation among the individual experimental units, the sales representatives in the previous example, may mask the variation due to the factor, the compensation plans in the previous example. A second experimental design might be used to circumvent this problem. It is called a randomized block design. Its use is analogous to the use of a paired t-test (see Section 5.4 of Chapter 5) instead of a t-test for independent samples (Section 5.2) when testing the equivalence of two population means. Just as the paired t-test provides a more precise test than the t-test for independent samples, the randomized block design provides a more precise test than that of the completely randomized design. Excel's ANOVA: TWO-FACTOR WITHOUT REPLICATION analysis tool is used to analyze the results from randomized block design.

For our previous Eves Valves example, suppose it is known that the sales representatives with the most experience will sell more regardless of the compensation plan used. Thus, we might make the statistical test more sensitive if we would block the representatives into eight groups of three each according to their experience. We would designate the three representatives with the most experience as block one. Each of them would be randomly assigned to a different compensation plan. The next three most experienced representatives would constitute block two. Each of them would be randomly assigned to a different plan and so on until all 24 have been assigned to a compensation plan. As a result of this type of assignment process, the representatives in each block would have a similar amount of experience. This type of experimental design would help remove the effect of experience on the sales results and improve the likelihood of detecting the actual differences among the three compensation plans.

To analyze this type of design with Excel for Ms. Lynn proceeds as follows.

1. Start Excel, enter the **Identification Material**, and then enter the labels and data in columns A through D as shown in Figure 8.4. Note that we are using the second worksheet in the workbook named ANOVA. We selected the second worksheet by clicking on the tab towards the bottom of the Excel window labeled *Sheet2*. Save the workbook file with the name ANOVA.

Figure 8.4 Two-way ANOVA without Interaction Data

	A	B	C	D	E
1		Analysis of Variance Examples			
2		Your Name			
3	Today's Date			File: ANOVA.xls	
4					
5		COMPENSATION PLAN INCLUDES			
6	Experience	Salary	Sal.&Com.	Commissn	
7	Block 1	4860	5100	5810	
8	Block 2	5040	4920	6180	
9	Block 3	4740	4740	5420	
10	Block 4	4580	4830	5460	
11	Block 5	4410	4430	5100	
12	Block 6	4500	4530	4800	
13	Block 7	4320	4140	4680	
14	Block 8	4200	4320	4620	
15					

---

2. From the menu bar select **Tools**, from the subsequent pull-down menu select **Data Analysis** and from the Data Analysis dialog box select **ANOVA: Two-Factor Without Replication**.

3. Fill in the entries of the ANOVA: Two-Factor Without Replication dialog box as shown in Figure 8.5. Notice the input range includes the labels in the cells A6, B6, C6, D6, and A7 through A14.

Figure 8.5 ANOVA: Two-Factor Without Replication Dialog Box

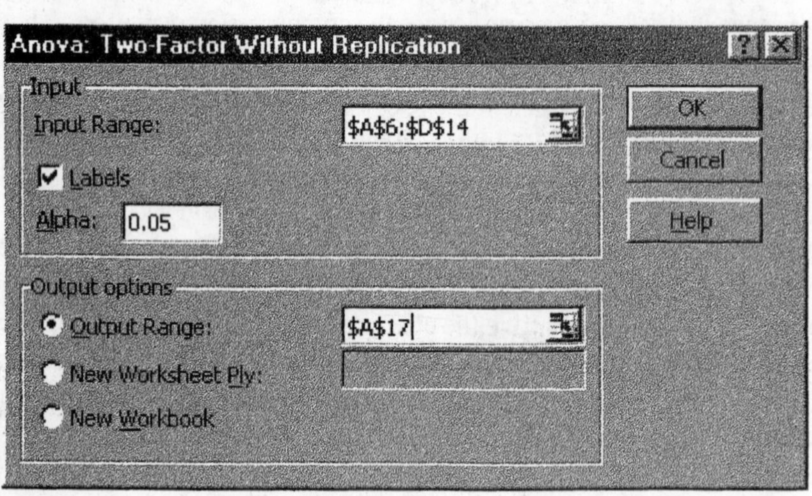

4. The output will appear as shown in Figure 8.6. In this figure column B has been widened to allow the display of the full labels.

Figure 8.6 Results for Two-way ANOVA without Interaction

	A	B	C	D	E	F	G	H
17		Anova: Two-Factor Without Replication						
18								
19		SUMMARY	Count	Sum	Average	Variance		
20		Block 1	3	15770	5256.67	244033		
21		Block 2	3	16140	5380	483600		
22		Block 3	3	14900	4966.67	154133		
23		Block 4	3	14870	4956.67	205633		
24		Block 5	3	13940	4646.67	154233		
25		Block 6	3	13830	4610	27300		
26		Block 7	3	13140	4380	75600		
27		Block 8	3	13140	4380	46800		
28								
29		Salary	8	36650	4581.25	80412.5		
30		Sal.&Com.	8	37010	4626.25	106170		
31		Commissn	8	42070	5258.75	313955		
32								
33								
34		ANOVA						
35		Source of Variatio	SS	df	MS	F	P-value	F crit
36		Rows	3017329	7	431047	12.4059	4.9E-05	2.7642
37		Columns	2296233	2	1148117	33.0439	5E-06	3.73889
38		Error	486433	14	34745.2			
39								
40		Total	5799996	23				

As with the one-way ANOVA results of Figure 8.3, Excel provides the means and variances for each of the three compensation plans. In addition, it presents the means and variances for each of the eight blocks. The ANOVA table at the bottom of the output provides sample statistics for conducting two separate F-tests. One is a test to determine if means for the compensation plans differ or not (labeled as **Rows** in cell B36). Specifically, the test hypotheses are

$$H_0: \mu_1 = \mu_2 = \mu_3$$
$$H_a: \text{not all } \mu\text{'s are equal}$$

The second F test is a test of whether there is a significant difference in the means of the eight blocks, that is, is there a block effect or not. For this example, the block effect would be the effect of sales experience on sales level (labeled as **Columns** in cell B37). The test hypotheses for block effect are

$$H_0: \mu_1 = \mu_2 = \mu_3 \ldots = \mu_8$$
$$H_a: \text{not all } \mu\text{'s are equal}$$

The **CRITICAL F-VALUE APPROACH** for both these tests requires you to compare the computed value for the F-statistic to the critical value for F. If the computed F is greater than the critical value of F, the null hypothesis is rejected. Otherwise the null hypothesis is not rejected. The critical value is the value from the F distribution that corresponds to the alpha value specified in Figure 8.5 and the degrees of freedom for the numerator and the denominator of the F statistic.

From cell F36 of Figure 8.6 we note that the computed value for F is 12.4059 and from cell H36 the critical value is 2.7642 for the first F test, that is, the test to determine the effect of the compensation plans. Accordingly, we would reject the null hypothesis and conclude the compensation plans did have an effect. In a similar manner, we note the for the second F test that the computed value is 33.0439 in cell F37 and the critical value is 3.73889 in cell H37. Again the null hypothesis is rejected and we conclude there is definitely a block effect. The experience level of the sales representative does affect the sales level.

For the **p-VALUE APPROACH** for the two tests, you will need to refer to Table 5.3 (or 5.5) to categorize the results. For this example the p-value for the first test is given in cell G36 of Figure 8.6 as 4.9E-05 (or 0.000049). The categories of Figure 5.3 would classify the results as *very highly significant*. Accordingly, we would again reject the null hypothesis that the means for the three compensation plans are equal. Similarly, the p-value for the second test in cell G37 is 5E-06 (0.000005) so again we would reject the null hypothesis that the means for the eight blocks are equal.

8.3 THE ANOVA: TWO-FACTOR WITH REPLICATION ANALYSIS TOOL ———

The ANOVA: TWO-FACTOR WITH REPLICATION analysis tool is used to analysis the results from a *two-way factorial experimental design*. This design is used to explore the effect of two variables. It is somewhat like the randomized block design of Section 8.2. However for the randomized block design the focus is on one variable and a blocking variable for improving the precision of the test. It requires only one measurement for each of the cells in the design. For the two-way factorial experiment, the focus is on determining the effect of each of two separate variables and an interaction effect of the two variables. It requires two or more measurements for each of the cells.

Let us continue our example with Brearbert Lynn of Eves Valves, Inc. Suppose for sales purposes Eves Values has the country divided into four sales regions, Northeast, Southeast, Midwest and West. Furthermore, suppose Brearbert not only is interested in exploring the effect of the three compensation plans but she is also interested in the effect of the four sales regions and in the combined effect of compensation plan and geographic region. In order to test the significance of these three possible effects, Brearbert randomly selects 24 sales representatives. She then randomly assigns two representatives to each of the twelve possible combinations of compensation plan and geographic region. The total sales for the next 6 months are recorded for each of the 24 representatives.

To analyze the results using Excel you would proceed as follows.

1. Start Excel, enter the **Identification Material**, and then enter the labels and data in columns A through D as shown in Figure 8.7. Note that we are using the third worksheet in the workbook named ANOVA. We selected the third worksheet by clicking on the tab towards the bottom of the Excel window labeled *Sheet3*. Save the workbook file with the name ANOVA.

Figure 8.7 Two-way ANOVA with Interaction Data

	A	B	C	D	E
1		Analysis of Variance Examples			
2		Your Name			
3	Today's Date			File: ANOVA.xls	
4					
5	SALES	COMPENSATION PLAN			
6	REGION	Salary	Sal.&Com.	Commissn	
7	Norhteast	4500	4430	5810	
8		4580	4740	5420	
9	Southeast	4200	4530	4800	
10		4860	4830	5100	
11	Midwest	5040	5100	5460	
12		4740	4920	6180	
13	West	4320	4140	4680	
14		4410	4320	4620	
15					

---

2. From the menu bar select **Tools**, from the subsequent pull-down menu select **Data Analysis** and from the Data Analysis dialog box select **ANOVA: Two-Factor With Replication**.

3. Fill in the entries of the ANOVA: Two-Factor With Replication dialog box as shown in Figure 8.8. Notice that the input range includes the labels in the cells A6, B6, C6, D6, and A7 through A13.

4. Click on **OK** and the output will appear as shown in Figure 8.9.

These ANOVA results provide the means and variances for each of the twelve possible combinations of compensation plan and geographic region. The ANOVA table at the bottom of the output provides sample statistics for conducting three separate F-tests. The first is a test to determine if the four geographic regions (labeled as **Sample** in cell A52) have a significant effect. Specifically, the test hypotheses are

$$H_0: \mu_1 = \mu_2 = \mu_3 = \mu_4$$
$$H_a: \text{not all } \mu\text{'s are equal}$$

Figure 8.8 ANOVA: Two-Factor with Replication Dialog Box

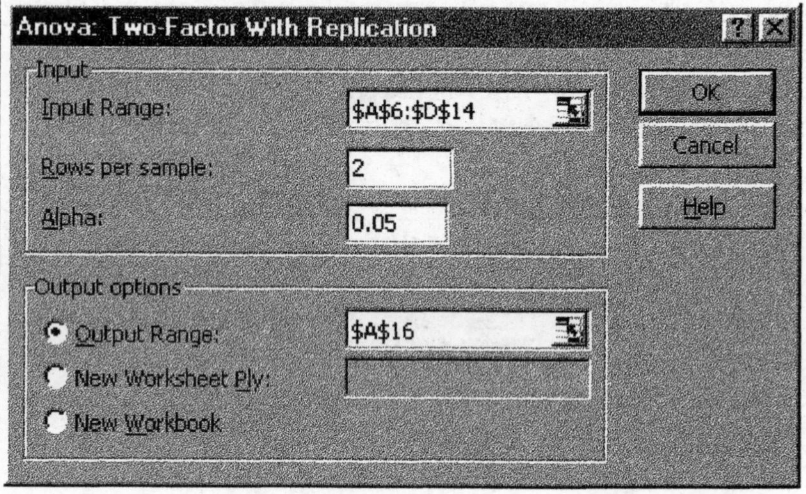

The second F-test is a test to determine if the three compensation plans (labeled as **Columns** in cell A53) have a significant effect. Specifically, the test hypotheses are

$$H_0: \mu_1 = \mu_2 = \mu_3$$
$$H_a: \text{not all } \mu\text{'s are equal}$$

The third F test is a test of whether there is a significant interaction or combined effect between the sales regions and compensation plans (labeled as **Interaction** in cell A54). The test hypotheses for the interaction effect are

$$H_0: \text{there is not an interaction effect between region and plan}$$
$$H_a: \text{there is an interaction effect between region and plan}$$

The **CRITICAL F-VALUE APPROACH** for these tests requires you to compare the computed value for the F-statistic to the critical value for F. If the computed F is greater than the critical value of F, the null hypothesis is rejected. Otherwise the null hypothesis is not rejected. The critical value is the value from the F distribution that corresponds to the alpha value specified in Figure 8.8 and the degrees of freedom for the numerator and the denominator of the F statistic.

We note in Figure 8.9 that the computed F values both for the sales region (11.08462 in cell E52) and for the compensation plan (17.71899 in cell E53) are greater than their corresponding *F crit* values in cells G51 and G53. Accordingly, we would reject the null hypothesis in both cases. In other words, we conclude that the sales region and the compensation plan both have a significant effect on the six months sales results. On the other hand, the computed F value for the interaction effect of these two variables is 1.470002 in cell E54. It is smaller than the critical F value of 2.996117 in cell F54 so we do not reject the null hypothesis for this test. We conclude there is not a significant combined effect of sales region and compensation plan.

Figure 8.9 Results for Two-way ANOVA with Interaction

	A	B	C	D	E	F	G
16	Anova: Two-Factor With Replication						
17							
18	SUMMARY	Salary	Sal.&Com.	Commissn	Total		
19	*Norhteast*						
20	Count	2	2	2	6		
21	Sum	9080	9170	11230	29480		
22	Average	4540	4585	5615	4913.333		
23	Variance	3200	48050	76050	321266.7		
24							
25	*Southeast*						
26	Count	2	2	2	6		
27	Sum	9060	9360	9900	28320		
28	Average	4530	4680	4950	4720		
29	Variance	217800	45000	45000	97800		
30							
31	*Midwest*						
32	Count	2	2	2	6		
33	Sum	9780	10020	11640	31440		
34	Average	4890	5010	5820	5240		
35	Variance	45000	16200	259200	268800		
36							
37	*West*						
38	Count	2	2	2	6		
39	Sum	8730	8460	9300	26490		
40	Average	4365	4230	4650	4415		
41	Variance	4050	16200	1800	41190		
42							
43	*Total*						
44	Count	8	8	8			
45	Sum	36650	37010	42070			
46	Average	4581.25	4626.25	5258.75			
47	Variance	80412.5	106169.6	313955.4			
48							
49							
50	ANOVA						
51	rce of Varia	SS	df	MS	F	P-value	F crit
52	Sample	2154713	3	718237.5	11.08462	0.000896	3.4903
53	Columns	2296233	2	1148117	17.71899	0.000262	3.88529
54	Interaction	571500	6	95250	1.470002	0.26801	2.996117
55	Within	777550	12	64795.83			
56							
57	Total	5799996	23				
58							

For the **p-VALUE APPROACH** to these tests, you will need to refer to Table 5.3 (or 5.5) to categorize the results. For this example the p value for the first test is given in cell F52 of Figure 8.9 as 0.000896 and that for the second test as 0.000262 in cell F53.   The categories of Table 5.3 (or 5.5) would classify both of these results as *very highly significant.* Accordingly, we would again reject the null hypothesis for both tests. The p value for the interaction effect test is 0.26801 in cell F52. We would categorize this as *not significant* and thus would not reject the null hypothesis.

This completes are discussion of the use of the three ANOVA data analysis tools provided by Excel. As mentioned in our introduction to this chapter, the F-test of this chapter is equivalent to the two-tailed t-test for population means of Chapter 5 for the two-population situation. In the next chapter we will explore a similar situation for population proportions. We will see that the χ^2 test is equivalent to the two-tailed z-test for two population proportions of Chapter 6. We will see that the χ^2 test can also be used if there are more than two population proportions. In addition, we will explore this test for another application, a test of independence.

CHAPTER 9. APPLICATIONS OF THE CHI-SQUARE STATISTIC

In Chapter 7 we showed how the chi-square statistic could be used for statistical estimation and testing for population variances. In this chapter we demonstrate two additional hypothesis testing procedures which are based on the chi-square statistic. The first, the goodness-of-fit test for a multinomial distribution, is discussed in **Section 9.1**. The second, the test for independence using contingency tables, is discussed in **Section 9.2**. Both of these tests are performed on frequency count data. The multinomial goodness-of-fit test requires frequency counts for one variable. On the other hand, the contingency table test of independence requires frequency counts for a cross-tabulation of all combinations of values for two variables. Sometimes the frequency values are readily available. At other times, it may be necessary to compute frequencies from a data set before conducting the test. For these instances, Excel provides a feature that makes the computation of frequencies somewhat easy. It is the PIVIOT TABLE WIZARD as presented in **Section 9.3**.

Before proceeding, we should mention that the tests of this chapter are generally used for **qualitative** or categorical data (measured on a nominal or ordinal measurement scale) as opposed to **quantitative** or numerical data (measured on an interval or ratio scale). However, they can also be applied to the analysis of quantitative data.

9.1 GOODNESS-OF-FIT TEST:
MULTINOMIAL DISTRIBUTION ———————

Excel provides two statistical functions for conducting the multinomial goodness-of-fit test. The function CHIINV facilitates the critical χ^2-value approach to the test and CHIDIST facilitates the p-value approach to the test. We will demonstrate both approaches with the following example.

> Kriti Waspork owns Bar-K Ranch, Inc., which produces hay for ranches deep in the heart of the state of Zexas. The ranch has thousands of customers to whom they provide five types of hay. In the past the proportion of their customers for the five types has been 0.16 for alfalfa, 0.09 for clover, 0.13 for timothy, 0.36 for mixture #1 and 0.26 for mixture #2. In planning for the upcoming season, they have asked a few of their customers their buying intentions. The result was 36 for alfalfa, 29 for clover, 27 for timothy, 55 for mixture #1 and 49 for mixture #2. Bar-K would now like to determine if these sample results indicate there has been a statistically significant change in their customers' requirements.

Bar-K's tabulation of their customers buying intentions could by done by hand. However, the PIVOT TABLE WIZARD of Excel can used to determine frequency counts such as this from a listing of the raw data. Thus, they could have used it as discussed in Subsection 9.3.1 to determine the necessary values.

We will develop a worksheet for computing the needed values for the hypothesis test. Proceed as follows.

1. Start Excel and enter the **Identification Material** in rows 1, and 2 of later Figure 9.2. Also enter the labels of rows 3, 10, 14 and 15 on the left-hand side of the worksheet and in rows 3 through 15 on the right-hand side of the worksheet. Enter the input values in cell C10, and cells A16 through A20, B16 through B20 and D16 through D20. Save the worksheet with the name CHI-SQR.

2. In cell H4 enter the formula to find the total observed frequencies. We will set this worksheet up to evaluate situations with up to 20 categories. Accordingly, the formula in cell H4 is **=SUM(B16:B35)** as shown in Figure 9.1.

3. Cell H5 is used to sum the hypothesized proportion inputs. These should sum to the value of 1.0. A value in this cell of something other than 1.0 indicates the proportions are not correct. The formula in cell H5 is **=SUM(D16:D35)** since we are allowing for up to 20 categories.

Figure 9.1 Formulas for Chi-square Goodness-of-Fit Test

	E	F	G	H
1				
2	Your Name		File: CHI-SQR.xls	
3	*STATISTIC*			
4		Observed Frequency Sum		=SUM(B16:B35)
5		Hypothesized Propor.Sum		=SUM(D16:D35)
6				
7		Number of Categories		=COUNTA(A16:A35)
8		Degrees of Freedom		=H7-1
9				
10		*Chi-square Test Statistic*		=SUM(G16:G35)
11		*Chi-square critical value*		=CHIINV(C10,H8)
12		*p-value for test*		=CHIDIST(H10,H8)
13				
14		Expected	Chi-square	
15		Frequency	Value	
16		=$H$4*D16	=IF(F16>0,(B16-F16)^2/F16,0)	
17		=$H$4*D17	=IF(F17>0,(B17-F17)^2/F17,0)	
18		=$H$4*D18	=IF(F18>0,(B18-F18)^2/F18,0)	
19		=$H$4*D19	=IF(F19>0,(B19-F19)^2/F19,0)	
20		=$H$4*D20	=IF(F20>0,(B20-F20)^2/F20,0)	
21		=$H$4*D21	=IF(F21>0,(B21-F21)^2/F21,0)	
22		=$H$4*D22	=IF(F22>0,(B22-F22)^2/F22,0)	
23		=$H$4*D23	=IF(F23>0,(B23-F23)^2/F23,0)	
24		=$H$4*D24	=IF(F24>0,(B24-F24)^2/F24,0)	
25		=$H$4*D25	=IF(F25>0,(B25-F25)^2/F25,0)	
26		=$H$4*D26	=IF(F26>0,(B26-F26)^2/F26,0)	
27		=$H$4*D27	=IF(F27>0,(B27-F27)^2/F27,0)	
28		=$H$4*D28	=IF(F28>0,(B28-F28)^2/F28,0)	

4. Cell H7 uses the function COUNTA to determine how many categories have been entered. The formula **=COUNTA(A16:A35)** counts the number of non-blank cells in the range A16 to A35.

5. The value for the degrees of freedom for the chi-square statistic is one less than the number of categories. The formula **=H7-1** in cell H8 computes this value.

6. In cell H10 we compute the value for the chi-square statistic the formula **=SUM(G15:G35)**.

7. In cell H11 we compute the critical value for the chi-square distribution. It depends on the significance level of the test in cell C10 and the degrees of freedom in cell H8. The formula is **=CHIINV(C10,H8)**.

8. The formula in cell H12 computes the p value for the test. Its value depends on the test statistic value in cell H10 and the degrees of freedom. The formula is **=CHIDIST(H10,H8)**.

9. Cells F16 through F35 compute the expected frequencies. In cell F16 enter the formula **=$H$4*D16**. The absolute cell reference is used for cell H4 so this formula can be correctly copied. Copy the formula to cells F17 through F35.

10. Finally cells G16 through G35 compute the chi-square value for each category. Since we are setting the worksheet up to use an indefinite number of categories, we are forced to use an IF

statement to set the value equal to zero for the blank categories in the range. Thus, the IF statement computes the chi-square value for the non-blank categories. The formula for cell G16 is entered as =IF(F16>0,(B16-F16)^2/F16,0). Copy the formula into cells G17 through G35.

The result of your efforts should appear as given in Figure 9.2. We now have the values necessary to conduct the test both with the critical χ^2-value approach and the p-value approach.

Figure 9.2 Results for Chi-square Goodness-of-Fit Test

	A	B	C	D	E	F	G	H
1			MULTINOMIAL GOODNESS-OF-FIT TEST					
2	Today's Date				Your Name		File: CHI-SQR.xls	
3	INPUT DATA				STATISTICAL OUTPUTS			
4						Observed Frequency Sum		196
5						Hypothesized Propor.Sum		1.000
6								
7						Number of Categories		5
8						Degrees of Freedom		4
9								
10	Significance Level of Test 0.05					Chi-square Test Statistic		11.600
11						Chi-square critical value		9.488
12						p-value for test		0.021
13								
14		Observed		Hypthesized		Expected	Chi-square	
15	Category	Frequency		Proportion		Frequency	Value	
16	Alfalfa	36		0.160		31.36	0.6865	
17	Clover	29		0.090		17.64	7.3157	
18	Timothy	27		0.130		25.48	0.0907	
19	Mixture #1	55		0.360		70.56	3.4313	
20	Mixture #2	49		0.260		50.96	0.0754	
21						0	0.0000	

The null and the alternative hypotheses for this test are the following.

H_0: $p_1 = 0.16$, $p_2 = 0.09$, $p_3 = 0.13$, $p_4 = 0.36$, $p_5 = 0.26$,
H_a: at least one of these proportions is incorrect

The **CRITICAL χ^2-VALUE APPROACH** requires you to compare the computed value for the chi-square statistic to the critical value for chi square. If the computed value is greater than the critical value, the null hypothesis is rejected. Otherwise the null hypothesis is not rejected. From Figure 9.2 we note that the computed chi-square value of cell H10 is 11.600 and the critical value of cell H11 is 9.488. Thus, we would conclude that not all the proportions are correct. In other words we would conclude that there has been a statistically significant change in Bar-K's customers' requirements.

For the **P-VALUE APPROACH** to the test, you need to refer to Table 5.3 (or 5.5) of Chapter 5 to categorize the results. For our example here the p-value given in cell H12 is 0.021. The categories of Table 5.3 (or 5.5) would classify these results as *significant*. Accordingly, we would again reject the null hypothesis. We would conclude there has been a change in the customers' requirements.

You should save your completed worksheet for future use. Although you developed it for a particular test situation, it is completely general. Thus, you can use it for testing any specified set of proportion values. To use the worksheet, you only need to enter

1. The significance value in cell C10.

2. The categories beginning in cell A16. Since the worksheet is set up to utilize data in rows 16 through 35, all cells in column A through row 35 which **do not represent a category should be blank**. If not, the number of categories computed in cell H5 will be incorrect.

3. The observed frequencies beginning in cell B16.

4. The hypothesized proportions beginning in cell D16. These should sum to 1.0. Cell H5 computes the sum of these so you may easily see if this is true or not.

Your worksheet will provide you with the values for conducting the hypothesis test for both the critical χ^2-value and the p-value approaches.

Before concluding this section let us point out ***TWO SPECIAL APPLICATIONS*** of this test. **First**, it is commonly used to test for the **equivalence of a set of proportions**. The hypotheses for this situation are

$$H_0: p_1 = p_2 = p_3 = p_4 = p_5 = \ldots = p_k = 1/k$$
$$H_a: \text{at least one of the proportions is not equal}$$

The entries for the worksheet are as before with one exception. It is that the *Hypothesized Proportion* values are all equal to one divided by the number of proportions (i.e., 1/k).

The **second** special application is for the **two-category situation**. For it the hypotheses are

$$H_0: p_1 = \text{a specified value}, \quad p_2 = 1\text{- the specified value}$$
$$H_a: p_1 \neq \text{a specified value}, \quad p_2 \neq 1\text{- the specified value}$$

These are equivalent to the **Two-Tailed** form for testing one population proportion as given in Subsection 6.1.2 of Chapter 6. Thus, this situation can be tested using either the z statistic as in Chapter 6, or the chi-square statistic of this chapter. The two tests will always yield the same result.

9.2 TEST OF INDEPENDENCE: CONTINGENCY TABLES ──────

Three of Excel's statistical functions are useful for conducting the contingency table test of independence. The function CHIINV facilitates the critical χ^2-value approach to the test. Both the functions CHIDIST and CHITEST can be used to compute the p-value for the test. We will demonstrate the use of these functions by continuing the Bar-K Ranch example of Section 9.1.

As you may recall Kriti produces hay for ranches deep in the heart of Zexas. In order to predict her customers' needs for the upcoming year she is attempting to determine if the type of hay a customer purchases is related to the primary type of livestock the customer has. She has analyzed data for a sample of her customers noting the type of hay and the primary livestock for each customer. These results are shown in Table 9.1. She would now like to use the χ^2 test of independence to determine if there is a significant relationship between the two qualitative variables *type of hay* and *type of livestock*.

Table 9.1 Number of Customers Classified by Type of Hay and Type of Livestock

TYPE OF HAY	PRIMARY TYPE OF LIVESTOCK			
	Cattle	Horses	Emus	Sheep
Alfalfa	6	14	11	5
Clover	5	11	12	1
Timothy	2	7	9	9
Mixture #1	16	10	7	22
Mixture #2	14	16	9	10

Before developing our worksheet to conduct the test, we should make one comment regarding the data of Table 9.1. Bar-K would have had to analyze a list of customers in order to determine the number for each cell in the table. They might do this by hand. However, Excel provides an analysis feature that can be used to determine frequency count data from a listing of data. It is called the PIVOT TABLE WIZARD and is discussed in Section 9.3. Thus, Bar-K could have used the procedure of Subsection 9.3.2 to compute the values for Table 9.1

We will now develop a worksheet for computing the needed values for the contingency table test of independence. You should continue with the CHI-SQR workbook from Section 9.1 but on *Sheet2*.

1. Enter the **Identification Information** in rows 1, and 2 of later Figure 9.5. Also enter the labels in rows 3 through 29, and the labels for cells A31 and A45. Enter the input values in cell E4, and in cells B9 through E13. Save the workbook CHI-SQR.

2. In cell E21 enter the formula to find the total observed frequencies. We will set this worksheet up to evaluate situations with up to 10 categories for each of the two variables. Accordingly, the formula in cell E21 is **=SUM(B9:K18)** as shown in Figure 9.3.

Figure 9.3 Beginning Formulas for Chi-square Test of Independence

	A	B	C	D	E
19					
20	*STATISTICAL OUTF*				
21		Observed Frequencies Sum			=SUM(B9:K18)
22					
23		Number of First Category			=COUNTA(A9:A18)
24		Number of Second Category			=COUNTA(B8:K8)
25		Degrees of Freedom			=(E23-1)*(E24-1)
26					
27		*Chi-square Test Statistic*			=SUM(B48:K57)
28		*Chi-square Critical Value*			=CHIINV(E4,E25)
29		*p-Value for Test*			=CHIDIST(E27,E25)
30					

---

3. Cell E23 uses the Excel function COUNTA to determine how many categories have been entered for the first variable. The formula **=COUNTA(A9:A18)** counts the number of non-blank cells in the range A9 through A18.

4. Cell E24 determines how many categories have been entered for the second variable. The formula is **=COUNTA(B8:K8)**.

5. The number of degrees of freedom for the chi-square statistic is one less than the number of categories for the first variable times one less than the number of categories for the second variable. The formula **=(E23-1)*(E24-1)** in cell E25 computes this value.

6. In cell E27 we compute the value for the chi-square statistic. The formula is **=SUM(B48:K57)**. As before this formula is set up to evaluate situations with up to 10 categories for each of the two variables. We will create the table in the range B47 through K56 later in this procedure.

7. In cell E28 we compute the critical value for the chi-square distribution. It depends on the significance level of the test in cell E4 and the degrees of freedom in cell E25. The formula is **=CHIINV(E4,E25)**.

8. The formula in cell E29 computes the p value for the test. Its value depends on the test statistic value in cell E27 and the degrees of freedom. The formula is **=CHIDIST(E27,E25)**.

9. As shown in Figure 9.4, Rows 31 through 43 present a table for computing the expected frequencies. To begin developing this table copy the contents of cells A7 through K18 to cells A32

through K43.   Also, copy cells A7 through K18 to cells A46 through K57 to provide the structure for the *Chi-Square Values Table* shown at the bottom of Figure 9.4.

Figure 9.4   Additional Formulas for Chi-square Test of Independence

	A	B	C
32	**First**		**Second Category**
33	**Category** =B8		=C8
34	=A9	=SUM(B$9:B$18)*SUM($B9:$K9)/$E$21	=SUM(C$9:C$18)*SUM($B9:$K9)/$E$21
35	=A10	=SUM(B$9:B$18)*SUM($B10:$K10)/$E$21	=SUM(C$9:C$18)*SUM($B10:$K10)/$E$21
36	=A11	=SUM(B$9:B$18)*SUM($B11:$K11)/$E$21	=SUM(C$9:C$18)*SUM($B11:$K11)/$E$21
37	=A12	=SUM(B$9:B$18)*SUM($B12:$K12)/$E$21	=SUM(C$9:C$18)*SUM($B12:$K12)/$E$21
38	=A13	=SUM(B$9:B$18)*SUM($B13:$K13)/$E$21	=SUM(C$9:C$18)*SUM($B13:$K13)/$E$21
39	=A14	=SUM(B$9:B$18)*SUM($B14:$K14)/$E$21	=SUM(C$9:C$18)*SUM($B14:$K14)/$E$21
40	=A15	=SUM(B$9:B$18)*SUM($B15:$K15)/$E$21	=SUM(C$9:C$18)*SUM($B15:$K15)/$E$21
41	=A16	=SUM(B$9:B$18)*SUM($B16:$K16)/$E$21	=SUM(C$9:C$18)*SUM($B16:$K16)/$E$21
42	=A17	=SUM(B$9:B$18)*SUM($B17:$K17)/$E$21	=SUM(C$9:C$18)*SUM($B17:$K17)/$E$21
43	=A18	=SUM(B$9:B$18)*SUM($B18:$K18)/$E$21	=SUM(C$9:C$18)*SUM($B18:$K18)/$E$21
44			
45	*Table 3–C*		
46	**First**		**Second Category**
47	**Category** =B8		=C8
48	=A9	=IF(B34>0,(B9-B34)^2/B34,0)	=IF(C34>0,(C9-C34)^2/C34,0)
49	=A10	=IF(B35>0,(B10-B35)^2/B35,0)	=IF(C35>0,(C10-C35)^2/C35,0)
50	=A11	=IF(B36>0,(B11-B36)^2/B36,0)	=IF(C36>0,(C11-C36)^2/C36,0)
51	=A12	=IF(B37>0,(B12-B37)^2/B37,0)	=IF(C37>0,(C12-C37)^2/C37,0)
52	=A13	=IF(B38>0,(B13-B38)^2/B38,0)	=IF(C38>0,(C13-C38)^2/C38,0)
53	=A14	=IF(B39>0,(B14-B39)^2/B39,0)	=IF(C39>0,(C14-C39)^2/C39,0)
54	=A15	=IF(B40>0,(B15-B40)^2/B40,0)	=IF(C40>0,(C15-C40)^2/C40,0)
55	=A16	=IF(B41>0,(B16-B41)^2/B41,0)	=IF(C41>0,(C16-C41)^2/C41,0)
56	=A17	=IF(B42>0,(B17-B42)^2/B42,0)	=IF(C42>0,(C17-C42)^2/C42,0)
57	=A18	=IF(B43>0,(B18-B43)^2/B43,0)	=IF(C43>0,(C18-C43)^2/C43,0)
58			

10. In cell A34 enter the equation **=A9** so the contents of A34 will always be the entry in cell A9.

11. Copy the formula in cell A34 into cells A35 through A43. Note the cells corresponding to blank cells in the Observed Frequency Table will display a 0 (zero).

12. In cell B33 enter the formula **=B8**.

13. Copy the formula in cell B33 into cells C33 through K33. Note the cells corresponding to blank cells in the Observed Frequency Table will display a 0.

14. The cells within the *Expected Frequencies Table* are equal to the corresponding row total of the *Observed Frequencies Table* times the corresponding column total divided by the total of all the observed frequencies. We begin by entering in cell B34 an appropriate formula for copying into the remaining cells of the table. The appropriate formula requires that we used **mixed relative and absolute references** for computing the row sums and the column sums. The formula for cell B34 is **=SUM(B$9:B$18)*SUM($B9:$K9)/$E$21**. Note the first sum involves a relative row

reference and an absolute column reference. The second sum has an absolute row reference and a relative column reference. Finally, the reference to cell E21 has absolute references for both row and column. (Note: if you are using the **F4** key to change a relative reference to an absolute reference, one click will change both row and column to absolute, two clicks will change just the column and three clicks will change just the row.)

15. Next copy the contents of cell B34 into all the remaining cells in the range from B34 through K43. This completes the development of the Expected Frequency Table.

16. As shown in Figure 9.4, Rows 45 through 57 present a table for computing the chi-square values for each of the individual terms. The structure of this table was copied in Step 9 above. In cell A48 enter the equation **=A9** so the contents of A48 will always be the entry in cell A9.

17. Copy the formula in cell A48 into cells A49 through A57. Note the cells corresponding to blank cells in the Observed Frequency Table will display a 0.

18. In cell B47 enter the formula **=B8**.

19. Copy the formula in cell B47 into cells C47 through K47. Note the cells corresponding to blank cells in the Observed Frequency Table will display a 0.

20. The computation within this table finds the difference between the observed frequency and the expected frequency for each cell. It then squares this difference and divides the result by the expected frequency. However, we are setting this worksheet up to use an indefinite number of categories. This requires that we use an IF statement to set the value equal to zero if the expected frequency is zero. Otherwise the computation would result in an invalid division by zero. The formula for cell B48 should be entered as **=IF(B34>0,(B9-B34)^2/B34,0)**.

21. Next copy the contents of cell B48 into all the remaining cells in the range from B48 through K57.

The result of your efforts should appear as given in Figure 9.5. If you successfully developed this worksheet yourself, you should have a feeling of accomplishment. You now have the values necessary to conduct the test of independence with both the critical χ^2-value approach and the p-value approach.

The null and the alternative hypotheses for this test are the following.

H_0: Type of hay is independent of type of livestock
H_a: Type of hay is not independent of type of livestock

The **CRITICAL χ^2-VALUE APPROACH** requires you to compare the computed value for the chi-square statistic to the critical value for chi square. If the computed value is greater than the critical value, the null hypothesis is rejected. Otherwise the null hypothesis is not rejected. From Figure 9.5 we note that the computed chi-square value in cell E27 is 32.43923 and the critical value in cell E28 is

Figure 9.5 Results for Chi-square Test of Independence

	A	B	C	D	E	F	G	H	I	J	K
1			**CONTINGENCY TABLE TEST OF INDEPENDENCE**								
2	Today's Date				Your Name					File: CHI-SQR.xls	
3	**INPUT DATA**										
4			Significance Level of Test=		0.05						
5											
6	**Table 1--Observed Frequencies**										
7	**First**		**Second Category**								
8	**Category**	Cattle	Horses	Emus	Sheep						
9	Alfalfa	6	14	11	5						
10	Clover	5	11	12	1						
11	Timothy	2	7	9	9						
12	Mixture #1	16	10	7	22						
13	Mixture #2	14	16	9	10						
14											
15											
16											
17											
18											
19											
20	**STATISTICAL OUTPUTS**										
21		Observed Frequencies Sum			196						
22											
23		Number of First Category			5						
24		Number of Second Category			4						
25		Degrees of Freedom			12						
26											
27		**Chi-square Test Statistic**			32.43923						
28		**Chi-square Critical Value**			21.02606						
29		**p-Value for Test**			0.00118						
30											
31	**Table 2--Expected Frequencies**										
32	**First**		**Second Category**								
33	**Category**	Cattle	Horses	Emus	Sheep	0	0	0	0	0	0
34	Alfalfa	7.898	10.653	8.816	8.633	0.000	0.000	0.000	0.000	0.000	0.000
35	Clover	6.362	8.582	7.102	6.954	0.000	0.000	0.000	0.000	0.000	0.000
36	Timothy	5.923	7.990	6.612	6.474	0.000	0.000	0.000	0.000	0.000	0.000
37	Mixture #1	12.066	16.276	13.469	13.189	0.000	0.000	0.000	0.000	0.000	0.000
38	Mixture #2	10.750	14.500	12.000	11.750	0.000	0.000	0.000	0.000	0.000	0.000
39	0	0.000	0.000	0.000	0.000	0.000	0.000	0.000	0.000	0.000	0.000
40	0	0.000	0.000	0.000	0.000	0.000	0.000	0.000	0.000	0.000	0.000
41	0	0.000	0.000	0.000	0.000	0.000	0.000	0.000	0.000	0.000	0.000
42	0	0.000	0.000	0.000	0.000	0.000	0.000	0.000	0.000	0.000	0.000
43	0	0.000	0.000	0.000	0.000	0.000	0.000	0.000	0.000	0.000	0.000
44											
45	**Table 3--Chi-Square Values**										
46	**First**		**Second Category**								
47	**Category**	Cattle	Horses	Emus	Sheep	0	0	0	0	0	0
48	Alfalfa	0.456099	1.051529	0.540864	1.528634	0	0	0	0	0	0
49	Clover	0.291676	0.681514	3.377903	5.097882	0	0	0	0	0	0
50	Timothy	2.598749	0.122618	0.862245	0.985128	0	0	0	0	0	0
51	Mixture #1	1.282394	2.419711	3.107267	5.886648	0	0	0	0	0	0
52	Mixture #2	0.982558	0.155172	0.75	0.260638	0	0	0	0	0	0
53	0	0	0	0	0	0	0	0	0	0	0

21.02606. Thus, we would conclude that the type of hay is not independent of type of livestock. In other words, there appears to be a statistically significant relationship between the type of hay and the type of livestock for Bar-K's customers.

For the **P-VALUE APPROACH** to the test, you need to refer to Table 5.3 (or 5.5) of Chapter 5 to categorize the results. For our example here the p value given in cell E29 is 0.00118. The categories of Figure 5.3 would classify these results as *highly significant*. Accordingly, we would again reject the null hypothesis. We would conclude there is a statistically significant relationship.

You should save your completed worksheet for future use. Although you developed it for a particular test situation, it is completely general. Thus, you can use it for conducting any test of independence between two variables. To use the worksheet, you only need to enter

1. The significance value in cell E4.

2. The categories for the first variable beginning in cell A9. The worksheet is set up to utilize data in rows 9 through 18 so all cells in column A through row 18 **which do not represent a category should be blank**. Otherwise the computation of cell E23 will be incorrect.

3. The categories for the second variable beginning in cell B8. The worksheet is set up to utilize data in columns B through K so all cells in row 8 through column K **which do not represent a category should be blank** so the value in cell E24 is correct.

4. The observed frequencies beginning in cell B9.

Your worksheet will provide you with the values for conducting the hypothesis test for both the critical χ^2-value and the p-value approaches.

Step 8 of the above procedure used the function CHIDIST to determine the p value of the test. Excel also provides the function CHITEST for determining the p value. This function has only two arguments, the range of the observed frequencies and the range of the expected frequencies. Accordingly, the use of this function would eliminate the need to explicitly compute (1) the degrees of freedom, (2) the chi-square values of the third table of Figure 9.5 and (3) the chi-square test statistic value. The function would implicitly perform all these computations. However such an approach would not provide the chi-square test statistic value for conducting the critical χ^2-value approach. To obtain this value it would be necessary to compute the degrees of freedom. Then you could use the CHIINV function with the p value and the degrees of freedom to find the chi-square test statistic value.

9.3 THE PIVOT TABLE WIZARD

Many statistical procedures previously studied require frequency count data for qualitative variables. For example, the descriptive procedures of Subsections 2.2.2 and 2.2.3 in Chapter 2 and the inferential procedures of Chapter 6 and the two prior sections of the current chapter. Excel provides a feature that easily computes frequency values from raw data. The feature is a special type of table called a *Pivot Table*. It is developed using the PIVOT TABLE WIZARD. This wizard presents a series of dialog boxes which has the user specify (1) the location of the source data for the table, (2) the structure of the *Pivot Table* and (3) the format for the output.

To demonstrate, we will continue with the Bar-K Ranch example of the prior two sections of this chapter. To make the example manageable for you we will only use the small customer list given in Figure 9.6. This list has only three variables, customer number, type of hay and type of livestock, for only 20 customers. However, the procedures that follow would still be appropriate if we had many more variables and thousands of customers. We will use these data first to obtain a one variable frequency count as required for the test of Section 9.1 and second to obtain a two variable frequency count as required for the test of Section 9.2.

Figure 9.6 Pivot Table Example Data

BAR-K RANCH DATA FOR PIVOT TABLE

CUSTOMER	HAY	LIVESTOCK
1453	Clover	Cattle
1454	Mixture #1	Emus
1455	Alfalfa	Sheep
1456	Clover	Horses
1457	Mixture #2	Horses
1458	Alfalfa	Sheep
1459	Mixture #1	Cattle
1460	Mixture #1	Emus
1461	Mixture #2	Sheep
1462	Mixture #2	Sheep
1463	Timothy	Cattle
1464	Alfalfa	Horses
1465	Mixture #1	Sheep
1466	Mixture #2	Sheep
1467	Clover	Horses
1468	Mixture #1	Horses
1469	Timothy	Cattle
1470	Mixture #2	Emus
1471	Timothy	Cattle
1472	Clover	Horses

Today's Date — Your Name — File: CHI-SQR.xls

9.3.1 One Variable Frequency Count

Suppose we wish to determine the frequency count data for a multinomial goodness-of-fit test such as conducted in Section 9.1. In particular, suppose we need to compute the frequency values from the customer list of Figure 9.6 to be entered in cells B16 through B20 of Figure 9.2.

We will continue with the CHI-SQR workbook from Section 9.2 but move to *Sheet3*.

1. Enter the **Identification Material** information in rows 1, and 2 of Figure 9.6. Also enter the labels in row 3 and the data in cells B4 through D23. Save the workbook CHI-SQR.

2. From the menu bar select **Data** and from the subsequent pull-down menu select **PivotTable and PivotChart Report** as shown in Figure 9.7.

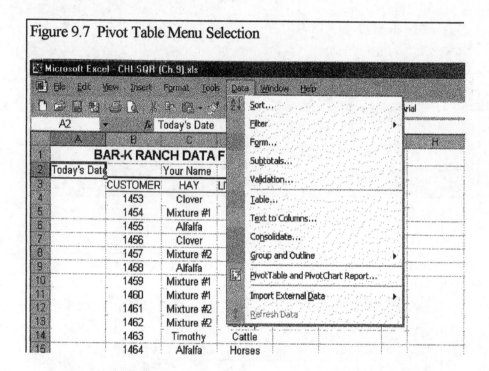

Figure 9.7 Pivot Table Menu Selection

3. The result will be the Step 1 dialog box for the PivotTable and PivotChart Wizard as shown in Figure 9.8. It asks for the source of the data. Since we are creating a Pivot Table from the data within our Excel worksheet, click on the option button for **Microsoft Excel list or database.** It also asks the kind of report is wanted so click on **PivotTable**. Click on **Next**.

4. The Step 2 dialog box of Figure 9.9 will be displayed. It asks for the range of the source data. Either drag to highlight the data or key it into the *Range* textbox. **It is necessary that the top row of the list, which contains the headings, be included in the range**. Click on the **Next.**

5. The result will be the Step 3 dialog box as given in Figure 9.10. This step specifies the location of the resulting Pivot Table either on a new worksheet or on an existing specified worksheet. To have the table presented on the worksheet with the data, select the option button for **Existing worksheet**. Next move the mouse pointer to a cell within the worksheet to denote the upper left corner of the Pivot Table and click the left mouse button. In Figure 9.10, this action as resulted in the **Sheet3!$F$4** textbox entry.

Figure 9.8 PivotTable and PivotChart Wizard Step 1

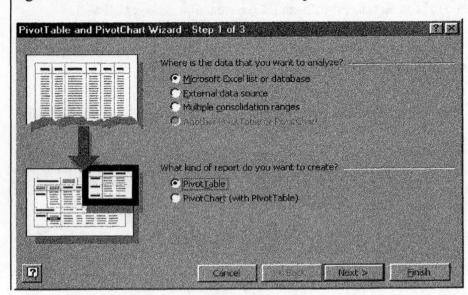

Figure 9.9 PivotTable and PivotChart Wizard Step 2

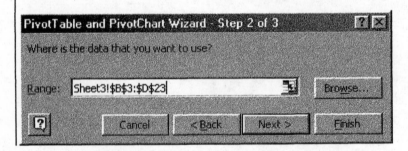

Figure 9.10 PivotTable and PivotChart Wizard Step 3

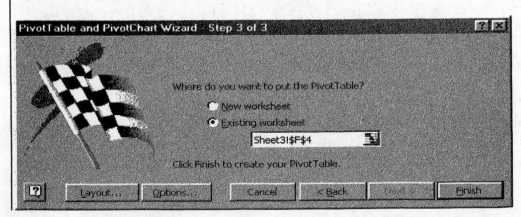

6. Next we need to specify the table layout by first clicking on the **Layout** command button of the dialog box of Figure 9.10 to yield the dialog box of Figure 9.11.

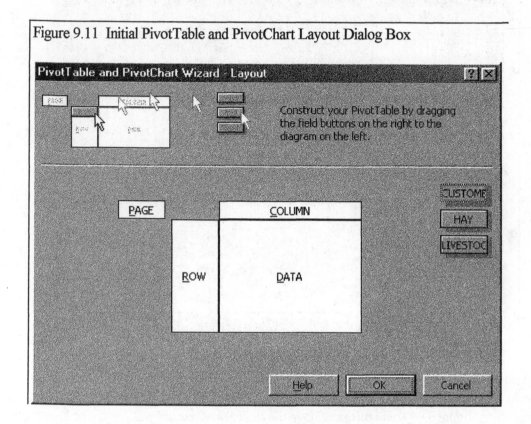

Figure 9.11 Initial PivotTable and PivotChart Layout Dialog Box

7. Figure 9.11 shows two general items for structuring the Pivot Table. On the right side it displays three buttons, one for each of the three variables. These are called a *field buttons*. In the center it displays a Pivot Table with its four possible parts: *Page, Row, Column* and *Data*. The top one-third of the dialog box tells you how to layout the table. Namely, you are to click and drag a field button to one of the four parts of the Pivot Table in the center of the dialog box.

8. For our example, we wish to determine the number of customers for each of the five types of hay. To specify this we would move the mouse pointer to the **Hay** button, hold down the left mouse button, move the mouse pointer (which becomes a small rectangular button) to the *Row* part of the pivot table and release the mouse button. The label *Hay* will appear above *Row* in the pivot table as shown in Figure 9.12. We repeat this dragging operation of the **Hay** button but release it on the *Data* part of the pivot table. The label *Count of Hay* will usually appear above *Data* in the table (see Figure 9.12). Excel has guessed that we wish to display the count of the number of hay customers. If it had guessed wrong, we proceed to Step 9 below to modify it. If it guessed right we proceed to Step 10 below by clicking on the **OK** button of Figure 9.12.

Figure 9.12 Completed PivotTable and PivotChart Layout Dialog Box

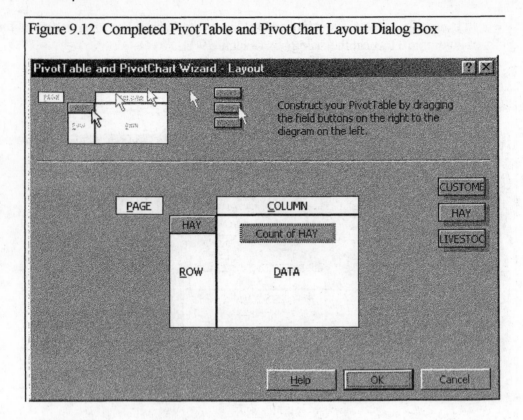

9. If *Data* section shows some summary measure other than *Count of Hay* as shown in Figure 9.12, double click on the summary measure shown. The result will be the *Pivot Table Field* dialog box as shown in Figure 9.13 (only the part above the label *Show data as* will usually be shown initially). The scrolling list box labeled as *Summarize by* shows 11 possible summary measures provided by the PivotTable and PivotChart Wizard. We would select **Count,** and click on **OK** to yield the results of Figure 9.12.   Next click on **OK** in the dialog box of Figure 9.12.

In passing we might note that you can modify the pivot data in additional ways. If you click on the **Options** button from the *Pivot Table Field* dialog box of Figure 9.13, an extension to the dialog box will be displayed (that of Figure 9.13 beginning with the label *Show data as*). It includes a scrolling list of nine modifications that can be made to the data. For example, it allows you to convert the frequency counts to percentages.

10.   A click on OK from the dialog box of Figure 9.12 will return you to the *Step 3 of 3* dialog box of Figure 9.10.   Click the **Options** button to yield the Pivot Table Options dialog box of Figure 9.14.

11.   You do not have to be concerned with most of the options shown in Figure 9.14. However, you usually will want the total count for each row and column that represents one of the variables. For this one-variable example, we will want the *Grand totals for columns*. Accordingly, we would select this check box as shown and then click on **OK** to return to the *Step 3 of 3* dialog box of

Figure 9.10. A subsequent click on **Finish** will result in the display of the Pivot Table within the worksheet with the data as shown in Figure 9.15.

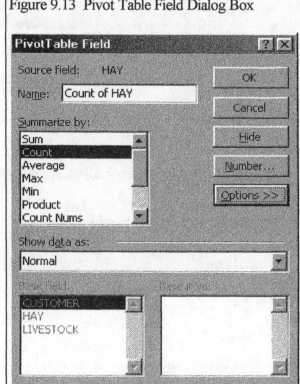

Figure 9.13 Pivot Table Field Dialog Box

As you will note in Figure 9.15, the worksheet includes a Pivot Table summarizing the original data. In addition, the *Pivot Table* toolbar and the *Pivot Table Field List* are displayed to facilitate further revisions and extensions to the table. The frequency values in cells G6 through G10 of the *Pivot Table* can now be copied to *Sheet1* of the CHI-SQR workbook to compute the values for the Multinomial Goodness-of-Fit test. When this is done the results of Figure 9.16 are obtained.

9.3.2 Two Variable Frequency Count

The pivot table feature of Excel can also be used to produce a cross-tabulation for all combinations of values for two variables. These results can than be copied to the contingency table test of independence worksheet, such as Figure 9.5, to compute the values for the test.

Suppose we wish to determine the frequency count for the test conducted in Section 9.2. In particular, suppose we need to compute the frequency values for cells B9 through E13 of Figure 9.5 from the data of the customer list of Figure 9.6.

Figure 9.14 Pivot Table Options Dialog Box

PivotTable Options

Name: PivotTable1

Format options

☑ Grand totals for columns
☐ Grand totals for rows
☑ AutoFormat table
☐ Subtotal hidden page items
☐ Merge labels
☑ Preserve formatting
☑ Repeat item labels on each printed page
☑ Mark Totals with *

Page layout: Down, Then Over

Fields per column: 0

☐ For error values, show:
☑ For empty cells, show:
☐ Set print titles

Data options

Data source options:
☑ Save data with table layout
☑ Enable drilldown
☐ Refresh on open
☐ Refresh every 60 minutes

External data options:
☑ Save password
☐ Background query
☐ Optimize memory

OK   Cancel

Figure 9.15 Pivot Table Final Results for One-Variable Example

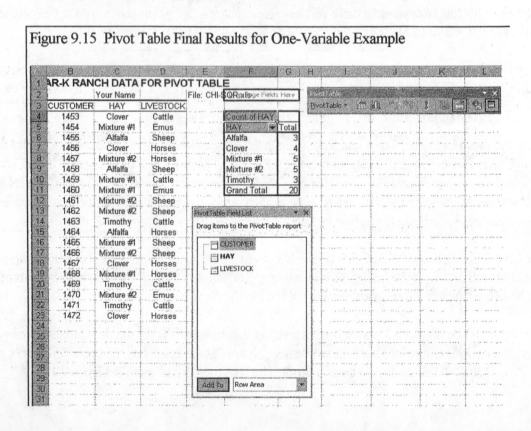

Figure 9.16 Pivot Table Chi-square Goodness-of-Fit Test Results

	A	B	C	D	E	F	G	H	I
1	MULTINOMIAL GOODNESS-OF-FIT TEST								
2	Today's Date				Your Name		File: CHI-SQR.xls		
3	INPUT DATA				STATISTICAL OUTPUTS				
4						Observed Frequency Sum		20	
5						Hypothesized Propor.Sum		1.000	
6									
7						Number of Categories		5	
8						Degrees of Freedom		4	
9									
10	Significance Level of Test 0.05					Chi-square Test Statistic		6.520	
11						Chi-square critical value		9.488	
12						p-value for test		0.164	
13									
14		Observed		Hypthesized		Expected	Chi-square		
15	Category	Frequency		Proportion		Frequency	Value		
16	Alfalfa	3		0.160		3.2	0.0125		
17	Clover	4		0.090		1.8	2.6889		
18	Timothy	5		0.130		2.6	2.2154		
19	Mixture #1	5		0.360		7.2	0.6722		
20	Mixture #2	3		0.260		5.2	0.9308		
21						0	0.0000		

The procedure for this two-variable table will be quite similar to that given above for the one-variable situation. We will move to *Sheet4* of the CHI-SQR workbook for this procedure.

1. Copy the data and labels in cells A1 through E23 of *Sheet3* (see Figure 9.6) to cells A1 through E23 of *Sheet4*. We could have continued on *Sheet3* for this example. However, a new worksheet will facilitate a clearer explanation.

2. From the menu bar select **Data** and from the subsequent pull-down menu select **PivotTablet and PivotChart Report** as previously shown in Figure 9.7. The result will be the Step 1 dialog box as previously shown in Figure 9.8. For this step, click on the option button for **Microsoft Excel List or Database** to indicate the data are internal to the current workbook and are located in one list on one worksheet. Click on the option button for **PivotTable** and click on **Next**.

3. The Step 2 dialog box of Figure 9.9 will be displayed. It asks for the range of the source data. Drag through or key in the range. **It is necessary that the top row of the list, which contains the headings, be included in the range**. Click on the **Next** button.

4. The result will be the Step 3 dialog box as given in Figure 9.10. As for the one-variable example, select the option button for **Existing worksheet** and designate cell **F4** as the upper left corner of the Pivot Table. Click on the **Layout** button. The result will be as given in Figure 9.11.

5. For our example, we wish to determine the number of customers for each of the twenty combinations of five types of hay and four types of livestock. To specify this we would move the mouse pointer to the **Hay** button, hold down the left mouse button, move the mouse pointer (which becomes a small rectangular button) to the *Row* part of the pivot table and release the mouse button. The label *Hay* will appear above *Row* in the pivot table as shown in Figure 9.17. Next we would drag the **Livestock** button to the *Column* part of the pivot table. The label *Livestock* will appear to the left of *Column* in the pivot table. Next we would repeat this dragging operation of the **Livestock** button but release it on the *Data* part of the pivot table (we could have used the *Hay* button a second time instead of the *Livestock* button a second time to obtain the same numerical results). The label *Count of Livestock* will appear above *Data* in the table (see Figure 9.17). Excel has guessed that we wish to display the count of the number of customers. If it had guessed wrong we would proceed to Step 6 below to modify it. If it guessed right we would proceed to Step 7 by clicking on the **OK** button of the dialog box in Figure 9.17.

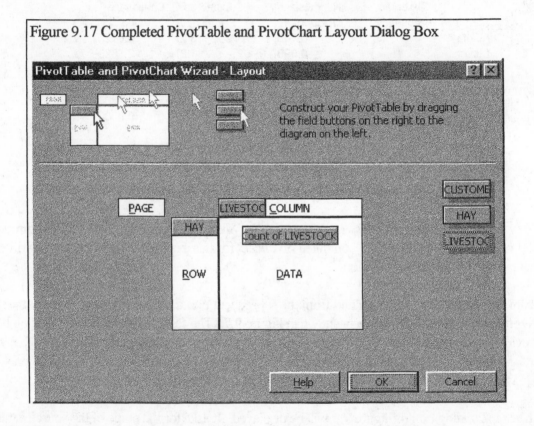

Figure 9.17 Completed PivotTable and PivotChart Layout Dialog Box

6. If the *Data* section shows some summary measure other than *Count of Livestock* as shown in Figure 9.17, double click on the summary measure shown. The result will be the *Pivot Table Field* dialog box as shown in Figure 9.13 (only the part above the label *Show data as* will usually be shown initially). The scrolling list box labeled as *Summarize by* shows 11 possible summary measures provided by the PivotTable Wizard. We would select **Count,** click on **OK** to yield the results of Figure 9.17.   Next click on **OK** of the dialog box in Figure 9.17.

In passing we might note that you can modify the pivot data in additional ways. If you click on the **Options** button from the *Pivot Table Field* dialog box, an extension to the dialog box will be displayed (that of Figure 9.13 beginning with the label *Show data as*). It includes a scrolling list of nine modifications that can be made to the data. For example, it allows you to convert the frequency counts to percentages.

7. A click on **OK** from the dialog box of Figure 9.17 will return you to the *Step 3 of 3* dialog box of Figure 9.10. Click the **Options** button to yield the *Pivot Table Options* dialog box of Figure 9.14.

8. You do not have to be concerned with most of the options shown in Figure 9.14. However, you usually will want the total count for each row and column that represents one of the variables. For this two-variable example, we will want the grand totals for the columns and the rows. Accordingly, we would select these check boxes and then click on **OK** to return to the *Step 3 of 3* dialog box of Figure 9.10. A subsequent click on **Finish** will result in the display of the two-variable Pivot Table within *Sheet4* as shown in Figure 9.18.

Figure 9.18 Pivot Table Final Results for Two-Variable Example

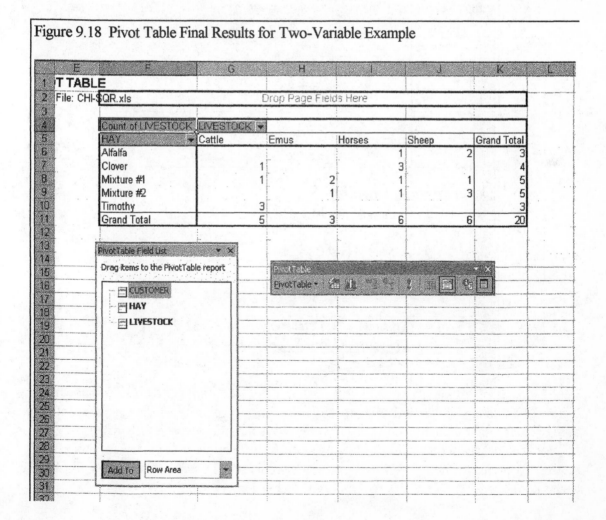

The frequency values in cells G22 through J26 can now be copied to *Sheet2* of the CHI-SQR workbook to compute the values for the Contingency Table Test of Independence. If you do this, the results of Figure 9.19 will be shown.

Figure 9.19 Pivot Table Test of Independence Results

	A	B	C	D	E	F
3	**INPUT DATA**					
4			Significance Level of Test=		0.05	
5						
6	**Table 1--Observed Frequencies**					
7	**First**		**Second Category**			
8	**Category**	Cattle	Horses	Emus	Sheep	
9	Alfalfa			1	2	
10	Clover	1		3		
11	Timothy	1	2	1	1	
12	Mixture #1		1	1	3	
13	Mixture #2	3				
14						
15						
16						
17						
18						
19						
20	**STATISTICAL OUTPUTS**					
21		Observed Frequencies Sum			20	
22						
23		Number of First Category			5	
24		Number of Second Category			4	
25		Degrees of Freedom			12	
26						
27		*Chi-square Test Statistic*			21.52222	
28		*Chi-square Critical Value*			21.02606	
29		*p-Value for Test*			0.04324	
30						

CHAPTER 10. REGRESSION ANALYSIS

10.1 Simple Linear Regression with TRENDLINE

10.2 Simple Linear Regression with the REGRESSION Analysis Tool

10.3 Multiple Regression with the REGRESSION Analysis Tool

10.4 Simple Non-linear Regression Analysis

Regression analysis may well be the most widely used statistical procedure in business and industry. It is a statistical method for studying the relationship between two or more variables. One objective of a regression analysis is to arrive at a mathematical relationship which will predict values for one variable, called the **dependent variable**, based on the values for the remaining variables, called the **independent variables**. Since most business, industrial, governmental and social organizations need to forecast values for such things as demand, interest rates, inflation rates, prices, costs and so on, there is great interest in the use of regression analysis. Regression analysis with only one independent variable is called **simple regression**. On the other hand, if the analysis includes two or more independent variables, it is called **multiple regression**.

As a result of the widespread use of regression analysis, Excel includes a number of resources for performing the required computations and charting. These resources can be categorized into three groups: (1) the trendline feature for charts, (2) three data analysis tools and (3) twelve statistical functions.

The trendline feature for charts facilitates the visual development of relationships for simple regression, that is, with one independent variable. The trendline feature can be used to develop relationships which are either linear or nonlinear. In addition, Excel includes three data analysis tools for performing regression analysis and the closely associated procedure called correlation analysis. These tools are the REGRESSION Analysis Tool, the CORRELATION Analysis Tool and the COVARIANCE Analysis Tool. Finally, Excel includes twelve functions that facilitate the computations for regression analysis and correlation analysis through the use of the INSERT FUNCTION facility. (For a description of these functions refer to the last twelve functions summarized in Appendix B.)

The capabilities of these three groups of resources duplicate each other in many aspects. The approach we take here is to introduce the student to those features that are the quickest and easiest to use for each part of the analysis. Accordingly, we first introduce in **Section 10.1** the use of the TRENDLINE feature for performing a simple linear regression analysis. We then consider in **Section 10.2** the added statistical results of the REGRESSION Analysis Tool for simple linear regression analysis. We continue with the use of the REGRESSION Analysis Tool in **Section 10.3** but for multiple regression. Finally in **Section 10.4,** we use both the TRENDLINE feature and the REGRESSION Analysis Tool for non-linear simple regression. Other resources are used in these four sections as needed to complete our analysis. For example, the function TREND is discussed in sections 10.1, 10.2 and 10.3 for forecasting values for the dependent variable, and the CORRELATION Analysis Tool is used in Section 10.3 to test for the condition called multicollinearity.

10.1 SIMPLE LINEAR REGRESSION WITH TRENDLINE———

We will begin our consideration of regression analysis with the following example.

Ms. Lore Ran is the product manager for Nutrecal, a food supplement product. In order to prepare her marketing plan for next year, she needs to predict the demand for Nutrecal. She feels the best predictor of demand for Nutrecal is the amount spent on advertising. Accordingly, she has gathered data from eight test markets that show the advertising level in thousands of dollars and the corresponding sales level in thousands of dollars. She first wishes to find a simple linear relationship that will allow her to predict sales as a function of advertising level. To analyze her results using the trendline feature of Excel you would proceed as follows.

1. Start Excel, enter the **Identification Material** in rows 1,2 and 3 of Figure 10.1. . Next enter the labels and data in columns B and C. Save the workbook with the file name REGRESS.

2.   As was noted in Section 2.2 of Chapter 2, Excel's Chart Wizard can be used to create many types of charts. The **XY (Scatter)** type will be used to plot the data and compute the regression equation for this example. Move the pointer to the CHART WIZARD icon on the standard

toolbar and click once. (Note: If you have not used the Chart Wizard before you may wish to refer to the discussion for Figures 2.8 through 2.12 given in Chapter 2.)

Figure 10.1 Simple Linear Regression Example Data

	A	B	C	D	E
1		Regression Analysis Examples			
2		Your Name			
3	Today's Date			File: REGRESS.xls	
4					
5		ADVERT.	SALES		
6		74.0	900.0		
7		27.5	266.4		
8		169.0	1555.2		
9		497.0	4320.0		
10		270.5	2707.2		
11		44.5	439.2		
12		63.0	1209.6		
13		189.5	2966.4		
14					

3.   The *Chart Wizard—Step 1 of 4—Chart Type* dialog box will appear as shown in Figure 10.2. If the **Standard Types** tab is not in front, click it.

4.   Use the mouse to select the **XY (Scatter)** chart and then select the chart sub-type at the top as shown in Figure 10.2. Click on the **Next** button. The *Chart Wizard—Step 2 of 4—Chart Source Data* dialog box will be displayed as given in Figure 10.3.

5.   If the **Data Range** tab is not in front, click it. Enter the range B5:C13 in the *Data Range* text box either by keying or by dragging. Click on **Next**. *The Chart Wizard—Step 3 of 4—Chart Options* dialog box will appear (an example is shown in Figure 2.11 in Chapter 2).

6.   The five dialog boxes of this step, allow you to format your chart as you would like it. For the **Titles** tab, we have entered a *Chart title* of *NUTRECAL SALES vs. ADVERTISING* and the titles for the *Value (X) axis* and *Value (Y) axis* as shown in Figure 10.4. For the **Axes** tab, we have selected the check boxes for both the *Value (X) axis* and *Value (Y) axis*. For the **Gridlines** tab, we have checked **Major gridlines** for both the *Value (X) axis* and *Value (Y) axis*. For the **Legends** tab, we have not selected the check box for *Show legend*. Finally for the **Data Labels** tab, none of the options under the *Label Contains* have been selected **(Excel 2000-App. D)**.

7.   Click on the **Next** button. *The Chart Wizard--Step 4 of 4—Chart Location* dialog box will appear (an example is shown in Figure 2.12 in Chapter 2). Click on *As object in* and click on the **Finish** button. The result will be as shown in Figure 10.4

Figure 10.2 Chart Wizard Step 1: XY(Scatter) Chart Sub-types

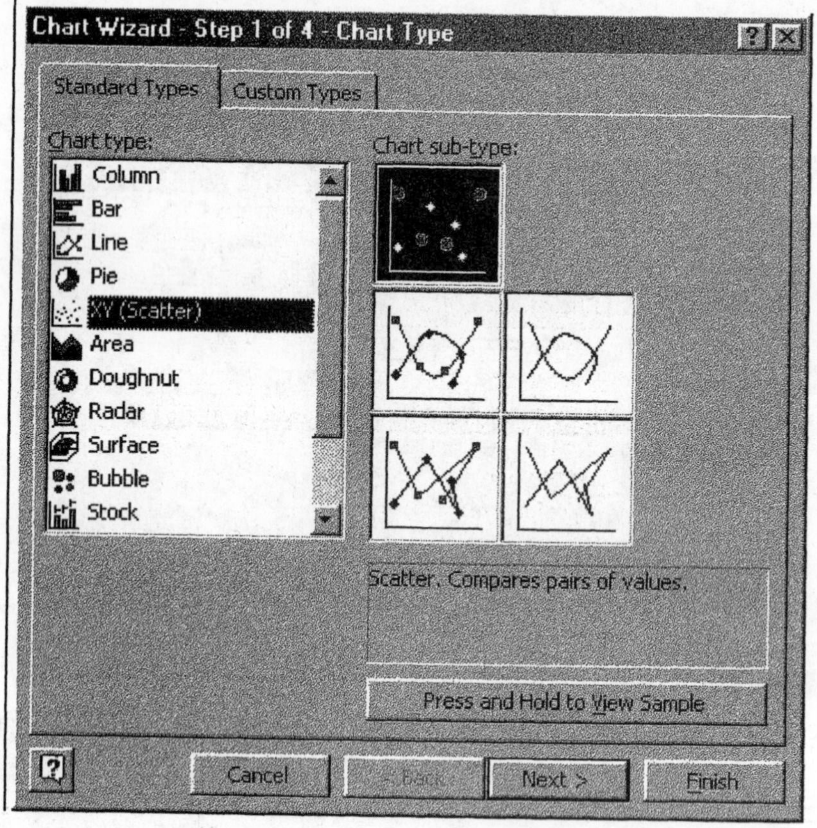

8. Next we will use the trendline feature for charts to find the linear regression equation for these data. Click inside the chart. This will activate the chart for editing as is indicated by the eight sizing handles on the border of the chart as seen in later Figure 10.7.

9. To superimpose a line of regression on this scatter diagram, click on **Chart** on the menu bar. On the subsequent pull-down menu, select **Add Trendline**.   The *Add Trendline Type* dialog box of Figure 10.5 will be displayed.

10. Click on **Linear** for the *Trend/Regression Type*. Click on the **Options** tab to obtain the dialog box of 10.6.

11. Put checks in the two check boxes labeled as **Display Equation on Chart** and **Display R-squared Value on Chart**. Click on **OK** and the results of Figure 10.7 will result.

What do the results of Figure 10.7 mean? First, the best linear relationship for these data is the equation

$$y = 8.4858x + 379.44$$

Figure 10.3 Chart Wizard Step 2: Chart Source Data

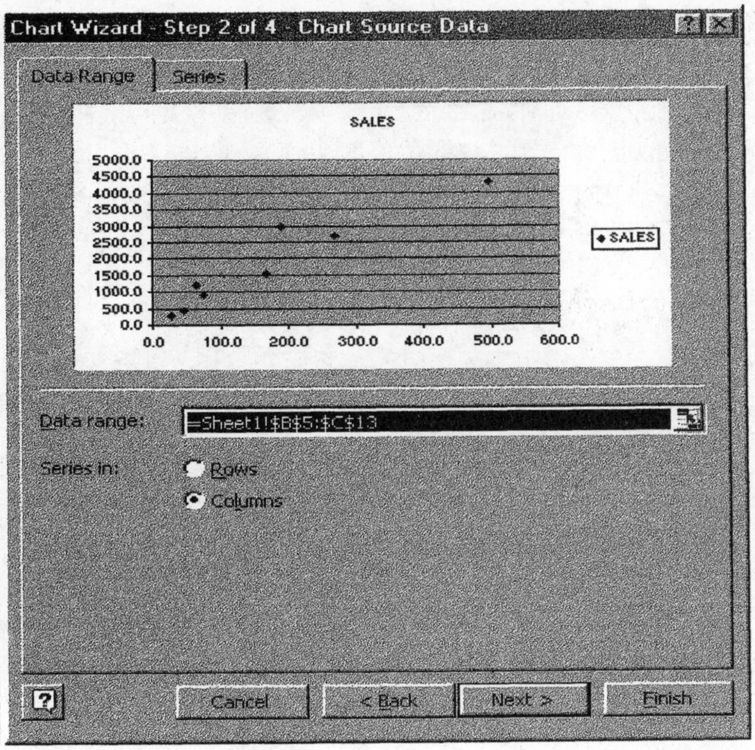

Figure 10.4 Scatter Diagram Final Results

	A	B	C	D	E
1		Regression Analysis Examples			
2			Your Name		
3	Today's Date			File: REGRESS.xls	
4					
5		ADVERT.	SALES		
6		74.0	900.0		
7		27.5	266.4		
8		169.0	1555.2		
9		497.0	4320.0		
10		270.5	2707.2		
11		44.5	439.2		
12		63.0	1209.6		
13		189.5	2966.4		

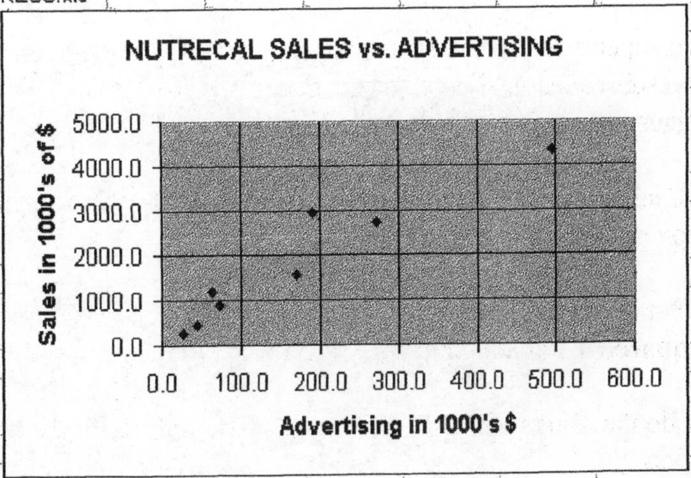

Figure 10.5 Trendline Type Dialog Box

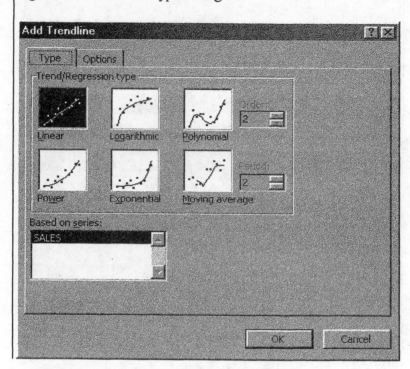

Figure 10.6 Trendline Options Dialog Box

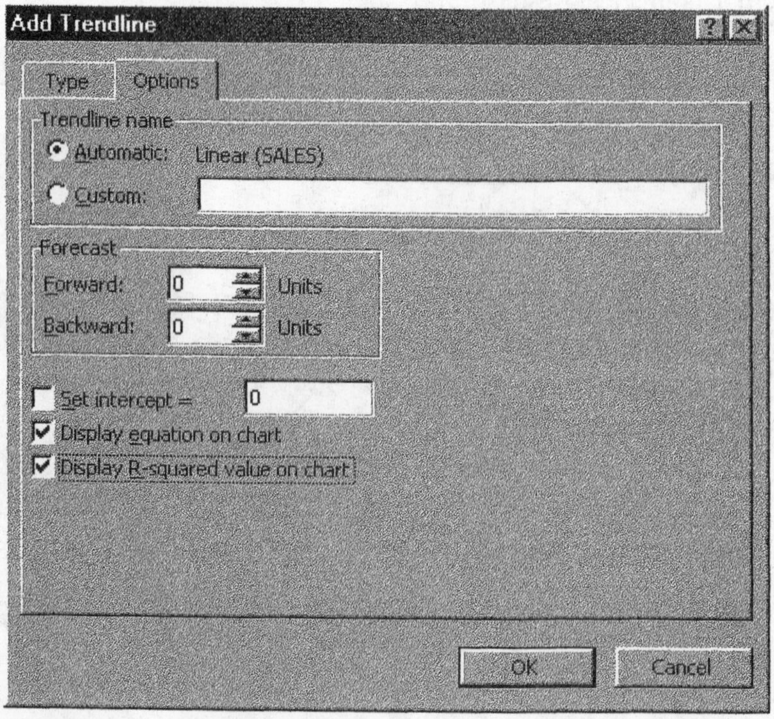

Figure 10.7   Scatter Diagram with Trendline, Regression Equation and R^2 Value

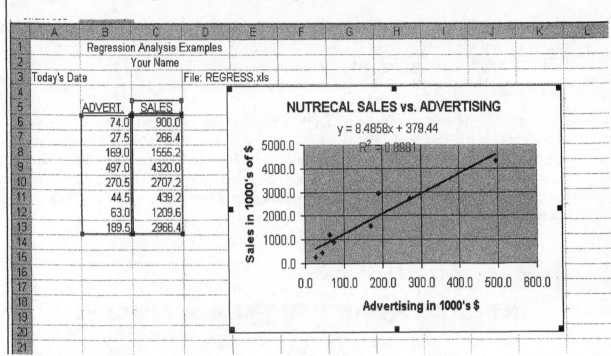

where x is the advertising level in 1000's of dollars and y is sales in 1000's of dollars. Second, $R^2 =$ 0.8981 suggests that 89.81% of the variability of the sales values about their average can be explained by changes in advertising. This indicates that the equation fits the data very well. There are more precise statistical measures of the goodness of fit of an equation to the data as we will see in the next section. However, R^2, called the coefficient of determination, is a good single measure of the strength of the relationship.

In summary, this approach to simple linear regression analysis rather easily yields (1) a scatter diagram providing a visual interpretation of the relationship between two variables, (2) the equation for the best straight line relationship and (3) R^2, a good measure of the strength of the linear relationship.

Once a good fitting relationship has been found, it can be used to predict the average value for y for a specified value of x. There are a number of ways of doing this in Excel. One approach would be to enter the regression formula in a worksheet cell and insert the value or cell location of the value for the independent variable, x, into the formula. The cell would then display the predicted y value.

We will demonstrate a second approach for predicting through the use of the statistical function called TREND. The general format for this function is

=TREND(range of y values, range of x values, range of x values to be used for predicting)

Suppose we wish to make predictions for the above example for advertising levels of 100, 200, 300 and 400 thousand dollars. We would continue as follows with the worksheet REGESS.

1. Enter values 100, 200, 300 and 400 in cells B18 through B21. *Move the cell pointer to cell C18.*

2. Click on the INSERT FUNCTION icon, *fx*, next to the *Formula box*. The result will be the *Insert function* dialog box (see Figure 3.7 in Chapter 3). Select **Statistical** from the drop-down list box labeled *Or select a category,* and click on **Trend** in the scrolling list box labeled *Select a function.* Click on the **OK**. The TREND function dialog box as shown in Figure 10.8 will be displayed.

3. As shown in Figure 10.8, enter the range for the *y values (Known_y's)*, the range for the *x values (Known_x's)*, and the range of *x values to be used for predicting (New_x's)*. The fourth text box labeled as *Const* can be left blank to indicate the constant is not to be forced to a value of zero (alternatively the word **True** or the number **1** can be entered for it). Click on the **OK** button. The result will be the predicted y value for the first x value. To obtain functions for the remaining x values, we need to edit the function so it is treated as an array.

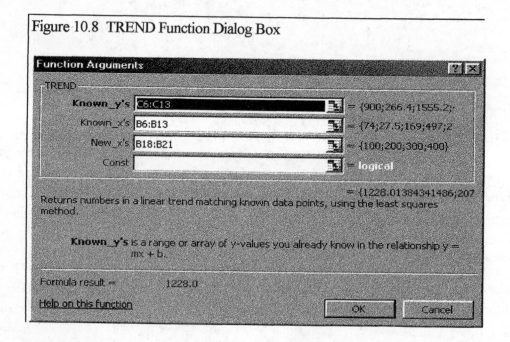

Figure 10.8 TREND Function Dialog Box

4. *Select the predicted y value cells C18 through C21* and press the **F2** key to enter the **Edit** mode. Notice the word *Edit* appears in the status bar on the far left below the worksheet.

5. Press and hold the **Ctrl** and **Shift** keys and then press the **Enter** key. Curly brackets will be added around the TREND function statement indicating it is a function for an array. The second and subsequent predicted y values will be computed. See Figure 10.9 for the predictions.

The above procedure provides the predicted y values for a number of specified x values. If you only wished to make a prediction for one x value, steps 4 and 5 would not be needed.

Figure 10.9 Predicted y Value Results

	A	B	C	D
1		Regression Analysis Example		
2		Your Name		
3	Today's Date			File: RI
4				
5		ADVERT.	SALES	
6		74.0	900.0	
7		27.5	266.4	
8		169.0	1555.2	
9		497.0	4320.0	
10		270.5	2707.2	
11		44.5	439.2	
12		63.0	1209.6	
13		189.5	2966.4	
14				
15				
16				
17				
18		100	1228.0	
19		200	2076.6	
20		300	2925.2	
21		400	3773.7	
22				

10.2 SIMPLE LINEAR REGRESSION WITH THE REGRESSION ANALYSIS TOOL

The TRENDLINE feature for charts is a quick and easy method for obtaining a regression analysis as demonstrated in the prior section. However, its analysis results are rather limited, and it is only useful if there is one independent variable. In this section, we wish to demonstrate a second Excel resource for conducting a regression analysis, the REGRESSION analysis tool. It provides more complete results, and as we will see in Section 10.3, it can be used with two or more independent variables.

Let us return to the Nutrecal problem of Ms. Lore Ran from the prior section. As before she wishes to find a simple linear regression relationship that will allow her to predict sales as a function of advertising level. To analyze her results using the regression analysis tool you would proceed as follows after you have selected *Sheet2* in the REGRESS workbook.

1. Enter the **Identification Material** in rows 1, 2 and 3, and then enter the labels and data in columns B and C as previously shown in Figure 10.1. (Alternatively, you could use Excel's **Copy** and **Paste** commands to copy the inputs of Figure 10.1 from *Sheet1* to *Sheet2*.) Save the workbook.

2. From the menu bar select **Tools**, from the subsequent pull-down menu select **Data Analysis** (see Figure 2.2 of Chapter 2). From the *Data Analysis* dialog box select, **Regression**.

3. Fill in the entries of the *Regression* dialog box as shown in Figure 10.10. Notice that the input range includes the labels in the cells B5 and C5, and the **Labels** check box has a check in it. All four check boxes in the Residuals section are checked.

4. Click on **OK** and the numerical output shown in Figure 10.11 will be presented on the screen. In addition, two charts or plots will be shown to the right of the numerical output. These are shown in Figures 10.12 and 10.13. The two charts are shown in a cascading format in which the plot title may be the only visible part of the bottom chart. You may move the top chart by dragging it with the mouse to an unused part of the worksheet so both can be viewed at once. These two charts have been edited for readability so the appearance of yours will be slightly different.

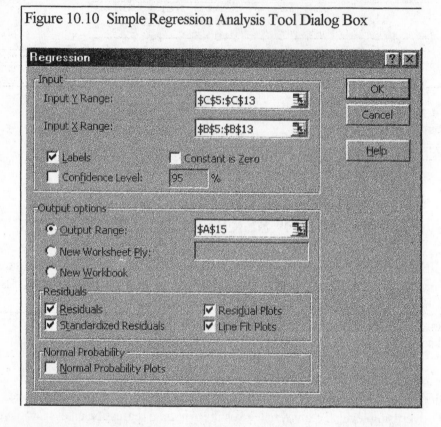

Figure 10.10 Simple Regression Analysis Tool Dialog Box

The numerical output of Figure 10.11 is presented in four parts from top to bottom. The top part labeled **Regression Statistics** presents the values for the coefficient of correlation, r, labeled as **Multiple R**, for the coefficient of determination, r^2, labeled as **R Square**, the *adjusted r^2* labeled as **Adjusted R Square**, the *standard error of the estimate* labeled as **Standard Error**, and the *sample size* labeled as **Observations**. The second part is found under the label **ANOVA.** It provides an *analysis of variance table* output for the regression. The third part presents the *regression coefficients* together with statistics for evaluating the significance of the coefficients, such as the *t statistic* values, *p values* and *confidence intervals*. Finally, the bottom part labeled **Residual Output** provides the *predicted y values* for each of the data points in the sample along with the *residuals* and *standardized residuals*.

Figure 10.11 Regression Analysis Tool Results

	A	B	C	D	E	F	G	H	I
15	SUMMARY OUTPUT								
16									
17	*Regression Statistics*								
18	Multiple R	0.947662558							
19	R Square	0.898064324							
20	Adjusted R Square	0.881075045							
21	Standard Error	486.9306154							
22	Observations	8							
23									
24	ANOVA								
25		df	SS	MS	F	Significance F			
26	Regression	1	12533335.05	12533335.05	52.86065	0.000344486			
27	Residual	6	1422608.545	237101.4242					
28	Total	7	13955943.6						
29									
30		Coefficients	Standard Error	t Stat	P-value	Lower 95%	Upper 95%	Lower 95.0%	Upper 95.0%
31	Intercept	379.436413	259.9462655	1.459672492	0.194671	-256.6296498	1015.502	-256.62965	1015.502476
32	ADVERT.	8.485774304	1.167146127	7.270532892	0.000344	5.629868526	11.34168	5.62986853	11.34168008
33									
34									
35									
36	RESIDUAL OUTPUT								
37									
38	Observation	Predicted SALES	Residuals	Standard Residuals					
39	1	1007.383712	-107.3837115	-0.238201627					
40	2	612.7952064	-346.3952064	-0.768383777					
41	3	1813.53227	-258.3322704	-0.573040048					
42	4	4598.866242	-276.8662421	-0.614152835					
43	5	2674.838362	32.36163774	0.071785513					
44	6	757.0533695	-317.8533695	-0.705071456					
45	7	914.0401942	295.5598058	0.655619234					
46	8	1987.490644	978.9093564	2.171444796					

Figure 10.12 Regression Analysis Tool Line Fit Plot

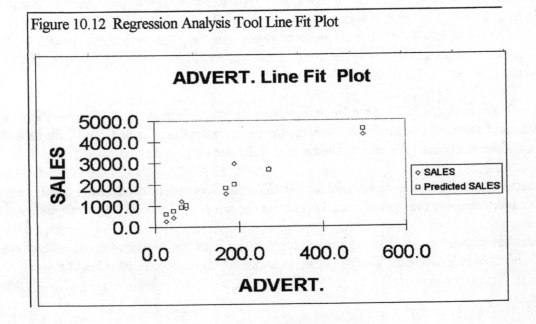

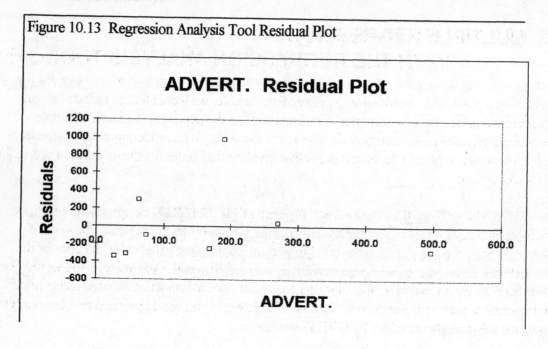

Figure 10.13 Regression Analysis Tool Residual Plot

Statistical values are given for testing the significance of the relationship with the p-value approach. From the ANOVA table we see the value for the F statistic is 52.86 in cell E26 with a corresponding *Significance F* value of 0.000344 in cell F26. The **Significance F** is the *p value* for the overall regression relationship. Using the categories of Table 5.3 (or 5.5) in Chapter 5 we would categorize the relationship as *Very Highly Significant*. Thus, we would reject the null hypothesis. That is, we would conclude it is a good relationship based on the data we have.

Since this is a simple linear regression analysis, we can reach the same conclusion based on the *t statistic* for the regression coefficient for advertising. We note from Figure 10.11 the advertising coefficient is 8.485774 in cell B32 with a t-statistic value of 7.270533 in cell D32 and a corresponding p value of 0.000344 in cell E32. For simple linear regression, the p values for this t statistic and for the prior F statistic will always be exactly the same. Thus, our conclusion is the same as in the prior paragraph. The relationship is statistically significant.

The line fit plot of Figure 10.12 is similar to the scatter diagram of Figure 10.7. However, Figure 10.12 doesn't show a line of predicted y values. Instead it shows the predicted y value for each of the x values of the input data. We can edit the chart to add a line if one is desired.

The residual plot of Figure 10.13 is useful for identifying outliers and for determining whether the assumptions underlying the regression analysis are met or not as discussed in your textbook.

As in the last section, predicted average values for y can be found by inserting the regression formula in a worksheet cell or by using the TREND function as previously demonstrated in Section 10.1.

10.3 MULTIPLE REGRESSION
WITH THE REGRESSION ANALYSIS TOOL ——

In developing a prediction equation for the dependent variable, we would like to include as many independent variables as can be shown to significantly affect the dependent variable. Multiple regression analysis allows any number of independent variables. By considering more independent variables, we would expect to develop a predictive equation that better fits the data than a simple linear regression equation.

For example let us reconsider the Nutrecal problem of Ms. Lore Ran. Suppose she feels there are independent variables other than advertising that are important in predicting the sales of Nutrecal. Suppose she identifies the other important independent variables as the price of the product and the number of sales representatives who sell Nutrecal. Accordingly, she would like to develop an equation that would allow her to predict sales as a function of advertising, price and number of sales representatives. To analyze her results you would proceed as follows after you have selected *Sheet3* of the REGRESS workbook.

1. Enter the **Identification Material** of rows 1, 2 and 3, and then enter the labels and data in columns B through E as shown in Figure 10.14. **Note that the columns for the three independent variables are contiguous (next to each other) as is required by Excel's Regression Analysis Tool**. Save the workbook file with the name REGRESS.

Figure 10.14 Multiple Regression Example Data

	A	B	C	D	E	F
1		Regression Analysis Examples				
2			Your Name			
3	Today's Date			File: REGRESS.xls		
4						
5		SALES	ADVERT.	PRICE	SALE REPS.	
6		900.0	74.0	475	4	
7		266.4	27.5	475	7	
8		1555.2	169.0	450	5	
9		4320.0	497.0	400	5	
10		2707.2	270.5	400	4	
11		439.2	44.5	475	12	
12		1209.6	63.0	450	7	
13		2966.4	189.5	400	10	
14						

2. From the menu bar select **Tools**, from the subsequent pull-down menu select **Data Analysis** (see Figure 2.2). From the Data Analysis dialog box select **Regression**.

3. Fill in the entries of the Regression dialog box as shown in Figure 10.15. Notice that the input range includes the labels in the cells B5 through E5, and the **Labels** check box has a check in it. All four check boxes in the *Residuals* section have been checked.

4. Click on **OK** and the numerical output shown in Figure 10.16 will be presented on the screen. In addition, six charts are shown to the right of the numerical output. These are given in Figure 10.17. The charts are shown in a cascading format in which the chart title may be the only visible part of all six except the top chart.

5. You can view each chart by bringing it to the top of the cascade stack. For example, click on the chart titled *SALES REPS. Residual Plot* to bring it to the front as shown in Figure 10.18.

Figure 10.15 Multiple Regression Analysis Dialog Box

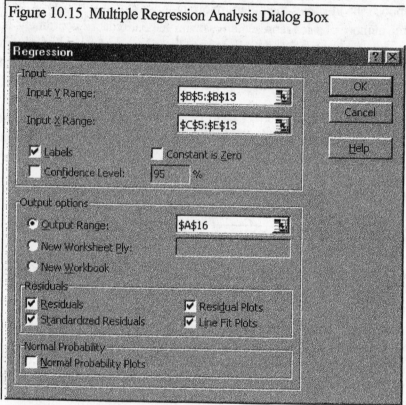

The numerical output of Figure 10.16 again includes four parts: *Regression Statistics, ANOVA,* regression coefficients with their statistics and *Residual Output.* From these results we conclude that the best linear relationship is given by

Sales = 9063.101 + 5.199 * Advertising - 18.7265 * Price + 17.19767 * Sales Reps.

This equation suggests that *Advertising* increases and *Sales Reps* increases will result in increased *Sales.* On the other hand, it also indicates that a *Price* increase will result in a *Sales* decrease.

Figure 10.16 Multiple Regression Analysis Example Results

	A	B	C	D	E	F	G	H	I
16	SUMMARY OUTPUT								
17									
18	*Regression Statistics*								
19	Multiple R	0.988169138							
20	R Square	0.976478246							
21	Adjusted R Square	0.958836931							
22	Standard Error	286.4735026							
23	Observations	8							
24									
25	ANOVA								
26		*df*	*SS*	*MS*	*F*	*Significance F*			
27	Regression	3	13627675.33	4542558.443	55.35178	0.001029217			
28	Residual	4	328268.2707	82067.06768					
29	Total	7	13955943.6						
30									
31		*Coefficients*	*Standard Error*	*t Stat*	*P-value*	*Lower 95%*	*Upper 95%*	*Lower 95.0%*	*Upper 95.0%*
32	Intercept	9063.100802	2688.436758	3.371141529	0.028014	1598.788265	16527.413	1598.78827	16527.4133
33	ADVERT.	5.199447488	1.304658803	3.985292917	0.016329	1.577126437	8.8217685	1.57712644	8.82176854
34	PRICE	-18.72645189	5.485416832	-3.413861237	0.026932	-33.95644215	-3.4964616	-33.956442	-3.49646163
35	SALE REPS.	17.1976686	41.53410263	0.414061398	0.700069	-98.11972621	132.51506	-98.119726	132.515063
36									
37									
38									
39	RESIDUAL OUTPUT								
40									
41	*Observation*	*Predicted SALES*	*Residuals*	*Standard Residuals*					
42	1	621.5859421	278.4140579	1.285658799					
43	2	431.4046397	-165.0046397	-0.761957455					
44	3	1600.892419	-45.69241938	-0.210998186					
45	4	4242.63379	77.36620995	0.357261229					
46	5	3047.761265	-340.5612654	-1.572641809					
47	6	605.78359	-166.58359	-0.769248722					
48	7	1084.146323	125.4536772	0.579319253					
49	8	2729.79203	236.6079695	1.09260689					

The R-Squared value of 0.976478 suggests that about 97.65% of the variability of the *sales* values about their average can be explained by changes in *advertising, price* and *sales representatives*. This is very high.

From the ANOVA table of Figure 10.16, we note the F statistic value is 55.35 in cell E27 with a corresponding *Significance F* value of 0.001029 in cell F27. As before the *Significance F* is the p value. Using the categories of Table 5.3 (or 5.5) of Chapter 5, we would categorize the relationship as *Highly Significant*. Thus, we would reject the null hypothesis that the relationship is not significant. That is, we would conclude we have found a good relationship based on the data we have.

However, we also need to examine the p-values for the individual regression coefficients to determine which of the independent variables are statistically different from zero. The p value in cell E33 for advertising is 0.016329. This value is *Significant*. That for price in cell E34 is 0.026932 and also *Significant*. On the other hand, the p value in cell E35 for sales representatives is 0.700069. It is *Not Significant*. Accordingly, we should re-run the regression with just the two independent variables, *advertising* and *price*.

An examination of the three line fit plots results in similar conclusions. While the plots for advertising and for price suggest a linear relationship may be present, the plot for sales representatives does not suggest a relationship at all.

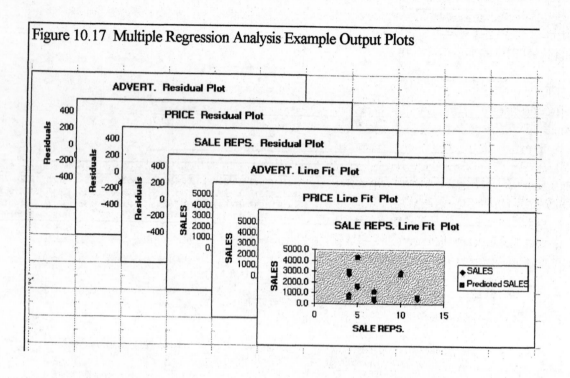

Figure 10.17 Multiple Regression Analysis Example Output Plots

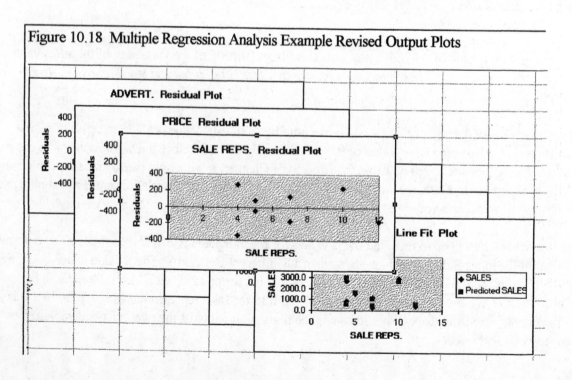

Figure 10.18 Multiple Regression Analysis Example Revised Output Plots

A final result that is important is the residual plots. As discussed in your textbook, these are useful for identifying outliers and for testing compliance with the assumptions underlying regression analysis.

Once we have found a statistically useful relationship, we will want to use it to predict values for the dependent variable for specified values of the independent variables. As in the two prior sections, predicted average *y values* can be made by entering the regression formula into a worksheet cell or by using the TREND function.

As a last consideration of multiple regression analysis, let us consider a problem called **multicollinearity**. This condition is present if two or more of the independent variables are positively or negatively correlated. One approach used to overcome the problem of multicollinearity begins with an examination of the simple correlation coefficients between all the variables in the multiple regression analysis. An Excel data analysis tool called CORRELATION easily obtains these correlation coefficient values (this tool was discussed in the last subsection of Chapter 3). To use CORRELATION for our current example we would proceed as follows.

1. Select **Tools** from the menu bar, **Data Analysis** from the subsequent pull-down menu, and **Correlation** from the resulting dialog box. The result will be the dialog box of Figure 10.19.

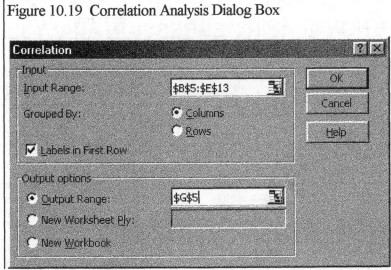

Figure 10.19 Correlation Analysis Dialog Box

2. Fill in the input range for all the variables including the labels. Click on **Columns** for the *Grouped By* selection, click on **Labels in First Row**, click on **Output Range** and enter **G5** as the upper left cell for the output range.

3. Click on **OK** and the matrix of correlation coefficients as shown in Figure 10.20 will be displayed in the worksheet.

Figure 10.20 Correlations for Multiple Regression Example

	G	H	I	J	K
4					
5		SALES	ADVERT.	PRICE	ALE REPS.
6	SALES	1			
7	ADVERT.	0.94766	1		
8	PRICE	-0.93386	-0.81554	1	
9	SALE REF	-0.27366	-0.38555	0.18272	1
10					

The correlation coefficient of 0.94766 in cell H7 between sales and advertising, and that of -0.93386 in cell H8 between sales and price suggest there is a significant relationship between the dependent variable *sales* and these two independent variables. This is consistent with the previous regression results of Figure 10.16 and with the line plots between these variables. However, the correlation coefficient value between advertising and price is given in cell I8 as -0.81554. This suggests these two independent variables may be colinear and may require further analysis as discussed in your textbook.

10.4 SIMPLE NON-LINEAR REGRESSION ANALYSIS

Oftentimes a scatter plot of a dependent variable, y, and an independent variable, x, will suggest the relationship between the two variables is not linear. For such situations Excel provides a feature for easily exploring the nature of the relationship. You may have noticed it while you were working through Section 10.1. Specifically in Figure 10.5, the **Trendline Type** dialog box includes *logarithmic, polynomial, power* and *exponential* relationships in addition to the *linear* relationship we used in Section 10.1. Accordingly, you may try various relationships through the trendline feature. (Note: the sixth option shown in Figure 10.5, *Moving Average*, is method for time series forecasting.)

To demonstrate how this is to be done we will continue with the example from Section 10.1. In that section we showed that a linear relationship fit the data very well. However, we can very easily evaluate the four other relationship forms available through the trendline feature in order to try to develop a better fit to the data. We can begin our investigation of non-linear relationships by returning to the scatter diagram of Figure 10.4.

1. Click on the *Sheet1* tab of the workbook named REGRESS.

2. Next click inside the chart to activate it for editing. The eight sizing handles will appear around the chart as was shown previously in Figure 10.7.

3. Remove the linear relationship line by first clicking on the line and then pressing the **Del** (delete) button.

4. To superimpose another line of regression on this scatter diagram, click on **Chart** on the menu bar. On the subsequent pull-down menu, select **Add Trendline**. The *Trendline Type* dialog box of previous Figure 10.5 will be displayed.

5. Click on **Logarithmic** for the Trend/Regression Type.

6. Click on the **Options** tab. Select **Automatic** for the *Trendline Name* option and click to add check marks to the **Display Equation on Chart** and the **Display R-squared Value on Chart** check boxes (see Figure 10.6). Click on **OK** to obtain the results of Figure 10.21. (Note the scatter diagram has been increased in size, and the *equation-R^2* box has been relocated for readability.)

Figure 10.21   Scatter Diagram with Logarithmic Trendline, Regression Equation and r^2

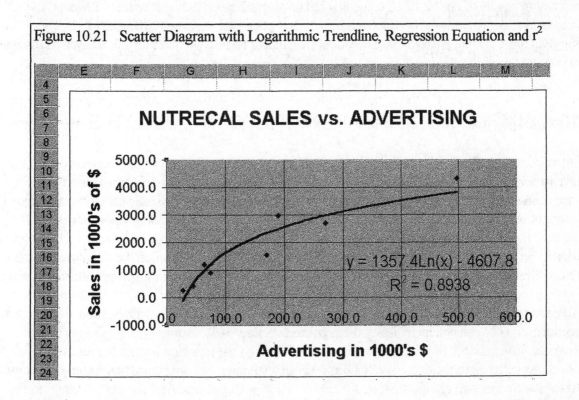

As shown in figure 10.21, the relationship found is

$$y = 1357.4*Ln(x) - 4607.8$$

where Ln(x) is the natural logarithm of the advertising level in 1000's of dollars and y is sales in 1000's of dollars. Also, $R^2 = 0.8938$ suggests that 89.38% of the variability of the sales values about their average can be explained by changes in advertising. Although this indicates that the equation fits the data very well, it is slightly less than the 89.81% given in Figure 10.7 for the linear relationship.

By changing our selection in Step 5 above, we can also develop a *polynomial* relationship, a *power* relationship and an *exponential* relationship for these data. Moreover, the polynomial relationship option allows you to specify a quadratic relationship (order 2), a cubic relationship (order 3), a quartic relationship (order 4), and on to order 6.

You may wish to try these other relationship forms on your scatter diagram. To do so, first move the mouse pointer so it is touching the line on the scatter diagram for the logarithmic curve. Then press the **Del** key to eliminate (1) the curve, (2) the equation and (3) the R^2. Then repeat steps 4, 5 and 6 above for the other relationship forms.

So that you may ascertain the correctness of your efforts, the results for four other forms is as follows.

Polynomial (order 2): $\quad y = -0.0107\,x^2 + 13.938\,x + 0.0966$ $\qquad\qquad R^2 = 0.9276$

Polynomial (order 3): $\quad y = 0.00006\,x^3 - 0.0578\,x^2 + 22.65\,x - 326.48$ $\quad R^2 = 0.9328$

Power: $\qquad\qquad\qquad y = 15.084\,x^{0.9401}$ $\qquad\qquad\qquad\qquad\qquad R^2 = 0.9178$

Exponential: $\qquad\qquad y = 543.7\,e^{0.0051\,x}$ $\qquad\qquad\qquad\qquad\qquad R^2 = 0.6931$

As demonstrated the trendline feature of Excel allows you to explore five different forms of a regression relationship quite easily. Relying on the scatter diagram to visually assess the fit and on the value of R^2 to numerically assess the fit, you may identify the relationship that appears to be best.

Once you have decided which regression formula appears to fit best, you can use it to predict values of y for specified x values. The TREND function cannot be used except for linear relationships. Thus the easiest approach for predicting with one of these non-linear relationships, is to enter the regression formula in a worksheet cell and insert the value or the cell location for the value of the independent variable, x. The cell will then display the predicted y value.

As discussed in Section 10.2, Excel's **REGRESSION Analysis Tool** provides many more analysis results then does the trendline feature for charts. Each of these non-linear regression relationships demonstrated above can also be obtained through the use of the REGRESSION tool. The general approach is to transform the original x values into appropriate altered values that are then used with REGRESSION.

For example, if we would add a column of x^2 values and run the regression of the y variable as a function of both the x and the x^2 values, we could obtain the polynomial (order 2) relationship. The results of this transformation process for the polynomial (order 2) are shown in Figure 10.22 (this was done on *Sheet4* of the workbook named REGRESS).

Figure 10.22   Regression Analysis Tool Results for Polynomial (order 2)

	A	B	C	D	E	F	G	H	I
4	Y	X	x^2						
5	SALES	ADVERT.	ADVERT--Squared						
6	900.0	74.0	5476.00						
7	266.4	27.5	756.25						
8	1555.2	169.0	28561.00						
9	4320.0	497.0	247009.00						
10	2707.2	270.5	73170.25						
11	439.2	44.5	1980.25						
12	1209.6	63.0	3969.00						
13	2966.4	189.5	35910.25						
14									
15	SUMMARY OUTPUT								
16									
17	*Regression Statistics*								
18	Multiple R	0.96312515							
19	R Square	0.92761005							
20	Adjusted R Square	0.89865408							
21	Standard Error	449.504173							
22	Observations	8							
23									
24	ANOVA								
25		df	SS	MS	F	Significance F			
26	Regression	2	12945673.59	6472837	32.03518	0.001409924			
27	Residual	5	1010270.01	202054					
28	Total	7	13955943.6						
29									
30		Coefficients	Standard Error	t Stat	P-value	Lower 95%	Upper 95%	Lower 95.0%	Upper 95.0%
31	Intercept	0.09664854	357.9064035	0.00027	0.999795	-919.9295478	920.122845	-919.92955	920.1228449
32	ADVERT.	13.9382584	3.965974198	3.51446	0.017019	3.743413805	24.133103	3.7434138	24.13310296
33	ADVERT--Squared	-0.01069558	0.007487056	-1.429543	0.212507	-0.029941638	0.00855048	-0.0299416	0.008550479
34									

We note that the results of Figure 10.22 are as previously given from the use of trendline. In particular, the regression equation and value for R^2 are

$$y = -0.01069558\ x^2 + 13.9382584\ x + 0.09664854$$

$$R^2 = 0.9276101$$

In addition, the results of Figure 10.22 show the overall regression relationship is *highly significant* (the *Significance F* value is 0.001409924). However, the p value for the x^2 term is 0.212507, *not significant*, and the p-value for the x term is 0.0107019, only *significant*.

We can use the REGRESSION Analysis Tool to obtain the results for polynomial relationships with higher order terms by including columns of x raised to the third power, x raised to the fourth power, and so on. Furthermore, we can use the tool to obtain the exponential relationship by including a column of the natural logarithm of each x value. We would then run the regression of the y variable as a function of the column of natural logarithm of the x values.

This completes our exploration of the regression capabilities of Excel. We have shown how to use the **trendline** feature, the **Regression Analysis Tool**, the **Correlation Analysis Tool** and the **Trend function**. We have not utilized a number of Excel's other regression functions that are summarized in Appendix B. However, those we have not used duplicate to a large degree the capabilities of the items we have demonstrated.

CHAPTER 11. TIME SERIES FORECASTING

11.1 Identification of Appropriate Forecasting Methods

11.2 The MOVING AVERAGE Analysis Tool

11.3 The EXPONENTIAL SMOOTHING Analysis Tool

11.4 Linear Trend Projection with TRENDLINE

11.5 Non-linear Trend Projection with TRENDLINE

11.6 Choosing the Best Forecasting Method

A time series consists of numerical data recorded over a period of time at regular intervals. Time series forecasting techniques are based on the premise that the factors that influenced patterns of activity in the past will continue to do so in the same manner in the future. Accordingly, time series forecasting techniques attempt to identify a pattern in the time series data that can be projected into the future.

Excel includes a number of resources for supporting time series forecasting. In **Section 11.1,** we discuss the use of CHART WIZARD for identifying forecasting methods that are appropriate for a particular time series. In sections 11.2 through 11.5, we present four time series forecasting methods that are readily available in Excel. **Section 11.2** presents the MOVING AVERAGE Analysis Tool and **Section 11.3** the EXPONENTIAL SMOOTHING Analysis Tool. In **Section 11.4,** we present the use of the TRENDLINE feature for charts for forecasting by linear trend projection. In **Section 11.5**, we present it for forecasting by non-linear trend projection. Finally in **Section 11.6,** Excel statistical functions are used to identify the best method for forecasting a time series.

11.1 IDENTIFICATION OF APPROPRIATE FORECASTING METHODS ———

Most well used time series forecasting methods consider a time series to be made up of the following four components.

1. Trend—a long-term upward or downward change in the time series
2. Cyclical—periodic increases and decreases that occur over a time period longer than a year
3. Seasonal—periodic increases and decreases that occur within a year
4. Irregular—remaining changes in the time series not attributable to the other three components

All time series forecasting methods assume there is an irregular component in the time series. In addition, some methods are appropriate when one or more of the first three components are also present. For example, some methods are appropriate when an irregular component and a trend component are present; others when an irregular and a cyclical component are present and still others when an irregular and a seasonal component are present. In addition, some are appropriate for an irregular component plus any combination of two or all three of the other components.

On the other hand, other methods are appropriate when only the irregular component is present. These methods are called smoothing methods. Both the *moving average method* of Section 11.2 and *simple exponential smoothing method* of Section 11.3 are smoothing methods. Thus, they are most effective for a time series that does not have a trend, cyclical or seasonal component.

The two trend projection methods of Section 11.4 and 11.5 are appropriate for time series with a trend component in addition to an irregular component. Thus, the determination of whether to use one of the two smoothing methods, moving average or simple exponential smoothing, as opposed to the two trend projection methods involves deciding whether a trend component is present or not.

The determination of the presence of a trend component should begin with a charting of the time series. A visual inspection of the time series plot can be used to ascertain whether a trend appears to be present or not. The chart is best created in Excel through the CHART WIZARD.

As an example, let us consider the situation of Riper's Donuts that has been in operation for the past 10 years in Murville. Mr. Riper needs to forecast weekly sales of donuts in order to determine the amount of ingredients to purchase. He has collected sales data for the past 20 weeks. These have been entered into an Excel worksheet as shown in Figure 11.1.

Figure 11.1 Riper's Donut Data and Time Series Chart

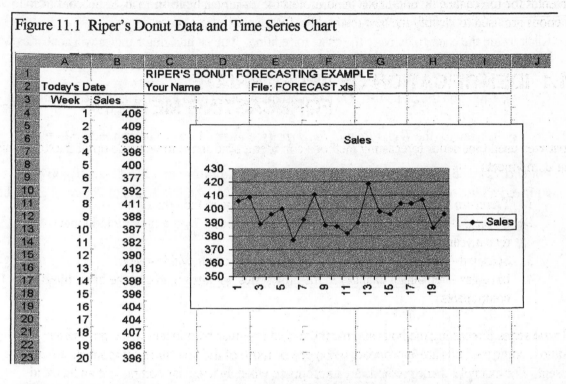

The time series chart of the sales data in Figure 11.1 is obtained using the CHART WIZARD. Briefly the procedure is as follows. (Note: Screen captures of the chart building process are shown in Figures 2.8 through 2.12 of Chapter 2.)

1. Use the mouse or the keyboard to highlight the sales data and label in cells B3 through B23 and click on the CHART WIZARD icon.

2. Click through the 4 steps of the Chart Wizard with the following.
    Step 1—Type = **Line,** *Sub-type* = **#4, Next**
    Step 2—**Next**
    Step 3—**Next**
    Step 4—**Finish**

3. Save the workbook using the name FORECAST.

With just 6 or so mouse clicks, we have obtained the line chart of the time series shown in Figure 11.1. Note we have not taken the steps necessary to provide a chart title, axes titles or other editing features. However, the resulting chart shows what we need to know. It presents a time series that does not appear to have either an increasing or decreasing long-term trend. The chart allows us to visually reach this conclusion although it wasn't apparent from an inspection of the numerical sales data.

The determination of the presence of a trend component can continue with the fitting of a straight line to the data of the time series plot. This will provide analytical support to our prior visual conclusion. As we learned in Section 10.1 of Chapter 10, the easiest procedure for fitting a straight line to data involves the use of the TRENDLINE feature. For the donut example, we should proceed as follows.

1. Click inside the chart to activate the chart for editing. The eight sizing handles will appear as was shown in Figure 10.7.

2. Click on **Chart** on the menu bar. On the subsequent pull-down menu, select **Add Trendline**.

3. Click on **Linear** for the *Trend/Regression Type* (see Figure 10.5). Click on the **Options** tab.

4. Put checks in the two check boxes labeled as **Display Equation on Chart** and **Display R-squared Value on Chart** (see Figure 10.6). Click on **OK** and the results of Figure 11.2 will be displayed.

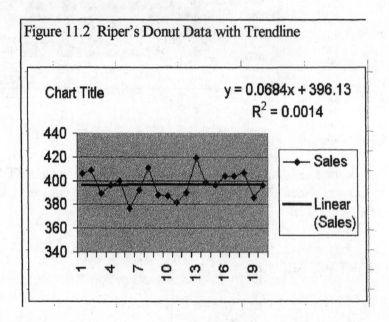
Figure 11.2 Riper's Donut Data with Trendline

The *linear (Sales)* line of Figure 11.2 clearly shows the lack of a significant trend. In addition, the equation shown at the top indicates the slope is only 0.064, almost zero. This reinforces are prior visual conclusion of the lack of a trend. Accordingly, we would recommend that either the moving average, simple exponential smoothing or some other smoothing method would be most appropriate for these data.

Now consider a second example. Sandy Guyer, the athletic director of Bubeye State University, is wishing to forecast the average attendance at their home football games for the upcoming year. She has obtained the average attendance for the last 8 years and entered these data into the *Sheet2* worksheet of the FORECAST workbook as shown in Figure 11.3.

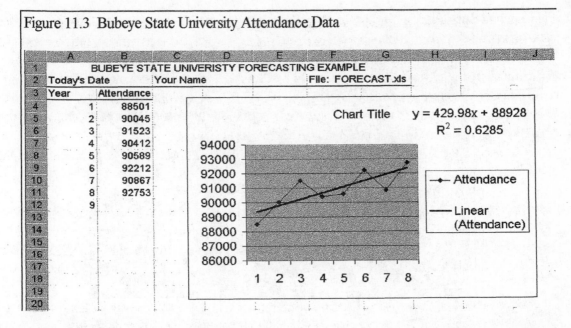

Figure 11.3 Bubeye State University Attendance Data

As for the first example, it is hard to draw a conclusion by viewing only the numerical values of columns A and B. If as before we use the CHART Wizard to create a time series plot, we can visually conclude there is an apparent long term increasing trend in the attendance data. If we go one step further and use TRENDLINE to fit a straight line to the data, we observe a linear line with a significant trend as shown in Figure 11.3. In addition, we note the equation for the line has a slope of 429.98, not near zero. Accordingly, we would recommend that either the linear trend projection, the non-linear trend projection or some other trend method would be the most appropriate for these data.

11.2 THE MOVING AVERAGE ANALYSIS TOOL

We will use the MOVING AVERAGE Data Analysis Tool to forecast for the Riper's Donut example of Figure 11.1. Begin by returning to *Sheet1* and then re-position the chart lower in the worksheet, say to row 26 or below.

The procedure for forecasting these data using a 4-point moving average is the following.

1. From the menu bar select **Tools**, from the subsequent pull-down menu select **Data Analysis** and from the *Data Analysis* list box select **Moving Average**.

2. Fill in the entries of the *Moving Average* dialog box as shown in Figure 11.4. Notice that the input range includes the label in cell B3, and the **Labels** check box has a check in it. The entry for **Interval** refers to the number terms in the moving average. For this example it has a value of **4**. Neither the *Chart Output* nor the *Standard Error* boxes are checked. Click **OK** and the numerical output shown in Column C of Figure 11.5 will be shown.

Figure 11.4 Moving Average Dialog Box

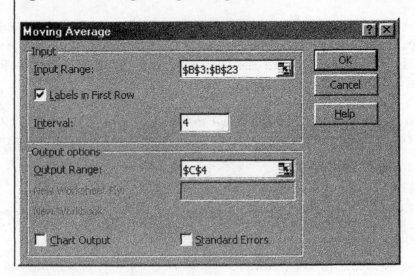

Figure 11.5 Moving Average Results

	A	B	C	D	E
2	Today's Date		Your Name		File: F(
3	Week	Sales	Moving Avg.	Forecast	
4	1	406	#N/A		
5	2	409	#N/A		
6	3	389	#N/A		
7	4	396	400.00		
8	5	400	398.50	400.00	
9	6	377	390.50	398.50	
10	7	392	391.25	390.50	
11	8	411	395.00	391.25	
12	9	388	392.00	395.00	
13	10	387	394.50	392.00	
14	11	382	392.00	394.50	
15	12	390	386.75	392.00	
16	13	419	394.50	386.75	
17	14	398	397.25	394.50	
18	15	396	400.75	397.25	
19	16	404	404.25	400.75	
20	17	404	400.50	404.25	
21	18	407	402.75	400.50	
22	19	386	400.25	402.75	
23	20	396	398.25	400.25	
24				398.25	
25					

3. Enter the label **Moving Avg** in Cell C3 and the label **Forecast** in Cell D3.

4. Each of the moving average values of Column C can be considered a forecast for the time period following it. These forecasts are shown in Column D. To obtain them, the entry =**C7** is placed in Cell D8. This entry is then copied to cells D9 through D24 to compute forecasts for the remaining time periods including that for the next time period, the 21st.

As shown in cell D24, the 4-point moving average forecast for the next period is 398.25. As discussed later we may want to explore values other than four for the number of points used in the moving average.

11.3 THE EXPONENTIAL SMOOTHING ANALYSIS TOOL ——

We will now use the EXPONENTIAL SMOOTHING Data Analysis Tool to forecast for the Riper's Donut example of Figure 11.2.

The procedure for forecasting these data using exponential smoothing with a smoothing constant value of 0.2 is the following.

1. From the menu bar select **Tools**, from the subsequent pull-down menu select **Data Analysis** and from the *Data Analysis* list box select **Exponential Smoothing**.

2. Fill in the entries of the *Exponential Smoothing* dialog box as shown in Figure 11.6. Notice that the input range includes the label in cell B3, and the **Labels** check box has a check in it. The entry for **Damping Factor** refers to the value of 1.0 minus the smoothing constant. Thus, its value is **0.8** for a smoothing factor of 0.2. Neither the *Chart Output* nor the *Standard Error* boxes are checked. Click on **OK** and the numerical output shown in Column F of Figure 11.7 will be obtained.

3. Enter the label **Expo.Sm.** in Cell E3 and the label **Forecast** in Cell F3.

4. The exponential smoothing values of column F are the forecasts for the next time period. The formula in Cell F23 has been copied into Cell F24 to provide a forecast for the 21st time period.

As shown in cell D24, the forecast for the next period is 397.63 based on simple exponential smoothing with a smoothing constant of 0.2. As discussed later, we may want to explore other values for the smoothing constant.

Figure 11.6 Exponential Smoothing Dialog Box

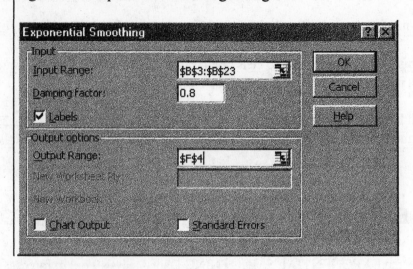

Figure 11.7 Simple Exponential Smoothing Results

	A	B	C	D	E	F	G
2	Today's Date		Your Name		File: FORECAST.xls		
3	Week	Sales	Moving Avg.	Forecast	Expo.Sm.	Forecast	
4	1	406	#N/A			#N/A	
5	2	409	#N/A			406.00	
6	3	389	#N/A			406.60	
7	4	396	400.00			403.08	
8	5	400	398.50	400.00		401.66	
9	6	377	390.50	398.50		401.33	
10	7	392	391.25	390.50		396.46	
11	8	411	395.00	391.25		395.57	
12	9	388	392.00	395.00		398.66	
13	10	387	394.50	392.00		396.53	
14	11	382	392.00	394.50		394.62	
15	12	390	386.75	392.00		392.10	
16	13	419	394.50	386.75		391.68	
17	14	398	397.25	394.50		397.14	
18	15	396	400.75	397.25		397.31	
19	16	404	404.25	400.75		397.05	
20	17	404	400.50	404.25		398.44	
21	18	407	402.75	400.50		399.55	
22	19	386	400.25	402.75		401.04	
23	20	396	398.25	400.25		398.03	
24				398.25		397.63	
25							

11.4 LINEAR TREND PROJECTION WITH TRENDLINE ─────

When a visual inspection of a time series plot and a straight line fit to the data indicate a trend component is present, neither the moving average nor the simple exponential smoothing method will be effective in forecasting. Both of these smoothing methods will result in forecasts that usually lag the actual time series values.

The Bubeye State University example shown in Figure 11.3 does exhibit an obvious trend component. For such a time series, a forecasting method that accounts for the trend is necessary. Excel's regression features facilitate the linear trend projection method of this section and the non-linear trend projection method of the next section.

Linear trend projection uses the method of least squares which is the basis for simple linear regression analysis. Excel has a number of resources for performing the computations for a least squares fit. These include the TRENDLINE feature for charts as previously demonstrated in this chapter, the REGRESSION data analysis tool demonstrated in Chapter 10, and functions such as TREND also used in Chapter 10.

Our feeling is that the most effective approach is based on the use of the **trendline** feature. It not only is quick and easy to use, it facilitates a visual and an analytical evaluation of the fit. In addition, the results are automatically updated as the data are changed.

To demonstrate this approach let us return to the Bubeye State University attendance example. Begin by returning to *Sheet2* of the FORECAST workbook. It should appear as shown in Figure 11.3. We can use the equation for the *linear fit* to the data to make a forecast for the next time period. We proceed as follows.

1. Key the label **Forecast** into Cell C3.

2. Key the formula **=429.98*A4+88928** in Cell C4.

3. Copy the contents of Cell C4 into cells C5 through C12. The results will appear as shown in Figure 11.8.

The result is an estimate of the attendance based on the least squares formula for all nine years including the next year's estimate of 92,797.8.

11.5 NON-LINEAR TREND PROJECTION
WITH TRENDLINE ─────

Frequently a time series plot will suggest a trend component that is not linear. For such situations Excel provides a resource for easily exploring the nature of the relationship. A reference to Figure 10.5

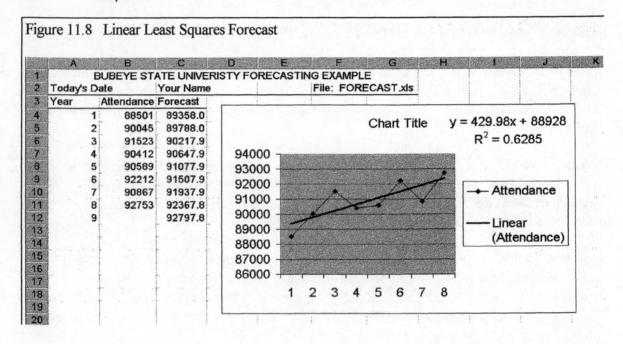

Figure 11.8   Linear Least Squares Forecast

of Chapter 10, shows that the TRENDLINE feature for charts includes *logarithmic, polynomial, power* and *exponential* relationships in addition to the *linear* relationship we used in Section 11.4. Accordingly, you may try any of these relationships through the trendline feature. (Note: the sixth option shown in Figure 10.5, Moving Average, could have been used in Section 11.2 above but we feel it is less effective than the data analysis tool used in that section.)

To demonstrate how this is to be done we will continue with the Bubeye State University example. We have shown that a linear trend fit the data quite well. However, we can very easily evaluate the four other relationship forms of **trendline** in order to try to develop a better fit to the data. To continue this example, we would proceed as follows.

1. Click on the linear relationship line in the chart. Remove it by pressing the **Del** button.

2. To superimpose another line of regression on this time series plot, click **Chart** on the menu bar. On the subsequent pull-down menu, select **Add Trendline**.

3. Click on the **Type** tab, click on **Logarithmic** for the *Trend/Regression Type* (see Figure 10.5).

4. Click on the **Options** tab. Select **Automatic** for the *Trendline Name* option (see Figure 10.6). Click to put checks in the **Display Equation on Chart** and **Display R-squared Value on Chart**. Click on **OK** to obtain the results of Figure 11.9.

5. In order to compute the forecasts shown in Figure 11.9, enter the formula from Figure 11.9, **=1573.5*LN(A4)+88777,** into Cell C4, and copy C4 into cells C5 through C12.

Figure 11.9 Logarithmic Least Squares Forecasts

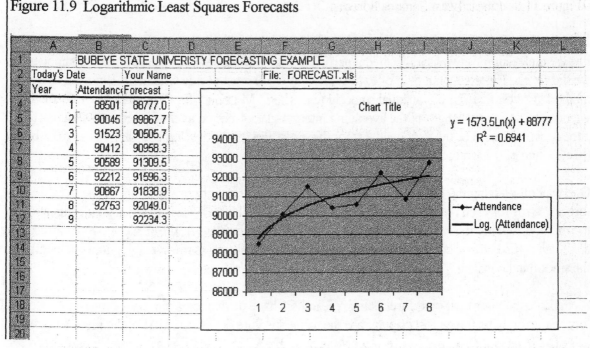

We can repeat the six steps above to develop a *polynomial* relationship, a *power* relationship and an *exponential* relationship for these data. Moreover, the polynomial relationship option allows you to specify a quadratic relationship (order 2), a cubic relationship (order 3), a quartic relationship (order 4), and so on up to order 6.

You may wish to try these other relationships on your time series plot by repeating steps 1 through 4 for other *Trend/Regression Types*. For comparison, the results for four other forms are the following.

Polynomial (order 2): $y = -38.81\ t^2 + 779.26\ t + 88346$

Polynomial (order 3): $y = 51.263\ t^3 - 730.85\ t^2 + 3419.3\ t + 85808$

Power: $y = 88783\ t^{\,0.0174}$

Exponential: $y = 88936\ e^{\,0.0047t}$

As demonstrated the trendline feature of Excel allows you to explore different forms of a least squares fit quite easily. In the following section we will consider how to decide what form best fits the data.

11.6 CHOOSING THE BEST FORECASTING METHOD

In sections 11.2 through 11.5 we have explored some forecasting methods. As we outlined in Section 11.1, the first consideration for choosing among them is whether the time series appears to have a trend component or not. However, you still have other decisions to be made regarding the forecast method to be used.

For example, suppose we have decided a particular time series does not include a trend component as we did for the Riper's Donut data of Figure 11.1. We still must decide whether the moving average method is better than the exponential smoothing method. Moreover for the moving average method, we need to decide the length of the averaging interval. Is a 4-period averaging interval superior to a 3-period, and so on? For the exponential smoothing method is a smoothing constant value of 0.2 better than a value of 0.3, and so on?

One way of selecting the *best* overall forecasting method is to compute a measure of the overall forecast error for each method. A comparison of the overall forecast error allows an identification of the method yielding the smallest forecasting error. In a similar manner, the smallest overall forecasting error can be used for selecting the *best* values for parameters such as the averaging interval length and the smoothing constant.

As indicated in your textbook, forecasting researchers have developed a number of measures of overall forecast error. The three most popular are the mean absolute deviation (MAD), the mean squared error (MSE) and the mean absolute percentage error (MAPE). MAPE is most appropriate for comparing the predictive accuracy of *two or more time series*. Since our interest instead is in comparing *two or more forecasting methods or* parameter values for one time series, MAPE is not appropriate here.

Of the remaining two measures, MAD computes the average of the absolute difference between the actual time series values and the corresponding forecast values. MSE computes the average of the square of the difference between the actual and forecast values. The choice between these two methods depends on the importance of large differences between actual and forecasted values. MSE should be used if it is important to avoid large differences. On the other hand, if you can afford to ignore a few extreme forecast errors provided the remaining forecast errors are small, than MAD should be used. The computations for MAD and MSE are almost identical. For MAD we find the absolute value of the forecast errors, and for MSE we square the forecast errors. We will demonstrate the use of MAD in our first example below and MSE in the second example.

Let us return to the Riper's Donut example by clicking on the *Sheet1* tab. We will pick it up where we last left it in Figure 11.7.

1. Enter the labels **MA Error, ES Error** and **MAD** = in cells H3, I3 and G25 respectively.

2. In cell H8 enter the formula **=ABS(B8-D8)** to compute the absolute value of the errors. Copy the formula in cell H8 to cells H9 through H23.

3. In cell H25 enter the formula **=AVERAGE(H8:H23)**

4. In cell I5 enter the formula **=ABS(B5-F5).** Copy the formula in cell I5 to cells I6 through I23.

5. In cell I25 enter the formula **=AVERAGE(I5:I23)**

The result will be as shown in Figure 11.10. Note that the two values for MAD are based on a different number of forecast errors. Each is the average of all the errors available for its specific forecast method.   For the moving average method there are 16 error values and for the exponential smoothing method there are 19 error values. There is no error value for the forecast for period 21.

Figure 11.10 Riper's Donut Example MAD Computations

	A	B	C	D	E	F	G	H	I	J
1			RIPER'S DONUT FORECASTING EXAMPLE							
2	Today's Date		Your Name		File: FORECAST.xls					
3	Week	Sales	Moving Avg.	Forecast	Expo.Sm.	Forecast		MA Error	ES Error	
4	1	406	#N/A			#N/A				
5	2	409	#N/A			406.00			3.00	
6	3	389	#N/A			406.60			17.60	
7	4	396	400.00			403.08			7.08	
8	5	400	398.50	400.00		401.66		0.00	1.66	
9	6	377	390.50	398.50		401.33		21.50	24.33	
10	7	392	391.25	390.50		396.46		1.50	4.46	
11	8	411	395.00	391.25		395.57		19.75	15.43	
12	9	388	392.00	395.00		398.66		7.00	10.66	
13	10	387	394.50	392.00		396.53		5.00	9.53	
14	11	382	392.00	394.50		394.62		12.50	12.62	
15	12	390	386.75	392.00		392.10		2.00	2.10	
16	13	419	394.50	386.75		391.68		32.25	27.32	
17	14	398	397.25	394.50		397.14		3.50	0.86	
18	15	396	400.75	397.25		397.31		1.25	1.31	
19	16	404	404.25	400.75		397.05		3.25	6.95	
20	17	404	400.50	404.25		398.44		0.25	5.56	
21	18	407	402.75	400.50		399.55		6.50	7.45	
22	19	386	400.25	402.75		401.04		16.75	15.04	
23	20	396	398.25	400.25		398.03		4.25	2.03	
24				398.25		397.63				
25							MAD =	8.58	9.21	
26										

Based on these results we would conclude the 4-point moving average method is slightly more accurate than the exponential smoothing method with a smoothing constant of 0.2. Of course, we can also use the computation of MAD to determine if there is a better value for the *number of points used in the moving average* and a better value for the *exponential smoothing constant.*

Let us now return to the Bubeye State University example as shown in Figure 11.9. For it we will compare the linear and a quadratic trend projection forecast methods using MSE as an error measure. We will first use the linear relationship found in Section 11.4 and the quadratic relationship given in Section 11.5 to make forecasts. Next we will find MSE for each of these two projection methods. We begin by clicking on *Sheet2* and then move the chart lower in the worksheet, say to row 16 or below.

1. Begin by entering the labels **LinearFore.**, **Quad.Fore.**, **Lin.Error**, **Quad.Error** and **MSE** in cells C3, D3, E3, F3 and D14 respectively.

2. In cell C4 enter the formula **=429.98*A4+88928** to compute the forecast of Figure 11.8.

3. In cell D4 enter the formula **=-38.81*A4^2+779.26*A4+88346** to compute the quadratic (polynomial—order 2) projection forecast equation given in Section 11.5.

4. Copy the contents of cells C4 and D4 to cells C5 through D12.

5. In cell E4 enter the formula **=(B4-C4)^2** to compute the error squared value for the linear forecast.

6. In cell F4 enter the formula **=(B4-D4)^2** to compute the error squared value for the quadratic forecast.

7. Copy the contents of cells E4 and F4 to cells E5 through F11 (Not F12).

8. In cell E14 enter the formula **=AVERAGE(E4:E11)** to compute the average of the linear errors.

9. Copy cell E14 to cell F14 to compute the average of the quadratic errors.

The results will be as shown in Figure 11.11. The MSE values suggest that the quadratic method is a slight improvement over the linear method. Its MSE value is somewhat smaller.

Figure 11.11 Bubeye Example MSE Computations

	A	B	C	D	E	F	G
1		BUBEYE STATE UNIVERISTY FORECASTING EXAMPLE					
2	Today's Date		Your Name			File: FORECAST.xls	
3	Year	Attendance	LinearFore.	Quad.Fore.	Lin.Error	Quad.Error	
4	1	88501	89358.0	89086.5	734414.7	342751.7	
5	2	90045	89788.0	89749.3	66069.6	87450.3	
6	3	91523	90217.9	90334.5	1703181.6	1412556.0	
7	4	90412	90647.9	90842.1	55658.2	184968.8	
8	5	90589	91077.9	91272.1	239023.2	466557.3	
9	6	92212	91507.9	91624.4	495785.0	345273.8	
10	7	90867	91937.9	91899.1	1146741.1	1065292.3	
11	8	92753	92367.8	92096.2	148348.2	431333.7	
12	9		92797.8	92215.7			
13							
14				MSE=	573652.7	542023.0	
15							

CHAPTER 12. STATISTICAL QUALITY CONTROL CHARTS

All processes in business and industry result in variation of the process outputs. In quality control, the causes of variation are classified either as **common (or chance) causes** or as **assignable (or special) causes**. Common causes are a number of randomly occurring events that are inherent to the process such as variations in materials, temperature, humidity and so on. Generally, these can be eliminated only by altering the process. On the other hand, assignable causes are specific events and factors which are usually temporary such as incorrect machine settings, cutting tool wear, operator error and so on. These causes can be identified and eliminated. The primary objective of quality control is to detect and eliminate the assignable causes of process variation.

If the variation in process outputs is due only to common causes the process is considered to be **in control**. On the other hand, if some of the variation is due to assignable causes, the process is considered to be **out of control**. A number of statistical techniques have been developed to determine if a process is out of control. One of these is the use of **control charts**.

A control chart consists of two major components. The first is a plot of a statistical value over time. The second component is three lines superimposed on the plot. One of these is the centerline, a second is an upper control limit and the third the lower control limit. The **centerline (CL)** indicates the most likely outcome for the statistical value, the **upper control limit (UCL)** the largest expected value and the **lower control limit (LCL)** the smallest expected value. If all the plotted statistical values are randomly distributed between the two control limits, the process is considered to be in control. If the points are not randomly distributed between the two limits, the process is considered to be out of control.

A number of types of control charts have been developed to detect an out of control situation for various process outputs. Some of the more useful charts are those for detecting an out of control situation in the process average ($\bar{x}$ **chart**), in the process variability (**R chart**), in the proportion of defective items produced by a process (**p chart**), in the number of defective items produced by a process (**np chart**) and in the number of defects per unit produced by a process (**c chart**).

All of these five types of charts are based on averages for the statistical value of interest. The Central Limit Theorem (see Section 4.3 of Chapter 4) states that the probability distribution of the possible values for averages is the normal distribution. Accordingly, all five of these types of charts are based on the normal distribution. For all of them, the centerline is defined as the average or mean, the upper control limit is defined as the mean plus three standard deviations, and the lower limit as the mean minus three standard deviations. For normal distribution, the probability that a value would fall outside these control limits can be found to be 0.0027 or about one-fourth of one percent. A very unlikely event when the process is in control.

The general process for constructing each of the five types of control charts is the same. It includes

1. Entering into a worksheet the values for the statistical output of interest ($\bar{x}$, R, p, np or c),
2. Computing an estimate of the mean and the standard deviation of the mean,
3. Setting the centerline (CL) equal to the mean, the upper control limit (UCL) equal to the mean plus three times the standard deviation, and the lower control limit (LCL) equal to the mean minus three times the standard deviation and
4. Charting the data values, centerline, upper control limit and lower control limit.

Accordingly, the five sections that follow present quite similar worksheets. In **Section 12.1** we construct an $\bar{x}$ chart for controlling a process average and in **Section 12.2** an R chart for controlling process variability. These two charts usually are used in conjunction with each other to control a process output measured on a quantitative scale such as time, length, weight, and so on. A p chart for controlling the proportion of defective items produced by a process is developed in **Section 12.3** and an np chart for controlling the number of defective items produced by a process in **Section 12.4**. These two charts provide the same type of results so usually either one or the other is used. Finally in **Section 12.5**, we demonstrate the use of Excel to develop a c chart for controlling the number of defects per unit produced by a process.

Since the development of these five charts is quite similar, we present the $\bar{x}$ chart in considerable detail. The subsequent four sections present primarily the differences from the discussion of this initial section.

12.1 $\bar{x}$ CHART FOR CONTROLLING PROCESS AVERAGE ————

We will use the following example to demonstrate the development of an $\bar{x}$ chart.

T&S Cakes, Inc., bakes and distributes cakes throughout the greater Terry Hut metropolitan area. The head baker, Granny Goose, attempts to produce cakes that weigh two pounds each. However, there is some variation in the cake weight that is monitored by Mr. Scotferd, T&S's quality control manager. During the most recent baking period, Scotferd took fifteen samples of four cakes each. The resulting 60 weights are given in cells B5 through E19 of the worksheet in Figure 12.1.

Figure 12.1 Data, Means and Ranges for T&S Cakes

Sample Number	\multicolumn{6}{c}{Sample Vaues}					Mean	Largest	Smallest	Range
	1	2	3	4	5	6	Mean	Largest	Smallest	Range
1	1.6	2.0	2.4	1.9			2.0	2.4	1.6	0.8
2	2.0	2.0	2.2	1.8			2.0	2.2	1.8	0.4
3	1.9	2.3	1.6	1.8			1.9	2.3	1.6	0.7
4	2.4	2.4	2.2	2.3			2.3	2.4	2.2	0.2
5	1.7	2.1	1.8	2.2			2.0	2.2	1.7	0.5
6	1.6	2.0	2.0	2.2			2.0	2.2	1.6	0.6
7	2.3	2.3	1.9	2.5			2.3	2.5	1.9	0.6
8	2.2	2.2	1.8	1.6			2.0	2.2	1.6	0.6
9	1.7	2.2	2.1	1.9			2.0	2.2	1.7	0.5
10	2.2	2.2	2.0	2.3			2.2	2.3	2.0	0.3
11	2.1	2.4	2.4	1.6			2.1	2.4	1.6	0.8
12	2.1	2.2	1.8	2.0			2.0	2.2	1.8	0.4
13	2.3	1.8	1.8	2.4			2.1	2.4	1.8	0.6
14	1.7	2.4	2.2	2.2			2.1	2.4	1.7	0.7
15	1.7	1.8	2.1	1.7			1.8	2.1	1.7	0.4
16										
17										
18										
19										
20										
21										

(Worksheet header: T & S CAKES, INC., EXAMPLE; Today's Date; Your Name; File: QUALITY.xls)

We have set the worksheet up to accommodate the most usual situations. Typically the number of samples will be from 20 to 25 and each sample will include 4, 5 or 6 values. Accordingly, the worksheet allows values to be entered into rows 5 through 29 and columns A through G. For our example, we have used only 15 samples with 4 values each to minimize the number of values you will need to enter into the worksheet.

Our analysis will utilize two worksheets. On *Sheet1* as shown in Figure 12.1, we include the raw data and the computations for finding the sample means and ranges. The remaining computations and the construction of the $\bar{x}$ chart are given on *Sheet2*. The second sheet begins with the values for the sample means and ranges. This two-sheet setup allows you to begin either by entering the raw data into *Sheet1* or by directly entering the sample means and ranges into *Sheet1* while bypassing the worksheet of Figure 12.1. The following procedure provides the steps for both approaches.

1. Start Excel and enter the **Identification Material** shown in rows 1 and 2 of Figure 12.1. Enter the labels and numbers in column A.

2. If you intend to enter the 60 data values, enter the remaining labels shown in rows 3 and 4 of Figure 12.1. Also enter the data values in the cells B5 through E19. If you wish to bypass entering the data and instead start by directly entering the sample means and ranges into the worksheet, you will be bypassing the worksheet of Figure 12.1. You should **skip to Step 7** below.

3. Enter the following formulas: **=AVERAGE(B5:G5)** in cell H5; **=MAX(B5:G5)** in cell I5; **=MIN(B5:G5)** in cell J5 and **=I5-J5** in cell K5 to find the mean and range for the first sample.

4. Copy the four formulas into rows 6 through 19 of their respective columns. The 15 sample means and 15 sample ranges will be computed for you.

5. Click on the *Sheet2* tab at the bottom of the worksheet. Enter the identification material in rows 1 and 2, and enter the labels and numbers in Column A as shown in Figure 12.2. (Alternatively, you may use the copy and paste commands to copy these labels from *Sheet1* to *Sheet2*.)

6. Enter the formula **=Sheet1!$K5** in cell B5 (the single dollar sign is needed to facilitate copying later for the R chart). Enter the formula **=Sheet1!H5** in cell H5. Copy these two formulas into rows 6 through 19 of their respective columns. You should now **skip to Step 8** below.

7. **This step is only for those who have skipped here from Step 2 above**. Your *Sheet1* will look like Figure 12.2. Enter the sample ranges in rows 5 through 19 of column B and the sample means in rows 5 through 19 of column H. Continue with **Step 8**.

8. Enter the remaining labels shown in row 4 of Figure 12.2.

9. Enter the six labels shown in cells D6 through D12 of Figure 12.2.

Figure 12.2 x̄ Chart Centerline and Control Limits for T&S Cakes

	A	B	C	D	E	F	G	H	I	J	K
1					T & S CAKES, INC., EXAMPLE						
2	Today's Date				Your Name					File: QUALITY.xls	
3	Sample										
4	Number	Range						Mean	LCL	CL	UCL
5	1	0.8						1.98	1.65	2.04	2.44
6	2	0.4		Avg.of Sample Means		2.0		2.00	1.65	2.04	2.44
7	3	0.7		Average Range		0.5		1.90	1.65	2.04	2.44
8	4	0.2		A2 Factor		0.729		2.33	1.65	2.04	2.44
9	5	0.5						1.95	1.65	2.04	2.44
10	6	0.6		Lower Control Limit		1.65		1.95	1.65	2.04	2.44
11	7	0.6		Centerline		2.04		2.25	1.65	2.04	2.44
12	8	0.6		Upper Control Limit		2.44		1.95	1.65	2.04	2.44
13	9	0.5						1.98	1.65	2.04	2.44
14	10	0.3						2.18	1.65	2.04	2.44
15	11	0.8						2.13	1.65	2.04	2.44
16	12	0.4						2.03	1.65	2.04	2.44
17	13	0.6						2.08	1.65	2.04	2.44
18	14	0.7						2.13	1.65	2.04	2.44
19	15	0.4						1.83	1.65	2.04	2.44
20	16										
21	17										

10. In cell F6 enter the formula **=AVERAGE(H5:H29)** in order to compute the average of the sample means. In cell F7 enter the formula **=AVERAGE(B5:B29)** to compute the average of the sample ranges.

11. Cell F8 contains the constant needed to convert the average of the sample ranges to the value for computing the 3-sigma control limits. It is the A_2 constant found in the table of control chart constants given in many business statistics textbooks. The value for A_2 depends on the number of observations in each sample. For four observations its value is 0.729 as indicated in Figure 12.2.

12. Cell F10 computes the lower control limit (LCL) with the formula **=F6-F8*F7**, cell F11 the centerline (CL) with the formula **=F6**, and cell F12 the upper control limit (UCL) with the formula **=F6+F8*F7**.

13. To facilitate the later plotting of LCL, CL and UCL, these values are to be repeated in columns I, J and K respectively. In cell I5 insert the formula **=$F$10**. We include the $ sign before the row and column designators to specify it as an absolute reference so it can be correctly copied later. In similar manner insert the formula **=$F$11** in cell J5 and **=$F$12** in cell K5.

14. Copy the formulas in cells I5, J5 and K5 into rows 6 through 19 of the respective columns. We now have the data for plotting the 15 means together with the LCL, CL and UCL in columns H, I, J and K.

15. We will use the CHART WIZARD to prepare the plot. As was noted in Section 2.2 of Chapter 2, Excel's CHART WIZARD can be used to create many types of charts. The **Line** type will be used to construct the x̄ chart. Begin by highlighting the cells H5 through K19.

16. Move the pointer to the CHART WIZARD icon on the standard toolbar and click once. (Note: If you have not used the CHART WIZARD before you may wish to refer to the discussion for Figures 2.8 through 2.12 given in Chapter 2.)

17. The *Chart Wizard—Step 1 of 4—Chart Type* dialog box will appear as shown in Figure 12.3. If the **Standard Types** tab is not in front, click on it.

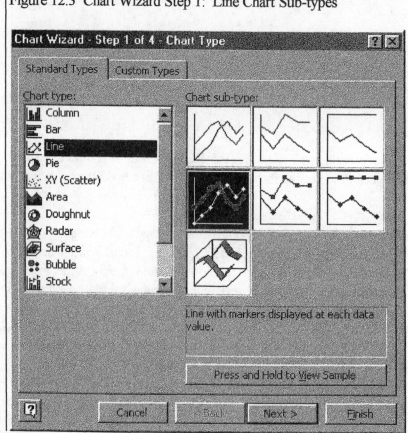

Figure 12.3 Chart Wizard Step 1: Line Chart Sub-types

18. Use the mouse to select the **Line** chart and then select the sub-type on the left of the second row as shown in Figure 12.3. Click on the **Next** button. The *Chart Wizard—Step 2 of 4—Chart Source Data* dialog box will be displayed as given in Figure 12.4.

Figure 12.4 Chart Wizard Step 2: Chart Source Data

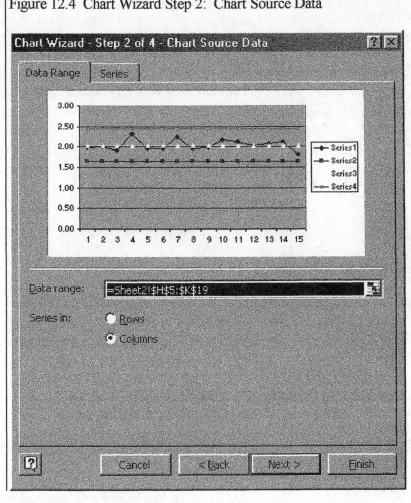

19. If the **Data Range** tab is not in front, click on it. Verify that the data range is correct and click on the **Next** button. The *Chart Wizard—Step 3 of 4—Chart Options* dialog box will appear as shown in Figure 12.5. If the **Titles** tab is not in front, click on it.

20. Enter the title *X-BAR CHART FOR T&S CAKES*. Enter *Sample Number* for the **Category (X) axis** and *Cake Weight in Pounds* for the **Value (Y) axis**

21. For the **Axes** tab, we have selected the check boxes for *Category (X) axis* and for *Value (Y) axis*. For the **Gridlines** tab, we have not selected any of the four check boxes. For the **Legends** tab, we have not selected the check box for *Show Legend*. Finally for the **Data Labels** tab, none of the options under *Label contains* has been selected **(Excel 2000-App. D)**.

22. Click on **Next**. *The Chart Wizard—Step 4 of 4—Chart Location* dialog box will appear. Click on *As object in* and click the **Finish** button. The result will be as shown in Figure 12.6.

Figure 12.5 Chart Wizard Step 3: Chart Options—Titles

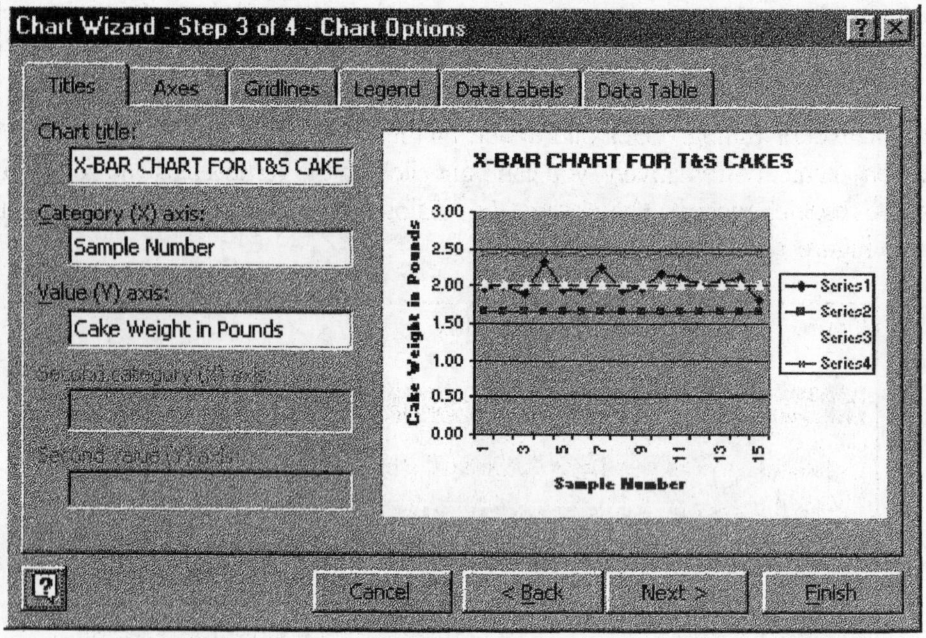

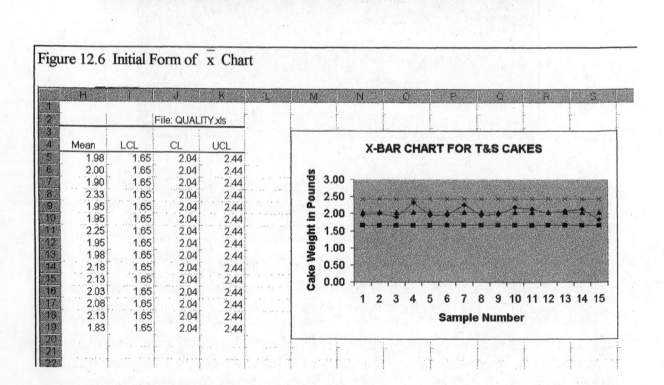

Figure 12.6 Initial Form of $\bar{x}$ Chart

File: QUALITY.xls

Mean	LCL	CL	UCL
1.98	1.65	2.04	2.44
2.00	1.65	2.04	2.44
1.90	1.65	2.04	2.44
2.33	1.65	2.04	2.44
1.95	1.65	2.04	2.44
1.95	1.65	2.04	2.44
2.25	1.65	2.04	2.44
1.95	1.65	2.04	2.44
1.98	1.65	2.04	2.44
2.18	1.65	2.04	2.44
2.13	1.65	2.04	2.44
2.03	1.65	2.04	2.44
2.08	1.65	2.04	2.44
2.13	1.65	2.04	2.44
1.83	1.65	2.04	2.44

Although the chart of Figure 12.6 presents all the data of a control chart, it could benefit from editing so it will appear as a usual control chart. We can make three types of changes. First we can change the y-axis scale so the four plotted lines aren't all bunched at the top of the chart. Second, we can remove the symbols (markers) from the LCL, CL and UCL lines. Third we can add a label to the LCL, CL and UCL lines. The result will be the form usually presented in textbooks. We demonstrate these editing changes by continuing with the procedure of this section.

23.   Click on the vertical axis. Black squares will be shown at the top and the bottom of the axis to indicate it is active for editing. Click on **Format** on the menu bar and click on **Selected Axis** on the subsequent menu. (Alternatively, you can right click on the vertical axis and select **Format Axis** from the resulting menu.) The *Format Axis* dialog box will be displayed. Click on the **Scale** tab to obtain Figure 12.7.

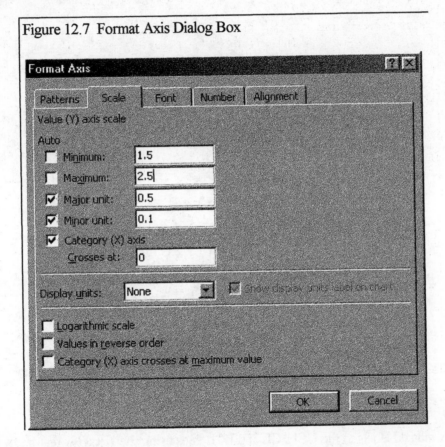

Figure 12.7 Format Axis Dialog Box

24.   Enter the number **1.5** in the minimum textbox and the number **2.5** in the maximum textbox as shown in Figure 12.7. Click on **OK**. The chart y-axis will be revised as shown in later Figure 12.9.

25.   Click on the UCL line. A number of squares will appear on it to indicate it is active for editing. Click on **Format** on the menu bar and click on **Selected Data Series** on the subsequent menu. (Alternatively, you can right click on the UCL line and select **Format Data Series** from the resulting menu.) The *Format Data Series* dialog box will be displayed. Click on the **Patterns** tab to obtain Figure 12.8.

26. For *Line,* click on the option button **Automatic** and for *Marker,* click on **None.** Click on **OK** and the UCL line will be displayed without symbols (markers) as shown in later Figure 12.9. (You may also want to change the color, style or weight of the line within this dialog box. Some textbooks use dashed lines for the control limits.)

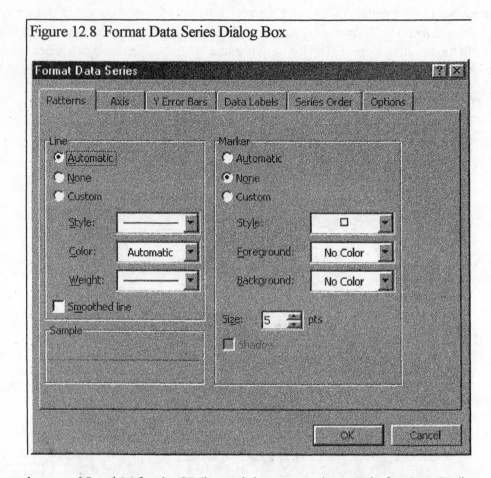

Figure 12.8 Format Data Series Dialog Box

27. Repeat the steps 25 and 26 for the CL line and then repeat them again for the LCL line.

28. Next we will add labels to the UCL, CL and LCL lines using the *Text Box* feature of the *Drawing* Toolbar. To display this toolbar click the **Drawing** icon on the *Standard* toolbar.

29. Click on the **Text Box** icon on the drawing toolbar. The mouse pointer will become a small cross. Locate it near the UCL line where you want the text box to begin. Then press the left mouse button and move the mouse to open the text box and then release the mouse button. You may need to practice this operation.

30. After the box is open, you can type the label **UCL** in it. If the box isn't large enough to display the entire label, click to activate the box and use the sizing handle to enlarge it.

31. Repeat steps 29 and 30 for the LCL line and the CL line. The final edited control chart is as shown in Figure 12.9.

This completes are discussion of the $\bar{x}$ chart. We will continue with this example in the next section for the development of an R chart for controlling process variability.

Figure 12.9 Final Edited Form of the $\bar{x}$ Chart

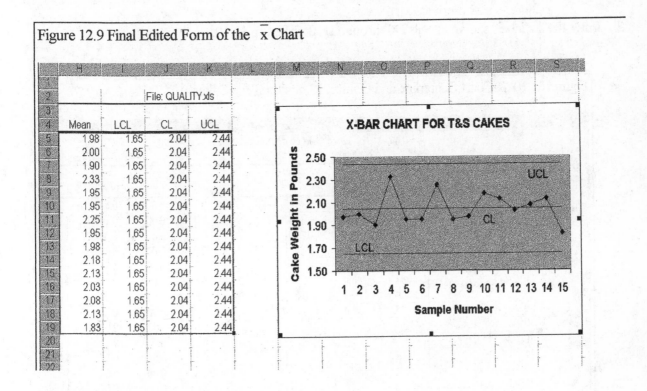

12.2 R CHART FOR CONTROLLING PROCESS VARIABLLILITY——————

The R chart is used to monitor the variability of a process output just as the $\bar{x}$ chart is used to monitor the average value for a process output. Sample values of the range are plotted on the R chart. We conclude the process variability is out of control if the plotted sample values are not randomly distributed between the lower and upper control limits.

The procedure needed to develop an R chart is very similar to that given in Section 12.1 for the $\bar{x}$ chart. Accordingly, our presentation here will primarily indicate the differences in the two procedures. We will continue with the example of T&S Cakes of the prior section. The procedure assumes you have developed the worksheets of Figure 12.1 (*Sheet1*) and Figure 12.2 (*Sheet2*). The R chart computations of Figure 12.10 will be shown on *Sheet3*. However if you entered directly the mean and range values into the $\bar{x}$ chart worksheet of Figure 12.2 thus bypassing the first worksheet of Figure 12.1, your R chart computations of Figure 12.10 will be shown on *Sheet2*. We proceed as follows.

1. Copy from *Sheet2* to *Sheet3* (from *Sheet1* to *Sheet 2* if you bypassed Figure 12.1) the following.
   a. Rows 1 and 2 into rows 1 and 2
   b. Cells A3 through A29 into A3 through A29
   c. Cells B4 through B19 into H4 through H19
   d. Cells I4 through K19 into I4 through K19

2. Enter the six labels shown in cells D6 through D12 of Figure 12.10.

Figure 12.10 R Chart Centerline and Control Limits for T&S Cakes

	A	B	C	D	E	F	G	H	I	J	K
1					T & S CAKES, INC., EXAMPLE						
2	Today's Date				Your Name					File: QUALITY.xls	
3	Sample										
4	Number							Range	LCL	CL	UCL
5	1							0.8	0.00	0.54	1.23
6	2			Avg.of Sample Range		0.54		0.4	0.00	0.54	1.23
7	3			D3 Factor		0.000		0.7	0.00	0.54	1.23
8	4			D4 Factor		2.282		0.2	0.00	0.54	1.23
9	5							0.5	0.00	0.54	1.23
10	6			Lower Control Limit		0.00		0.6	0.00	0.54	1.23
11	7			Centerline		0.54		0.6	0.00	0.54	1.23
12	8			Upper Control Limit		1.23		0.6	0.00	0.54	1.23
13	9							0.5	0.00	0.54	1.23
14	10							0.3	0.00	0.54	1.23
15	11							0.8	0.00	0.54	1.23
16	12							0.4	0.00	0.54	1.23
17	13							0.6	0.00	0.54	1.23
18	14							0.7	0.00	0.54	1.23
19	15							0.4	0.00	0.54	1.23
20	16										

3. In cell F6 enter the formula **=AVERAGE(H5:H29)** in order to compute the average of the sample ranges.

4. Cells F7 and F8 contain the constants needed to convert the average of the sample ranges to the value for computing the 3-sigma control limits. These are the D_3 and the D_4 constants found in the table of control chart constants given in many business statistics textbooks. These values depend on the number of observations in each sample. For four observations the values are 0.000 and 2.282 as given in Figure 12.10.

5. Cell F10 computes the lower control limit (LCL) with the formula **=F6*F7**, cell F11 the centerline (CL) with the formula **=F6**, and cell F12 the upper control limit (UCL) with the formula **=F6*F8**.

6. We will use the CHART WIZARD to construct a **Line** chart. Begin by highlighting the cells H5 through K19.

7. You now need to repeat steps *16 through 22 of Section 12.1* in order to produce the initial R Chart. In Step 20 you should use the appropriate titles for the chart and for the Y-axis. (See Figure 12.11.)

8. Repeat steps *25 through 31 of Section 12.1* (the scale adjustment of steps 23 and 24 is not needed for this plot) in order to edit your R chart into the final form as shown in Figure 12.11.

Figure 12.11 Final Edited Form of the R Chart

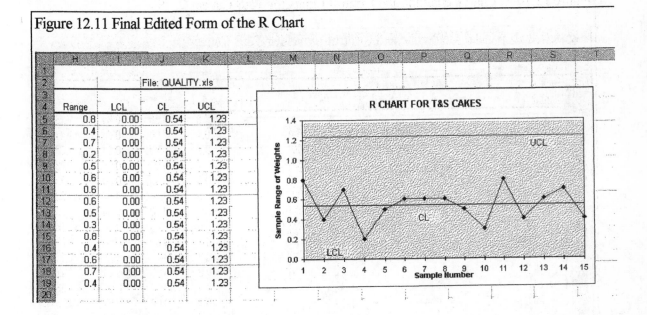

12.3 p CHART FOR CONTROLLING PROPORTION OF DEFECTIVE ITEMS———

Many times a quality characteristic for the output of a process cannot be measured on a quantitative scale such as time, length or weight. For such situations, each item of output from the process may be classified as **defective** (nonconforming to specifications) or **nondefective** (effective or conforming to specifications). We can then monitor the quality of the process by analyzing either the proportion of defective items in a sample or the number of defective items in a sample. The control chart appropriate for monitoring the proportion of defective items is called the **p chart** presented in this section. The closely related control chart appropriate for monitoring the number of defective items is called an **np chart** and is presented in the immediately following section.

The procedure needed to develop a p chart is very similar to that given for the $\bar{x}$ chart and the R chart. We plot sample values between 3-sigma control limits to determine if the sample values have a random pattern within the limits.

We will again return to T&S Cakes, Inc. The ever-discriminating Granny Goose wants every cake to have an acceptable frosting. However, it is not possible for her to personally inspect the large number of cakes produced each day by T&S. Consequently, she inspects a sample of 100 cakes each day and categorizes each cake as defective or not. Figure 12.12 presents the results for the last 15 days of her inspections. She would like to use these data to determine if the process is in control.

Figure 12.12 p Chart Centerline and Control Limits for T&S Cakes

	A	B	C	D	E	F	G	H	I	J	K
1					T & S CAKES, INC., EXAMPLE						
2	Today's Date				Your Name				File: QUALITY.xls		
3	Sample	Number						Proportion			
4	Number	Defective						Defective	LCL	CL	UCL
5	1	7		Size of Each Sample		100		0.070	0.0000	0.0607	0.1323
6	2	1		Number of Samples		15		0.010	0.0000	0.0607	0.1323
7	3	5		Total Defectives		91		0.050	0.0000	0.0607	0.1323
8	4	9		Average Proportion	0.060667			0.090	0.0000	0.0607	0.1323
9	5	10		Std. Dev. for Avg. Pro	0.023872			0.100	0.0000	0.0607	0.1323
10	6	8		Lower Control Limit	0.000000			0.080	0.0000	0.0607	0.1323
11	7	6		Centerline	0.060667			0.060	0.0000	0.0607	0.1323
12	8	9		Upper Control Limit	0.132282			0.090	0.0000	0.0607	0.1323
13	9	2						0.020	0.0000	0.0607	0.1323
14	10	3						0.030	0.0000	0.0607	0.1323
15	11	10						0.100	0.0000	0.0607	0.1323
16	12	8						0.080	0.0000	0.0607	0.1323
17	13	3						0.030	0.0000	0.0607	0.1323
18	14	9						0.090	0.0000	0.0607	0.1323
19	15	1						0.010	0.0000	0.0607	0.1323
20	16										

We will develop our p chart on *Sheet4* of the workbook QUALITY as shown on Figure 12.12 (*Sheet3* if you bypassed Figure 12.1). We proceed as follows.

1. Copy from *Sheet3* to *Sheet4* the following.
   a. Rows 1 and 2 into rows 1 and 2
   b. Cells A3 through A29 into A3 through A29
   c. Cells I4 through K19 into I4 through K19

2. Enter the labels in cells B3, B4, H3 and H4. Enter the data values in cells B5 through B19.

3. Enter the formula =**B5/$F$5** in cell H5. Copy this formula into cells H6 through H19.

4. Enter the eight labels shown in cells D5 through D12 of Figure 12.12.

5. Enter into cell F5 the number of observations in each sample, **100**, and into cell F6 the number of samples, **15**.

6. In cell F7 enter the formula =**SUM(B5:B29)** in order to compute the total number of defectives.

7. The contents of cell F8 depend on whether the value for the proportion defective items for the process when it is in control is known or not. If this value is known, it should be entered into cell F8. If it is not known (as assumed for Figure 12.12), enter the formula =**F7/F6/F5** to compute an estimate for it from the sample values.

8. The formula for cell F9 computes the estimate for the standard deviation for the proportion defective. It is found from the formula =**SQRT(F8*(1-F8)/F5)**.

9. The LCL is equal to the estimate of the average proportion defective minus three times the standard deviation of the average proportion defective. However, the LCL cannot be negative. Consequently, we must first determine if it is negative and set it equal to zero when it is. This can be accomplished with an **IF** function. The formula is =**IF(F8-3*F9<0,0,F8-3*F9)**.

10. Cell F11 computes the centerline (CL) with the formula =**F8**, and cell F12 the upper control limit (UCL) with the formula =**F8+3*F9**.

11. We will use the CHART WIZARD to prepare the p chart. Begin by highlighting the cells H5 through K19.

12. Repeat *steps 16 through 22 of Section 12.1* in order to produce the initial p Chart. In Step 20 you should use the appropriate titles for the chart and for the Y-axis. (See Figure 12.13.)

13. Repeat *steps 25 through 31 of Section 12.*1 (the scale adjustment of steps 23 and 24 is not needed for this plot) in order to edit your p chart into the final form as shown in Figure 12.13.

Our computations for the p chart have assumed that the number of observations in each sample is the same. However, a p chart can also be developed for situations when the number of observations is not the same for each sample. The worksheet of Figure 12.12 can be very easily modified to accommodate this. The modifications would include: (1) adding a column for sample size in column B, (2) finding the sum and the average for column B, (3) changing the formula in cell F8 to F7 divided by the sum of column B, (4) changing the denominator in cell F9 from F5 to the average for column B, and (5) changing the denominator in cell H5 from $F$5 to C5. Everything else would remain the same.

Figure 12.13 Final Edited Form of the p Chart

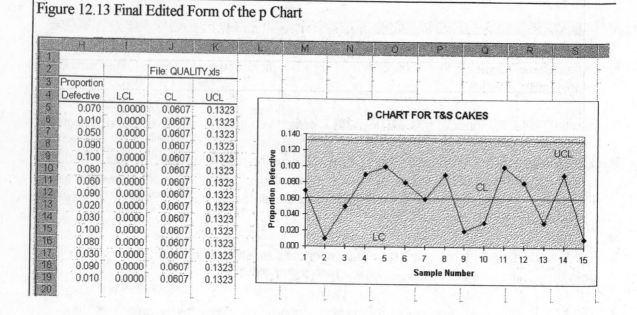

12.4 np CHART FOR CONTROLLING
NUMBER OF DEFECTIVE ITEMS

The np chart offers an alternative to the p chart if all the samples have the same number of observations. It provides exactly the same information as the p chart. The only difference is that the number of defective items is plotted instead of the proportion of defective items. If the number of observations is the same for all samples, the choice between the two charts is a matter of personal preference.

As for the p chart, the **np chart** is applicable for situations when each item of output from a process may be classified as **defective** (nonconforming to specifications) or **nondefective** (effective or conforming to specifications). One approach to monitoring the quality of the process is to analyze the number of defective items in a sample with an np chart. The procedure needed to develop an np chart is very similar to that previously given for the $\bar{x}$, R and p charts of the prior sections of this chapter. We plot sample values between 3-sigma control limits to determine if the sample values have a random pattern within the limits. Again we will consider the T&S Cakes example from the prior section.

The ever-discriminating Granny Goose wants every cake to have an acceptable frosting. However, it is not possible for her to personally inspect the large number of cakes produced each day by T&S. Consequently, she inspects a sample of 100 cakes each day and categorizes each cake as defective or not. Figure 12.14 presents the results for the last 15 days of her inspections. She would like to use these data to determine if the process is in control.

Figure 12.14 np Chart Centerline and Control Limits for T&S Cakes

	A	B	C	D	E	F	G	H	I	J	K
1					T & S CAKES, INC., EXAMPLE						
2	Today's Date				Your Name					File: QUALITY.xls	
3	Sample	Number						Number			
4	Number	Defective						Defective	LCL	CL	UCL
5	1	7		Number of Samples		15		7	0.0000	6.0667	13.2282
6	2	1		Total Defecitves		91		1	0.0000	6.0667	13.2282
7	3	5		Average No. Defectiv		6.06667		5	0.0000	6.0667	13.2282
8	4	9		Average Proportion		0.06067		9	0.0000	6.0667	13.2282
9	5	10		Std. Dev. for Avg. Pro		2.38718		10	0.0000	6.0667	13.2282
10	6	8		Lower Control Limit		0.00000		8	0.0000	6.0667	13.2282
11	7	6		Centerline		6.06667		6	0.0000	6.0667	13.2282
12	8	9		Upper Control Limit		13.22820		9	0.0000	6.0667	13.2282
13	9	2						2	0.0000	6.0667	13.2282
14	10	3						3	0.0000	6.0667	13.2282
15	11	10						10	0.0000	6.0667	13.2282
16	12	8						8	0.0000	6.0667	13.2282
17	13	3						3	0.0000	6.0667	13.2282
18	14	9						9	0.0000	6.0667	13.2282
19	15	1						1	0.0000	6.0667	13.2282
20	16										

We will develop our np chart on *Sheet5* of the QUALITY workbook as shown on Figure 12.14 (*Sheet4* if you bypassed Figure 12.1). We proceed as follows.

1. Copy from *Sheet4* to *Sheet5* the following.
   a. Rows 1 and 2 into rows 1 and 2
   b. Cells A3 through B29 into A3 through B29
   c. Cells I4 through K19 into I4 through K19

2. Enter the labels in cells H3 and H4. Enter the formula =**B5** in cell H5. Copy this formula into cells H6 through H19.

3. Enter the eight labels shown in cells D5 through D12 of Figure 12.14.

4. Enter into cell F5 the number of samples, **15**.

5. In cell F6 enter the formula =**SUM(B5:B29)** in order to compute the total number of defective items.

6. The average number defectives is computed in cell F7 with the formula =**F6/F5**, and the average number of proportion defective in cell F8 with the formula =**F7/100**.

7. The formula for cell F9 computes the estimate for the standard deviation for the number defective. It is found from the formula =**SQRT(F7*(1-F8))**.

8. The LCL is equal to the estimate of the number defective minus three times the standard deviation of the number defective but it cannot be negative. As before, we use an **IF** function to test for negativity. The formula for cell F10 is **=IF(F7-3*F9<0,0,F7-3*F9)**.

9. Cell F11 computes the CL with the formula **=F7**, and cell F12 the UCL with the formula **=F7+3*F9**.

10. We will use the CHART WIZARD to prepare the np chart. Highlight cells H5 through K19.

11. You now need to repeat *steps 16 through 22 of Section 12.1* in order to produce the initial np Chart. In Step 20 you should use the appropriate titles for the chart and for the Y-axis. (See Figure 12.15.)

12. Repeat *steps 25 through 31 of Section 12.1* (the scale adjustment of steps 23 and 24 is not needed for this plot) in order to edit your np chart into the final form as given in Figure 12.15.

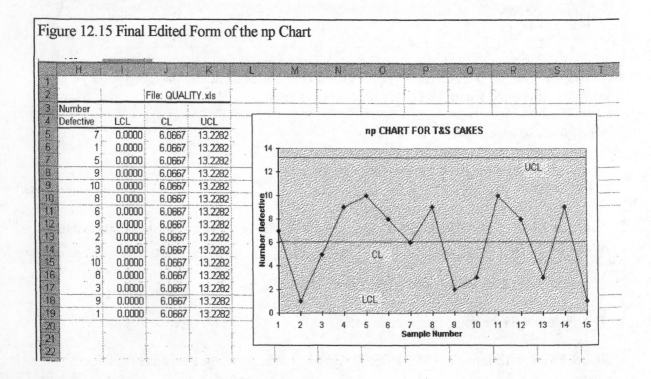

Figure 12.15 Final Edited Form of the np Chart

12.5 c CHART FOR CONTROLLING
NUMBER OF DEFECTS PER UNIT

The p and the np charts monitor the proportion or number of defectives. Each item such as a T&S cake is simply classified as either being defective or not. However for some processes, it is possible for an output item to have more than one defect. For example, each cake might have a number of defects that can be counted. Accordingly, we could monitor the quality based on the **number of defects per unit or per item** not the proportion or number defective items. This can be accomplished through a **c chart**.

Suppose the discriminating Granny Goose does count the number of defects she finds in each cake. The results she obtained for the last 15 samples are shown in column B of Figure 12.16. She would like to use these data to develop a c chart.

Again the basic procedure is to plot sample values between 3-sigma control limits to determine if the sample values have a random pattern within the limits. The primary way this chart differs from the four previously discussed is in the computation of the standard deviation for determining the LCL and UCL values. The basis for a c chart is that the Poisson distribution represents the number of defects per unit.

Figure 12.16 c Chart Centerline and Control Limits for T&S Cakes

	A	B	C	D	E	F	G	H	I	J	K
1					T & S CAKES, INC., EXAMPLE						
2	Today's Date				Your Name					File: QUALITY.xls	
3	Sample	Number of						Number of			
4	Number	Defects						Defects	LCL	CL	UCL
5	1	1						1	0.0000	1.7333	5.6830
6	2	2						2	0.0000	1.7333	5.6830
7	3	3			Average No. Defects	1.73333		3	0.0000	1.7333	5.6830
8	4	4			Std.Dev. No.of Defect	1.31656		4	0.0000	1.7333	5.6830
9	5	2						2	0.0000	1.7333	5.6830
10	6	1			Lower Control Limit	0.00000		1	0.0000	1.7333	5.6830
11	7	4			Centerline	1.73333		4	0.0000	1.7333	5.6830
12	8	1			Upper Control Limit	5.68302		1	0.0000	1.7333	5.6830
13	9	3						3	0.0000	1.7333	5.6830
14	10	2						2	0.0000	1.7333	5.6830
15	11	0						0	0.0000	1.7333	5.6830
16	12	0						0	0.0000	1.7333	5.6830
17	13	1						1	0.0000	1.7333	5.6830
18	14	2						2	0.0000	1.7333	5.6830
19	15	0						0	0.0000	1.7333	5.6830
20	16										

We will develop our c chart on *Sheet6* of the QUALITY workbook as shown on Figure 12.16 (*Sheet5* if you bypassed Figure 12.1). We proceed as follows.

1. Copy from *Sheet5* to *Sheet6* the following.
    a. Rows 1 and 2 into rows 1 and 2
    b. Cells A3 through A29 into A3 through A29
    c. Cells H4 through K19 into H4 through K19

2. Enter the labels in cells B3, B4, H3 and H4.

3. Enter the five labels shown in cells D7 through D12 of Figure 12.17.

4. Enter into cell F7 the formula **=AVERAGE(B5:B29)**.

5. In cell F8 enter the formula **=SQRT(F7)** to compute the standard deviation of the number of defects.

6. The LCL is equal to the estimate of the number of defects minus three times the standard deviation of the number of defects but it cannot be negative. The formula is **=IF(F7-3*F8<0,0,F7-3*F8)**.

7. Cell F11 computes the CL with the formula **=F7**, and cell F12 the UCL with the formula **=F7+3*F8**.

8. We will use the Chart Wizard to construct the c chart. Highlight cells H5 through K19.

9. Repeat *steps 16 through 22 of Section 12.1* in order to produce the initial c Chart. In Step 20 you should use the appropriate titles for the chart and for the Y-axis. (See Figure 12.17.)

10. Repeat *steps 24 through 31 of Section 12*.1 (the scale adjustment of steps 23 and 24 is not needed for this plot) in order to edit your c chart into the final form as shown in Figure 12.17.

Figure 12.17 Final Edited Form of the c Chart

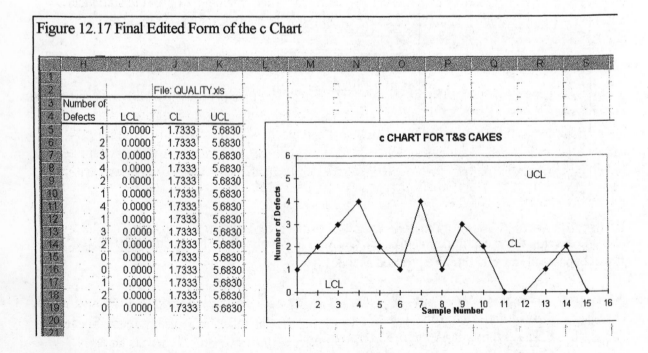

APPENDIX A. EXCEL DATA ANALYSIS TOOLS

1. What Are the Data Analysis Tools? Excel includes a collection of 19 data analysis tools. These provide analysis capabilities beyond Excel's inherent capabilities. One of them provides *Fourier analysis* for engineering applications. The remaining 18 provide statistical analyses. A discussion of the differences between these 18 statistical analysis tools and 80 statistical functions of Excel begins on the first page of Appendix B.

2. Where Can I Find the Data Analysis Tools? The data analysis tools are available in the component called the Analysis ToolPak that is an **add-in** program. Add-in programs are developed by organizations other than Microsoft and can be added to Excel to increase its capabilities. Microsoft includes a number of add-ins, such as the Analysis ToolPak, with the Excel software it distributes. These must be *added in* to Excel before they can be used within it.

3. Are the Data Analysis Tools Available on the Computer I am Using? The level of availability of the data analysis tools depends on the specific computer you are using. There are three possibilities.

a. The first possibility is that the Analysis ToolPak **(1) has been installed** and **(2) has been added** to the **Tools** pull-down menu. This means the data analysis tools are ready to use. To determine if this is your situation, click on **Tools** from the menu bar. If there is an entry usually near the bottom of the subsequent pull-down menu labeled **Data Analysis...**, the tools are ready to use. If it is not present, continue to the next possibility.

b. The second possibility is that the Analysis ToolPak **(1) has been installed** but **(2) has not been added** to the **Tools** menu. You must then add it to the menu. To determine if this is your situation and to add it to the menu, click on **Tools** from the menu bar. Then click on **Add-ins…** from the *Tools* pull-down menu. If the menu includes the selection **Analysis ToolPak** in the subsequent dialog box, you should click on the check box to its left to add a check mark to the box. (Note you are to add **Analysis ToolPak**, *not* **Analysis ToolPak-VBA**.) Next click on **OK** and the Analysis ToolPak will be added to the **Tools** menu and ready to use. If Analysis ToolPak is not an option on the add-ins dialog box, continue to the third possibility.

c. The third possibility is that the Analysis ToolPak **(1) has not been installed** and **(2) has not been added**. You must then first install it and second add it to the *Tools* menu. If this is your situation, you will need to exit from Excel and all other application programs and return to your computer's opening Windows screen.

Get your original CD for Microsoft Office (or Excel) and run the *Setup* program for it. Select the *Custom* installation option and select the **Analysis ToolPak** for installation in Excel. Once reinstallation is completed, launch Excel. You will next need to add *Analysis ToolPak* to the Tools menu. Select **Tools**, then **Add-Ins** and put a check mark in the **Analysis ToolPak** check box and select **OK**. The Data Analysis Tools will now be available from the Tools pull-down menu.

4. How Do I Use the Data Analysis Tools? Once you have the Analysis ToolPak installed and it has been added to the **Tools** pull-down menu, you are ready to use these analysis tools. First click on **Tools** from the menu bar and then click on **Data Analysis** on the subsequent pull-down menu. The result will be the *Data Analysis* dialog box with a scrolling list of the 19 data analysis tools (see Figure 1.5 of Chapter 1). You then click on the name of the tool you wish to use and click on **OK**. A dialog box will then appear which allows you to enter the input range, output options and any other options required for the tool you have selected. If you are uncertain of an entry for a tool's dialog box, first click on **Help** (this is the **Help** in the tool's dialog box, not the **Help** in the prior *Data Analysis* dialog box with the scrolling list of the 19 tools). Once the tool's dialog box is complete, click on **OK** and the output will appear. For example, you may refer to Figure 2.3 of Chapter 2 to view a completed *Histogram* data analysis tool dialog box.

5. For What Analyses Are the Data Analysis Tools Used? A presentation of the uses of the data analysis tools is perhaps most helpful if it is given by category of analysis. Accordingly, the following list of the 18 statistical tools is by the type of statistical analysis each supports. The six categories used are *Descriptive Statistics, Sampling, Hypothesis Testing, Analysis of Variance, Regression and Correlation,* and *Time Series Forecasting*. The order of presentation of the six categories is the order of a typical business statistics textbook. Within each category the tools are listed in the order they appear in this manual. The entry for each of the 18 statistical tools provides its name, its purpose and where its use is described within this manual. Further description of these is available through the Excel *help* facility. To access it, select **Tools** from the menu bar, **Data Analysis** from the subsequent pull-down menu, select the tool you wish to use from the resulting scrolling list, click on **OK** and click on **Help** in the next dialog box.

DESCRIPTIVE STATISTICS

Histogram—determines and graphs individual and cumulative frequencies for a one variable data set. It is presented in Section 2.1 of Chapter 2 and Section 4.3 of Chapter 4.

Descriptive Statistics—generates a report of the values for 16 descriptive statistics such as the mean, median, mode, standard deviation, range, skewness and kurtosis for a one variable data set. It is presented in Section 3.1 of Chapter 3.

Rank and Percentile—produces a table of the ordinal and percentage rank of each value in a one variable data set. It is presented in Section 3.2 of Chapter 3.

SAMPLING

Random Number Generation—generates random values drawn from one of six possible probability distributions (it also has a non-random selection called *patterned*). It is presented in Section 4.3 of Chapter 4.

Sampling—draws a random sample from a specified population for a single variable. This is the one statistical data analysis tool not used within this manual.

HYPOTHESIS TESTING

t-Test: Two Sample Assuming Unequal Variances—performs a t-test on two independent samples to determine if the difference in the two population means is equal to a specified value (such as zero). This test is conducted under the condition that the two population variances are not known to be equal. It is presented in Section 5.2 of Chapter 5.

t-Test: Two Sample Assuming Equal Variances—performs a t-test on two independent samples to determine if the difference in the two population means is equal to a specified value (such as zero). This test is conducted under the condition that the two unknown population variances are known to be equal. It is presented in Section 5.3 of Chapter 5.

z-Test: Two Sample for Means—performs a z-test on two independent samples to determine if the difference in the two population means is equal to a specified value (such as zero). This test is conducted under the condition that the values of the two population variances are known, or the sample sizes are large so the normal distribution can be used to approximate the t distribution. It is presented in Section 5.3 of Chapter 5.

t-Test: Paired Two Sample for Means—performs a t-test on two paired (matched) samples to determine if the mean of the differences between the two population is equal to a specified values (such as zero). It is presented in Section 5.4 of Chapter 5.

F-Test: Two-Sample for Variances—performs an F-test on two independent samples to determine if two population variances equal. It is presented in Section 7.2 of Chapter 7.

ANALYSIS OF VARIANCE

ANOVA: Single-Factor—performs a one-way analysis of variance to determine if two or more population means are equal. This test uses data from a *completely randomized* experimental design. It is presented in Section 8.1 of Chapter 8.

ANOVA: Two-Factor Without Replication—performs a two-way analysis of variance without interaction to determine if two or more population means are equal. This test uses data from a *randomized block* experimental design. It is presented in Section 8.2 of Chapter 8.

ANOVA: Two-Factor With Replication—performs a two-way analysis of variance with interaction to determine if two or more population means are equal. This test uses data from a *two-way factorial* experimental design. It is presented in Section 8.3 of Chapter 8.

REGRESSION AND CORRELATION

Covariance—creates a table of covariance values for all possible pairs of 2 or more independent variables. It is presented in Subsection 3.5.1 of Chapter 3.

Correlation—creates a table of correlation coefficients for all possible pairs of 2 or more independent variables. It is presented in Subsection 3.5.2 of Chapter 3, and in Section 10.3 of Chapter 10.

Regression—performs a simple linear regression analysis or a multiple regression analysis with up to 16 independent variables. It is presented in Sections 10.2, 10.3 and 10.4 of Chapter 10.

TIME SERIES FORECASTING

Moving Average—projects a time series based on the moving averages smoothing method. It is presented in Section 11.2 of Chapter 11.

Exponential Smoothing—projects a time series based on the simple exponential smoothing method. It is presented in Section 11.3 of Chapter 11.

APPENDIX B. EXCEL STATISTICAL FUNCTIONS

1. What Are the Statistical Functions? Excel includes hundreds of built-in functions. These are predefined formulas for performing frequently needed computations. Excel presents its functions in categories such as *Financial, Date & Time, Math &Trig,* and *Database*. One of the function categories is *Statistical*. The statistical category includes 80 statistical functions.

2. How Do the Statistical Functions and the Data Analysis Tools Differ? The statistical functions duplicate the capabilities of parts of the *Data Analysis Tools* discussed in Appendix A. However, there are differences in these two Excel features. The differences include the following.

- The results from the *Tools* usually are numbers, not formulas. Thus, a change in the input data analyzed by a *Tool* will not change the statistical results already computed by it. To get the new results the *Tool* will have to be initiated again through its dialog box. In contrast, the output from a *function* is a formula. Accordingly, whenever the input data for the *function* are changed, the numerical results computed by it are changed. (Note: Two of the *Data Analysis Tools*, MOVING AVERAGE and EXPONENTIAL SMOOTHING, are exceptions to this difference. These two tools do result in formulas, not numbers being entered into the worksheet. Also, the COVARIANCE tool results in formulas for some of its outputs, the variances for the input variables.)

- The output from a *Data Analysis Tool* is formatted and labeled whereas that from a function merely presents the numerical results. The user must provide labels and editing as needed.

- A *Tool* generally provides the results that would be obtained from more than one function.

- *Tools* cannot be used in Excel formulas but statistical functions can.

3. How Do I Use the Statistical Functions? Access to the statistical functions is facilitated through Excel's INSERT FUNCTION feature. When you click the icon labeled with the symbol *fx* next to the *Formula box,* you will be presented with the *Insert function* dialog box (see Figure 1.6 of Chapter 1 or Figure 3.7 of Chapter 3). The label *Or select a category* identifies a drop-down list box. It presents a list of the names of Excel's function categories plus the three categories of *Most Recently Used, All* and *User Defined.* If you click on the category **Statistical,** the scrolling list at the bottom of the dialog box presents the 80 statistical functions.

To select one of the statistical functions, highlight the function name by clicking on it. A brief description of the function will be displayed at the bottom of the dialog box. Much greater detail about the selected function can be obtained by clicking on the *Help on this function* label in the bottom left corner of the dialog box. This action will activate *Microsoft Excel Help* window.

If you click on the command button labeled **OK**, the dialog box for the function will be displayed (see Figure 3.8 of Chapter 3 for an example). Generally, this dialog box will present one or more text boxes for keying the required values. Again *help* is available through the *Help on this function* label. Once the required text boxes are completed, click on the **OK** button and the completed function will be entered into the active cell of the worksheet. The F2 key on the keyboard may be pressed in order to edit the function within the cell if it is necessary.

4. For What Analyses Are the Statistical Functions Used? The presentation of the uses of the statistical functions is perhaps most helpful if it is by category of analysis. Accordingly, the following list of the 80 Excel statistical functions is by the type of statistical analysis each supports. The 15 categories include six descriptive statistics categories, four probability distribution categories, one hypothesis testing and confidence interval category, and four regression and correlation categories.

The order of presentation of these 15 categories is that of a typical business statistics textbook. Within each category the functions are presented in alphabetical order. The entry for each of the statistical functions provides its name and purpose. The use of many of these is demonstrated throughout this manual. Refer to the index to find the specific location for each function. You may find further description of the functions with examples of their use through the Excel *help* facility. To access it, select the INSERT FUNCTION icon (that labeled with *fx* next to the formula box), next select the category **Statistical** and then select the specific function of interest. Finally, click on the *Help on selected function* label in the lower left corner of the dialog box. The result will be a detailed *help* window.

DESCRIPTIVE STATISTICS—MEASURES OF LOCATION

AVERAGE—computes the arithmetic average (the usual mean)

AVERAGEA— computes the arithmetic average but includes cells that contain text and the logical values FALSE and TRUE, not just numerical values. Cells that contain **text,** the word **FALSE** or are **empty** are evaluated as if they contained the number **zero**. Cells that contain the word **TRUE** are evaluated as if they contained the number **1**.

GEOMEAN—computes the geometric mean (used for ratios, rates of changes and so on)

HARMEAN—computes the harmonic mean (rarely used in business applications)

MEDIAN—computes the median

MODE—computes the mode

TRIMMEAN—computes the trimmed mean (removes unusually small and/or large values)

DESCRIPTIVE STATISTICS—MEASURES OF VARIABILITY

AVEDEV—computes the average of the absolute deviations about the mean (**MAD**)

DEVSQ—computes the sum of the squared deviations about the mean

STDEV—computes the sample standard deviation (**n -1** in the denominator)

STDEVA—computes the sample standard deviation but includes cells that contain text and the logical values FALSE and TRUE, not just numerical values. Cells that contain **text,** the word **FALSE** or are **empty** are evaluated as if they contained the number **zero**. Cells that contain the word **TRUE** are evaluated as if they contained the number **1**.

STDEVP— computes the population standard deviation (**N** in the denominator)

STDEVPA— computes the population standard deviation but includes cells that contain text and the logical values FALSE and TRUE, not just numerical values. Cells that contain **text,** the word **FALSE** or are **empty** are evaluated as if they contained the number **zero**. Cells that contain the word **TRUE** are evaluated as if they contained the number **1**.

VAR—computes the sample variance (**n -1** in the denominator)

VARA—computes the sample variance but includes cells that contain text and the logical values FALSE and TRUE, not just numerical values. Cells that contain **text,** the word **FALSE** or are **empty** are evaluated as if they contained the number **zero**. Cells that contain the word **TRUE** are evaluated as if they contained the number **1**.

VARP—computes the population variance (**N** in the denominator)

VARPA—computes the population variance but includes cells that contain text and the logical values FALSE and TRUE, not just numerical values. Cells that contain **text,** the word **FALSE** or are **empty** are evaluated as if they contained the number **zero**. Cells that contain the word **TRUE** are evaluated as if they contained the number **1**.

DESCRIPTIVE STATISTICS—MEASURES OF SHAPE AND POSITION

KURT—computes the coefficient of kurtosis

SKEW—computes the coefficient of skewness

STANDARDIZE—computes the standardized value or z-score for a number

DESCRIPTIVE STATISTICS—SPECIFIC VALUES

LARGE—determines the kth largest value in a range (determines largest value if k is 1, the second largest if k is 2, and so on)

MAX—determines the maximum (largest) value in a range

MAXA— determines the maximum (largest) value in a range but includes cells that contain text and the logical values FALSE and TRUE, not just numerical values. Cells that contain **text,** the word **FALSE** or are **empty** are evaluated as if they contained the number **zero**. Cells that contain the word **TRUE** are evaluated as if they contained the number **1**.

MIN—determines the minimum (smallest) value in a range

MINA— determines the minimum (smallest) value in a range but includes cells that contain text and the logical values FALSE and TRUE, not just numerical values. Cells that contain **text,** the word **FALSE** or are **empty** are evaluated as if they contained the number **zero**. Cells that contain the word **TRUE** are evaluated as if they contained the number **1**.

SMALL— determines the kth smallest value in a range (determines smallest value if k is 1, the second smallest if k is 2, and so on)

DESCRIPTIVE STATISTICS—COUNTING

COUNT—counts the number of cells in a range that contain numeric values

COUNTA—counts the number of cells in a range that are not blank

COUNTBLANK— counts the number of cells in a range that are blank

COUNTIF— counts the number of cells in a range that are not blank and meet a specified criterion

FREQUENCY—determines the frequency distribution for data in a range

PERMUT—computes the number of permutations of n items taken k at a time (Excel also includes a combinations function, **COMBIN**, it is in the **Math & Trig** category)

DESCRIPTIVE STATISTICS—PERCENTILES AND RANKS

PERCENTILE—determines the kth percentile value of the values in a range (determines 10th percentile value if k is 0.1, 20th percentile if k is 0.2, and so on)

PERCENTRANK—determines the percentage rank in a range for a specified value (this is the inverse of the **PERCENTILE** function)

QUARTILE—computes the minimum value, maximum value or one of the three quartile values for a range

RANK—determines the rank of a number in a range of numbers

DISTRIBUTIONS—DISCRETE PROBABILITY DISTRIBUTIONS

BINOMDIST—computes either the individual probability value or the cumulative probability value for a specified random variable value for the binomial probability distribution

HYPGEODIST— computes the individual probability value (but not the cumulative probability value) for a specified random variable value for the hypergeometric probability distribution

NEGBINOMDIST— computes the individual probability value (but not the cumulative probability value) for a specified random variable value for the negative binomial probability distribution

POISSON—computes either the individual probability value or the cumulative probability value for a specified random variable value for the Poisson probability distribution

PROB— computes either the individual probability value for a specified random variable value or the total probability for a specified range for the random variable for a given discrete probability distribution

DISTRIBUTIONS—EXPONENTIAL AND NORMAL PROBABILITY DISTRIBUTIONS

EXPODIST— computes either the individual probability value or the cumulative probability value for a specified random variable value for the exponential probability distribution

NORMDIST—computes either the individual probability value or the cumulative probability value for a specified random variable value for the normal probability distribution

NORMINV—computes the random variable value for a specified probability value for the cumulative normal probability distribution

NORMSDIST—computes the cumulative probability value for a specified random variable value for the standard normal (mean of zero and standard deviation of one) probability distribution

NORMSINV—computes the random variable value for a specified probability value for the cumulative standard normal (mean of zero and standard deviation of one) probability distribution

DISTRIBUTIONS—DERIVED DISTRIBUTIONS

CHIDIST— computes the probability value for a specified random variable value for the chi-square distribution

CHIINV— computes the random variable value for a specified probability value for the chi-square distribution

FDIST—computes the probability value for a specified random variable value for the F distribution

FINV—computes the random variable value for a specified probability value for the F distribution

TDIST—computes the probability value for a specified random variable value for the t distribution

TINV—computes the random variable value for a specified probability value for the t distribution

DISTRIBUTIONS—OTHER CONTINUOUS PROBABILITY DISTRIBUTIONS

BETADIST—computes the probability value for a specified random variable value for the cumulative beta probability distribution

BETAINV— computes the random variable value for a specified probability value for the cumulative beta probability distribution

GAMMADIST— computes either the individual probability value or the cumulative probability value for a specified random variable value for the gamma probability distribution

GAMMAINV—computes the random variable value for a specified probability value for the cumulative gamma probability distribution

GAMMALN—computes the natural logarithm of the gamma function (not the gamma distribution)

LOGINV— computes the random variable value for a specified probability value for the cumulative lognormal probability distribution

LOGNORMDIST— computes either the individual probability value or the cumulative probability value for a specified random variable value for the lognormal probability distribution

WEIBULL—computes either the individual probability value or the cumulative probability value for a specified random variable value for the Weibull probability distribution

HYPOTHESIS TESTING AND CONFIDENCE INTERVALS

CHITEST—computes the p-value for the chi-square test of independence

CONFIDENCE—computes the sampling (or maximum) error (the half-width of the confidence interval) for a population mean using the z (standard normal) distribution

CRITBINOM—computes the critical value for hypothesis tests based on the binomial distribution

FISHER—computes the Fisher transformation for hypothesis tests

FISHERINV—computes the inverse of the Fisher transformation

FTEST—computes the p-value for the F test of the equivalence of two population variances

TTEST—computes the p-value for the t test of the equivalence of two population means for paired samples, for independent samples with equal variance or for independent samples with unequal variance

ZTEST—computes the p-value for the z (standard normal) test of one population mean with the population standard deviation either known or not known

REGRESSION AND CORRELATION—ASSOCIATION BETWEEN TWO VARIABLES

CORREL—computes the table of correlation coefficients (Pearson product moment correlation coefficients) for two ranges (this function is identical to **PEARSON**)

COVAR—computes the table of covariance values for two ranges

PEARSON—computes the table of correlation coefficients (Pearson product moment correlation coefficients) for two ranges (this function is identical to **CORREL**)

REGRESSION AND CORRELATION—SIMPLE LINEAR REGRESSION ANALYSIS

FORECAST—computes an estimated dependent variable value for a specified independent variable value based on a simple linear regression relationship

INTERCEPT—computes the value of the intercept for a simple linear regression

RSQ—computes the value for the coefficient of determination (the square of the correlation coefficient) for a simple linear regression

SLOPE—computes the value of the slope for a simple linear regression

STEYX—computes the standard error of the estimated y values for a simple linear regression

REGRESSION AND CORRELATION—MULTIPLE REGRESSION ANALYSIS

LINEST—performs a multiple (or simple) regression analysis and displays the regression coefficients and the additional regression outputs of the standard error for each of the regression coefficients, the coefficient of determination, the standard error of the estimated y values, the F statistic value and degrees of freedom, the sum of squares due to the regression and the sum of squares due to the error

TREND—computes estimated dependent variable values for specified independent variable values based on a multiple (or simple) regression relationship

REGRESSION AND CORRELATION—EXPONENTIAL REGRESSION ANALYSIS

GROWTH— computes estimated dependent variable values for specified independent variable values based on an exponential regression relationship

LOGEST—performs an exponential regression analysis (similar to **LINEST**, however the **LOGEST** relationship has the independent variables as exponents for the regression coefficients not multiplied times the coefficients as for the standard regression relationship used in **LINEST**)

APPENDIX C. BOX PLOT PROCEDURES

Subsection 3.4.4 of Chapter 3 discusses the computation of a five-number summary with Excel. The discussion goes on to show how the workbook file *Boxplot.xls* can be used to convert a five-number summary into a box plot (sometimes called a box and whisker plot). This workbook file is included on the CD accompanying this manual. However, some readers may wish to develop their own box plot workbook. Accordingly, **Section C.1** below presents the procedure for developing the *Boxplot.xls* workbook.

Also in Subsection 3.4.4, we have suggested it is possible to save the *Boxplot.xls* file as a built-in custom chart in your copy of Excel. Thus, it would always be directly available to you through the CHART WIZARD. The procedure for saving this file as a custom chart, and the procedure for using the custom box plot chart are presented in **Section C.2** below.

C.1 CONSTRUCTING A BOX PLOT ────────────

The procedure for developing a box plot worksheet such as that contained in the file **Boxplot.xls** is the following.

1. Start Excel and enter your **Identification Material,** worksheet title, your name, the date and the file name, as shown in Figure C.1. Enter the label and data in Column A. The data are for the example of Section 3.1 of Chapter 3. The values may be found on Table 3.1 and Figure 3.1. Save the workbook with the file name *Boxplot.xls*.

Figure C.1 Example Data and Box Plot Computations

	A	B	C	D	E	F	G
1			WORKSHEET TO CONSTRUCT A BOX PLOT				
2			Your Name				
3	Today's Date				File: BOXPLOT.xls		
4							
5	FREIGHT		FIVE-NUMBER SUMMARY				
6	45		Smallest Value	35			
7	40		First Quartile	40.75			
8	44		Median	43.5			
9	39		Third Quartile	45			
10	40		Largest Value	48			
11	37						
12	41		LENGTHS FOR BOX PLOT				
13	43		First	35			
14	43		Second	5.75			
15	46		Third	2.75			
16	37		Fourth	1.5			
17	35		Fifth	3			
18	44						
19	44						
20	45						
21	44						
22	46						

2. Enter the labels for cells C5 through C17.

3. In cells D6 through D10 enter the five QUARTILE expressions.

=QUARTILE(A6:A105,0)
=QUARTILE(A6:A105,1)
=QUARTILE(A6:A105,2)
=QUARTILE(A6:A105,3)
=QUARTILE(A6:A105,4)

4. In cells D13 through D17 enter the following five formulas.

= D6
= D7 – D6
= D8 – D7
= D9 – D8
= D10 – D9

5. Drag through cells D13 through D 17 to highlight these five lengths.

6. Click on the CHART WIZARD icon on the standard toolbar. On the resulting dialog box as shown in Figure C.2, select **Bar** for *Chart type* and **Stacked Bar** for *Chart sub-type* (the sub-type in the middle of the top row). Click on the **Next** button.

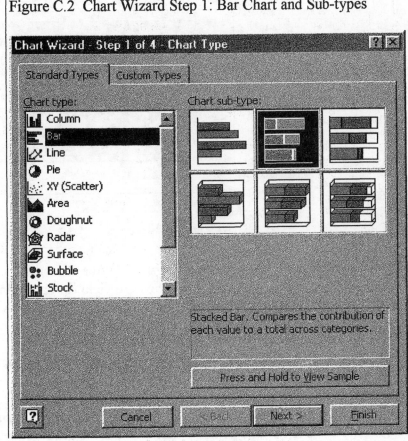

Figure C.2 Chart Wizard Step 1: Bar Chart and Sub-types

7. For Step 2 of 4 of the CHART WIZARD (see Figure 2.10 of Chapter 2), click the option button labeled as **Rows** for *Series in* option. Click on the **Next** button.

8. For Step 3 of 4 (see Figure 2.11), select the **Axes** tab. Click to eliminate the check for the check box labeled **Category (X) axis** under the label *Primary axis*.

9. Select the **Gridlines** tab for Step 3 of 4. Click to eliminate the checks for the two check boxes under the heading *Value (Y) axis*.

10. Select the **Legend** tab. Click to eliminate the check for *Show legend*. Click the **Finish** button for Step 3 of 4. Your stacked bar chart will appear as shown in Figure C.3. Note that the chart has been dragged to an unoccupied part of the worksheet.

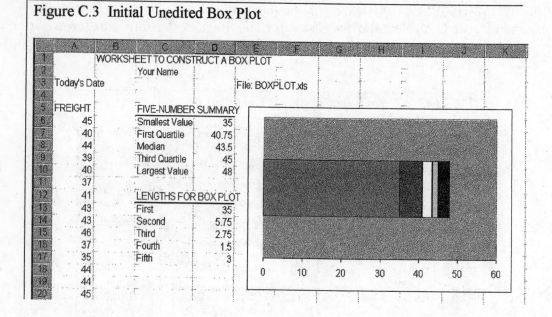

Figure C.3 Initial Unedited Box Plot

11. As you will note in Figure C.3, the bar chart is made up of five boxes. The lengths of each are shown to the left of the chart. The first has a length of 35, the second 5.75 and so on. We need to edit the two leftmost boxes and the rightmost box to yield the appearance of a box plot. Click on the first box (leftmost). Then **right click** the box and then click on **Format Data Series** from the subsequent shortcut menu.

12. Click on the **Patterns** tab. Select the **None** option button under the *Border* part of the dialog box and select **None** under the *Area* part. Click **OK.**

13. Click the second box and perform Step 12 above for it. Next select the **Y Error Bars** tab. Under the heading *Display*, click on the **Minus** option. Under the heading *Error amount* click the option button labeled **Percentage**. To the right of the word *Percentage*, click on the up arrow to change the spinner to read **100%**.

14. Perform steps 12 and 13 for the fifth box (rightmost).

15. Click on the axis labeled 0 to 60. Next **right click** it and select **Format Axis** from the resulting shortcut menu.

16. Click on the dialog box tab labeled as **Scale**. Change the minimum amount to 30 and the maximum amount to 50. Click on **Next** to obtain the final results of Figure C.4.

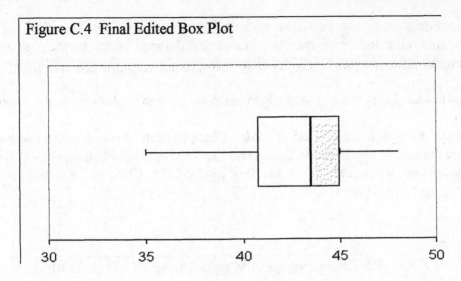

Figure C.4 Final Edited Box Plot

C.2 SAVING AND USING THE CUSTOM BOX PLOT CHART —

It is possible to add the box plot as a built-in custom chart to your copy of Excel. You can than create box plots without needing the *Boxplot.xls* file. The procedure for saving *Boxplot.xls* in your copy of Excel is the following.

1. Click on the border of the chart as given in Figure C.4 to activate it. Next click on **Chart** on the main menu bar (*not the Chart icon from the Standard Toolbar*). From the subsequent pull-down menu select **Chart Type** and then select the dialog box tab for **Custom Types**.

2. Click the option button for **User-defined** under the label *Select from*. Two command buttons will be added to the bottom right of the dialog box. As shown in Figure C.5, one is labeled *Add* and the other *Delete*.

3. Click on the Add command button and key in *Box Plot* for the name of the chart. If you would like you may add a description of this new chart type. The description is optional. Click on **OK**.

The Box Plot chart is now stored in your copy of Excel for future use. The procedure for using is quite simple.

1. Highlight the five lengths for the box plot (cells D13 through D17 of Figure C.1). Click on Chart icon on the Standard Toolbar and make these selections for Step 1 of 4 for the Chart Wizard. **Custom Types** tab, **User-defined** option button, **Box Plot** for *Chart type* and **Next**.

2. For the Step 2 of 4 for the Chart Wizard, select **Rows** for *Series in* and **Finish**.

3. The entire box plot may not be displayed for a particular set of data. It may be necessary to adjust the minimum and/or the maximum values for the axes. Click on the *X-axis* to ready it for editing.

4. Next **right click** the *X-axis* and select **Format Axis** from the resulting shortcut menu.

5. Click on the dialog box tab labeled as **Scale**. Change the minimum amount and the maximum amount to appropriate values. Use the *Smallest Value* and *Largest Value* given on the worksheet as guides (cells D6 and D10 of Figure C.1). Click on **Next** to obtain your final box plot as given in Figure C.4.

Figure C.5 Dialog Box for Adding or Deleting Custom Chart

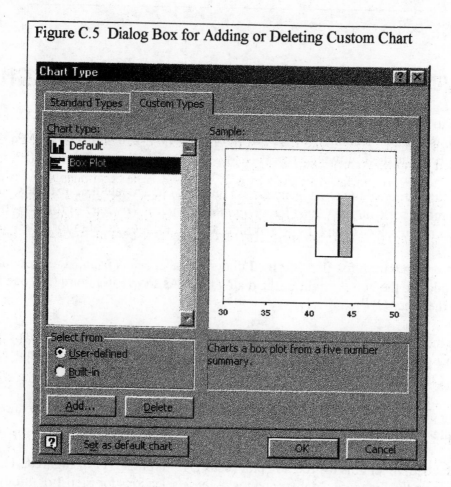

APPENDIX D. EXCEL 2000 DIFFERENCES

This manual has been developed with the most recent version of Excel for use on Microsoft Windows based computers. It is Excel 2002, which is a component of Microsoft Office XP. The prior version, Excel 2000, differs very little from Excel 2002. The functionality and capability of Excel 2000 is essentially the same as Excel 2002. However Excel 2002 has some new convenience features and a few redesigned dialog boxes. For those using Excel 2000, the following is a summary of how these small differences affect the content of this manual.

Chapter 1

1. Page 4, Figure 1.1 Excel 2000 does not include the *Ask a Question Box* to the right of the *Menu bar* and does not include the *Task Pane* to the right of the worksheet window. These two convenience features are not available in Excel 2000. Figure D.1 is the comparable figure for Excel 2000.

2. Page 8, Figure 1.2 The Excel 2000 *Options* dialog box only has eight tabs as opposed to the 13 shown in Figure 1.2. Figure D.2 is the comparable figure for Excel 2000.

3. Page 17, Subsection 1.4.2, Figure 1.6   For Excel 2000 the *Insert Function* is called *Paste Function*. The *fx* icon for Excel 2000 is located on the standard toolbar. In addition, the dialog box for Excel 2000 is as shown in Figure D.3 as compared to Figure 1.6 for Excel 2002.

Figure D.1 Excel Window for Excel 2000

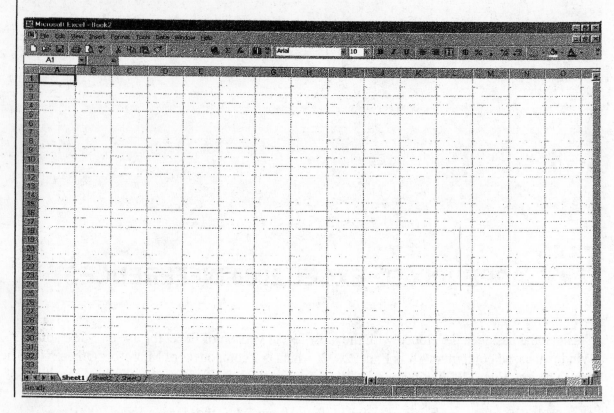

Chapter 2

For the *Chart Wizard Step 3: Chart Options*, the **Data Labels** dialog box is laid out differently in Excel 2000. It uses *Option Buttons* in place of *Check Boxes* for making selections. This requires a modification in four places in Chapter 2. One of the modifications required is the following:

The explanation *None of the boxes under the words* **Label Contains** *should be checked,* should be replaced for Excel 2000 with the words, *Select the option button for* **None**. This modification is to be made in the following three places:

     1. Page 36, Step 12.
     2. Page 40, Step 11.
     3. Page 46, Step 11.

The fourth modification is on

     4. Page 43, next to last paragraph.

The explanation *do check both* **Category Name** *and* **Percentage** *for the Data Label dialog box* should be replaced by *select the* **Show label and percent** *option*.

Figure D.2 Elements of Dialog Boxes for Excel 2000

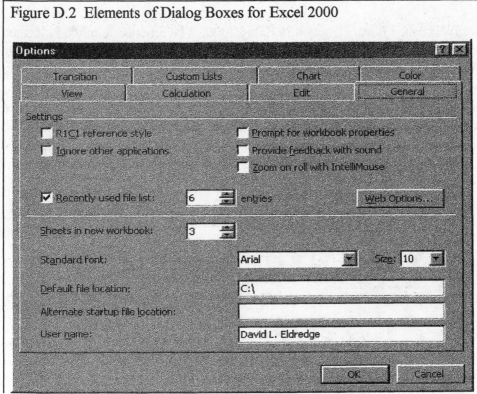

Figure D.3 Paste Function Dialog Box for Excel 2000

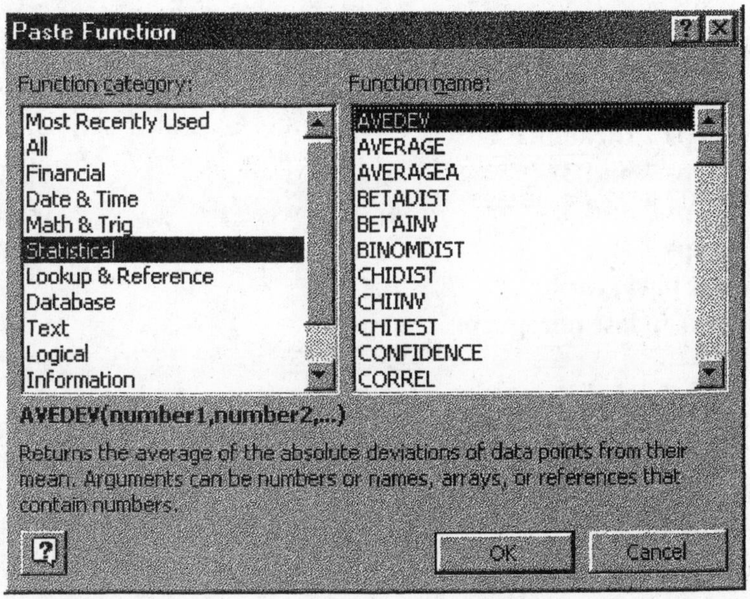

Chapter 3

Insert Function is called *Paste Function* in Excel 2000. The function icon, *fx*, is located on the standard toolbar, not next to the formula box. In addition, the dialog box for Excel 2000 is as shown in Figure D.3 as compared to Figure 3.7 for Excel 2002.

When a function is selected from the right list of the Paste Function dialog box, a subsequent dialog box appears for the selected function. These boxes differ slightly for Excel 2000. Figures 3.8, 3.10, 3.12 and 3.14 present dialog boxes for four Excel 2002 functions. Figure D.4 presents the Excel 2000 equivalent of Figure 3.8. As you will note, the changes are only cosmetic.

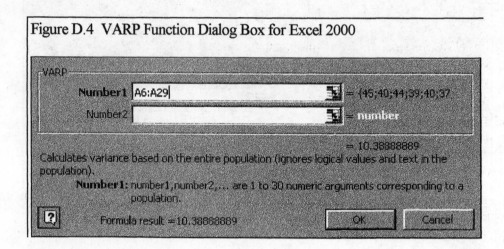

Figure D.4 VARP Function Dialog Box for Excel 2000

This altered treatment for inserting/pasting functions affects the explanations in the following places in Chapter 3.

1. **Page 54, Subsection 3.1.3, second paragraph.**
2. **Page 57, Steps 2 through 5.**
3. **Page 59, Steps 2 and 3.**
4. **Page 61, Steps 2 and 3.**
5. **Page 63, Steps 2 and 3.**
6. **Page 67, last paragraph.**
7. **Page 68, next to last paragraph.**

Chapter 4

There are two reasons for modifications in Chapter 4. The first involves functions and the second involves charting.

Functions. As discussed above for Chapter 3, *Insert Function* is called *Paste Function* in Excel 2000. The function icon, *fx*, is located on the standard toolbar, not next to the formula box. In addition, the dialog box for it is different. Whereas Figure 4.1 presents that for Excel 2002's *Insert Function*, the previous Figure D.3 is the dialog box for Excel 2000's *Paste Function*.

When a function is selected from the right list of the dialog box of Figure D.3, a subsequent dialog box appears for the selected function. These boxes differ slightly for Excel 2000. Figures 4.2 and 4.5, present dialog boxes for two Excel 2002 functions. Figure D.4 presents a dialog box for an Excel 2000 function. As you will note, the changes are only cosmetic.

This altered treatment for inserting/pasting functions affects the explanations in the following places in Chapter 4.

1. **Page 70, Section 4.1, first paragraph.**
2. **Page 71, Steps 6 through 9.**
3. **Page 75, Steps 4 through 6.**
4. **Page 77, Subsection 4.1.3, first and third paragraphs.**
5. **Page 79, Step 4.**
6. **Page 81, Step 2**

Charting. For the *Chart Wizard Step 3: Chart Options*, the **Data Labels** dialog box is laid out differently in Excel 2000. This requires a modification in two places in Chapter 4. The modification required is the following:

The explanation *None of the boxes under the words* **Label Contains** *should be checked,* should be replaced for Excel 2000 with the words, *Select the option button for* **None**.

This modification is to be made in the following two places:

1. **Page 73, Step 9.**
2. **Page 77, Step 9.**

Chapter 9

There is one minor modification for Chapter 9. For the Pivot Table results, the *Pivot Table* toolbar and the *Pivot Table Field List* are combined as one dialog box. This change appears in two places.

1. **Page 182, Figure 9.15 is replaced by Figure D.5.**
2. **Page 185, Figure 9.18 is replaced by Figure D.6.**

Figure D.5 Pivot Table Final Results for One-Variable Example

	A	B	C	D	E	F	G	H	I	J	K
1											
2							Drop Page Fields Here				
3		CUSTOMER	HAY	LIVESTOCK							
4		1453	Clover	Cattle			Count of HAY				
5		1454	Mixture #1	Emus			HAY	Total			
6		1455	Alfalfa	Sheep			Alfalfa	3			
7		1456	Clover	Horses			Clover	4			
8		1457	Mixture #2	Horses			Mixture #1	5			
9		1458	Alfalfa	Sheep			Mixture #2	5			
10		1459	Mixture #1	Cattle			Timothy	3			
11		1460	Mixture #1	Emus			Grand Total	20			
12		1461	Mixture #2	Sheep							
13		1462	Mixture #2	Sheep							
14		1463	Timothy	Cattle							
15		1464	Alfalfa	Horses							
16		1465	Mixture #1	Sheep							
17		1466	Mixture #2	Sheep							
18		1467	Clover	Horses							
19		1468	Mixture #1	Horses							
20		1469	Timothy	Cattle							
21		1470	Mixture #2	Emus							
22		1471	Timothy	Cattle							
23		1472	Clover	Horses							
24											

Figure D.6 Pivot Table Final Results for Two-Variable Example for Excel 2000

	E	F	G	H	I	J	K	L
1	PIVOT TABLE							
2	File: CHI-SQR.xls		Drop Page Fields Here					
3								
4	Count of LIVESTOCK	LIVESTOCK						
5	HAY	Cattle	Emus	Horses	Sheep	Grand Total	
6	Alfalfa			1	2	3	
7	Clover	1		3		4	
8	Mixture #1	1	2	1	1	5	
9	Mixture #2		1	1	3	5	
10	Timothy	3				3	
11	Grand Total	5	3	6	6	20	

Chapter 10

There are two reasons for modifications in Chapter 10. The first involves functions and the second involves charting.

Functions. As discussed above for Chapter 3, *Insert Function* is called *Paste Function* in Excel 2000. The function icon, *fx*, is located on the standard toolbar, not next to the formula box. In addition, the dialog box for it is different. Whereas Figure 3.7 presents that for Excel 2002's *Insert Function*, the previous Figure D.3 is the dialog box for Excel 2000's *Paste Function*.

When a function is selected from the right list of the dialog box of Figure D.3, a subsequent dialog box appears for the selected function. These boxes differ slightly for Excel 2000. Figure 10.8 presents a dialog boxes for Excel 2002. Figure D.4 presents a dialog box for an Excel 2000 function. As you will note, the changes are only cosmetic.

This altered treatment for inserting/pasting functions affects the explanation in the following place in Chapter 10.

      Page 194, Step 2

Charting. For the *Chart Wizard Step 3: Chart Options*, the **Data Labels** dialog box is laid out differently in Excel 2000. This requires a modification in Chapter 10. The modification required is the following:

The explanation *None of the boxes under the words* **Label Contains** *should be checked,* should be replaced for Excel 2000 with the words, *Select the option button for* **None**.

This modification is to be made on

      Page 189, Step 6.

Chapter 12

For the *Chart Wizard Step 3: Chart Options*, the **Data Labels** dialog box is laid out differently in Excel 2000. This requires a modification in Chapter 12. The modification required is the following:

The explanation *None of the boxes under the words* **Label Contains** *should be checked,* should be replaced for Excel 2000 with the words, *Select the option button for* **None**.

This modification is to be made on

      Page 229, step 21.

<u>Appendix B</u>

For the *Chart Wizard Step 3: Chart Options,* the **Data Labels** dialog box is laid out differently in Excel 2000. This requires a modification in two places in Apendix B. The modification required is the following:

The explanation *None of the boxes under the words* **Label Contains** *should be checked,* should be replaced for Excel 2000 with the words, *Select the option button for* **None**.

This modification is to be made in the following two places:

1. **Page 249, Item number 3, first paragraph.**
2. **Page 249, Item number 4, second paragraph.**

INDEX

Index